Law Enforcement
in American Cinema,
1894–1952

Law Enforcement in American Cinema, 1894–1952

George Beck

McFarland & Company, Inc., Publishers
Jefferson, North Carolina

ISBN (print) 978-1-4766-8022-4
ISBN (ebook) 978-1-4766-4065-5

LIBRARY OF CONGRESS AND BRITISH LIBRARY
CATALOGUING DATA ARE AVAILABLE

Library of Congress Control Number 2020041387

© 2020 George Beck. All rights reserved

No part of this book may be reproduced or transmitted in any form or by any means, electronic or mechanical, including photocopying or recording, or by any information storage and retrieval system, without permission in writing from the publisher.

On the cover: Robert Armstrong (left), James Cagney (center, holding phone) and Edward Pawley (slumped in background) in "*G*" *Men*, 1935 (Warner Bros./Photofest)

Printed in the United States of America

*McFarland & Company, Inc., Publishers
Box 611, Jefferson, North Carolina 28640
www.mcfarlandpub.com*

Table of Contents

Acknowledgments vii

Introduction 1

    I. Early Twentieth-Century Law Enforcement and Cinema   17

    II. Just the Facts: The Police in Short Early Silent-Era Film   34

    III. Cops in Silent-Era Feature Film: *Traffic in Souls* (1913), *Easy Street* (1917) and *Cops* (1922)   65

    IV. Enforcing the Law in the "Talkies"   82

    V. Shadows of Law Enforcement in Film Noir   103

Coda: Law Enforcement in Early Twentieth-Century Film: From a Subject of Suspicion to a Power for the Common Good   122

Filmography   131

Chapter Notes   137

Bibliography   153

Index   165

Acknowledgments

This book developed from many historical conversations with Drew University's associate dean William "Bill" Rogers (now retired). To my surprise, a study solely focusing on law enforcement in film during the first half of the twentieth century was yet to be written. Thank you, Dean Rogers, for your guidance and patience. You have had the most profound impact on my understandings of American history.

I also thank Dr. James O'Kane for being a part of this historical endeavor. Dr. O'Kane's *The Crooked Ladder: Gangsters, Ethnicity, and the American Dream* had a deep influence on this book, especially in Chapter IV. Dr. O'Kane's additional work *Wicked Deeds: Murder in America* also shaped my thinking on the subject and thus influenced my professional understandings as a police officer. Thank you, Dr. O'Kane, for our meaningful discussions on criminology and sociology.

Thank you to Dr. Jessica Hope Jordan for all your expertise in film that provided the necessary academic sustenance to push this book over the finish line. Dr. Jordan's work, *The Sex Goddess in American Film, 1930–1965: Jean Harlow, Mae West, Lana Turner, and Jayne Mansfield*, greatly influenced my thinking, especially in Chapter V's discussion of film noir.

I also thank my inspirations, Shamainie, and our children, Jordan, Karista, and Colton, for always supporting me to complete this book. Writing a book is no easy task. It requires long days that seemingly get longer and longer as the months go by. Without the support of my family, always encouraging me to push ahead, I would still be dreaming of this study and yet to write it. I endlessly thank them for always being here for me. I love you.

I conclude by thanking the person I was thinking of during my earlier mentioned discussions with Dean Rogers—my late grandfather Gerald "Jerry" J. Beck. He passed many years ago, yet continues to inspire me. Grandpa Jerry was a tough-as-nails Marine infantryman and Korean

Acknowledgments

War veteran who instilled lives of service into his children as well as his grandchildren. It is no surprise that my father George, my uncle Gregg, my brothers Chris and Michael, and myself all actively serve with either the police or fire departments. Grandpa Jerry embodied the strong patriotic American spirit of the 1950s I've discussed in this book. He routinely taught that challenges in life were meant to be overcome and to stand your ground at times when most people would turn and run. He was also an avid film collector who built custom cabinets to hold his massive collection of VHS tapes, making them easily accessible in his living room. Grandpa Jerry's collection of war films featured tough-guy lawmen like John Wayne and Gary Cooper, and I've captured many of these icons here. One of my earliest memories of watching a film with Grandpa Jerry was seeing *High Noon* in his living room as a young kid with my brothers. Thank you, Grandpa Jerry, for all you've done to shape my upbringing and for your influence on my life.

And to everyone along the way who either read drafts and offered criticism, or helped with copy editing and proofreading, I am forever grateful you were on this journey with me. As the saying holds, no man is an island; we all depend on others to achieve and advance professionally and personally.

Introduction

The widespread policing most are familiar with today began in America at the start of the twentieth century, just as American film moved from the nickelodeon to the big screen as a more developed art form. Thus, the history of modern law enforcement and American cinema, in many ways, both parallel and intersect each other. Most importantly for this study, since the inception of contemporary cinema, modern law enforcement has been an ongoing topic of entertainment in American film.

Therefore, this study asserts that the American public's changing perception of police officers in the first half of the twentieth century can be found by tracing their many manifestations in American film in this period. While it is important to note that a movie is an art form, and not history per se, it can, however, be asserted that, in many ways, film both shapes and refracts popular cultural perceptions, thereby allowing the historian to locate and analyze these perceptions within the film archive. To adequately represent the changes in on-screen depictions of law enforcement from the inception of American film up until the first half of the twentieth century, each chapter in this work analyzes numerous movies from several different, earlier eras of cinema. In particular, this study focuses on the ways filmmakers presented law enforcement's changing roles in society, and especially the portrayals of whether police were considered to be either effective or ineffective, and whether or not they were considered a force that was working for the greater good of the community.

The relative dearth of scholarly treatment specifically on early police representations in American film, and especially from a historiographical approach, makes this research a significant contribution. The closest work to this investigation is M. Ray Lott's broad discussion *Police on Screen: Hollywood Cops, Detectives, Marshalls, and Rangers*, wherein he covers approximately 100 years of film. However, Lott's extensive

Introduction

examination does not provide a precise focus on film's early years. While there is, of course, much scholarly research in the area of early film, when it comes to characterization, most film criticism focuses on civilians, including representations of criminals and ordinary folk, while what is absent are more delineated representations of law enforcement. One would expect the opposite, however, primarily because of the film industry's often rocky early relationship with the police, although, of course, much has been written about the film industry's grievances over issues of morality, law, and censorship.[1]

While Lott's aforementioned work influences this study, his broad-ranging coverage of the representations of law enforcement from cinema's inception through the 2000s is somewhat misleading because his work mainly analyzes films from the mid-twentieth to the twenty-first century, instead of the first half of the twentieth century. In addition, recent popular cultural studies provide scholarship that focuses on the figure of the American gangster. However, they do not examine representations of the antagonist to that gangster—the police officer. Therefore, it is fair to state that there has not yet been an in-depth study of law enforcement from the period of early film through the mid-twentieth century. This research thus aims to fill this gap in scholarship by tracing the evolution of police portrayals in early cinema because, as mentioned, film is a site where public sentiments toward the police are both created and reflected.

The changing representations of the police in American film additionally parallels America's challenges in the first half of the twentieth century, including rapidly changing technologies and the influx of immigrants. Silent films often depicted the police as sometimes good, albeit dense, guys, and they were portrayed with resentment or parodied, even in the protagonist role. They were also often depicted as heavy-handed, quick to use brutality, or quick to draw their pistol to force compliance. Police officers were additionally, at times, even seen as symbols of the government that were against the very people they served. For example, D.W. Griffith's *A Corner in Wheat* (1909) portrays police as agents of the government: two officers beat needy family members for arguing with a baker over the prohibitive rising prices of wheat while a greedy tycoon manipulates the world's wheat market for personal gain. This film both reflects the sentimentalism of American silent cinema and presents a clear message—the police are not on the side of the poor.

This rich-versus-poor theme, and the corresponding unfairness

Introduction

of the justice system, also appears in Edwin S. Porter's *The Kleptomaniac* (1905), which tells the tale of two women committing theft. One woman is wealthy and shoplifts from a department store, while the other woman is poor and steals bread to feed her hungry children; this contrast reflects the influence of the Reform movements in the nineteenth and early twentieth centuries. Both women are arrested and brought before the court. The police in this film are depicted purely in their procedural roles but are also reflections of the justice system. The wealthy woman is let go, while the poor woman who stole to feed her family is punished. This early silent film was another sign of the times, demonstrating a weary public attitude toward the police and a justice system that, at times, was unfair. These films appeared in the Progressive era (1890–1920), a period rife with social reform initiatives and accompanying trepidations in the forefront of American consciousness and which also influenced social perceptions of the police.

Silent film directors Wallace McCutcheon and Edwin S. Porter were concerned about an ambivalent perception of the police that circulated both in society and film, and thus they co-directed *Life of an American Policeman* (1905), a movie about the New York City Police Department. By following a day in the life of a policeman, the film intends to send a clear message that the police are concerned with wholesome family values, exist for the betterment of the community, and are a proper force to serve and protect the community. At a time when crime films that sympathized with the criminal appeared en masse, this film presented a much-needed alternative view. In its further effort to support law enforcement, *Life of an American Policeman* also raised money for the Police Relief Fund with two vaudeville showings in New York City.[2]

From the above examples, it is evident that the dualistic depictions of law enforcement officers in early American cinema are complicated in many ways, all of which this study seeks to explore. Chapter I analyzes the histories of both modern policing techniques and early silent film. By the early twentieth century, police reforms had already begun, such as required civil service, civilian oversight committees, and allowing women and minorities to serve in department jobs.[3] The rise of police unions also helped to contribute to this reform movement.[4] During this period, by creating a paid police force, federal, state, and local police departments ended the former days of volunteers and a reliance on vigilantes to enforce laws. Training and employment requirements were standardized. Law enforcement became an independent entity and potential career choice.

Introduction

During this same period, the former days of popular entertainment as primarily purveyed through vaudeville and live theater had given way to the cinema, which moved from shorts flickering dimly at nickelodeons to full-length narrative movies.[5] The days of live actors portraying a storyline on stage with props, where one show at a time took place, were now replaced with showing the same film in numerous theaters across the country. It was the invention of celluloid, which allowed the camera to record action, that moved live performances to recorded ones. In 1889, Thomas Edison and his assistant, William K.L. Dickson, invented a working moving picture camera. Their first film recorded a man bowing, smiling, and leaving the frame. From that moment on, film technology advanced briskly in rapid developments that continues today; similarly, technological advancements for law enforcement are also constantly progressing.

Chapter I also presents a discussion on early forms of film censorship, a result of local ordinances that provided police departments superior oversight to decide whether or not to issue a viewing license in their jurisdiction. Since these forms of censorship were interpretative, censorship arguments took place simultaneously in police stations across the country, while the film industry sought to remove the power from the police, opting instead for forms of self-regulation. These evolutions of censorship regarding police and self-regulation from inception through the first half of the twentieth century also appear in Chapter I.

Chapter II covers critical early films wherever law enforcement appears. For example, Edison's 1894 *Robetta and Doretto [No. 2]*, also known as *Chinese Laundry*, is where the first visual portrayal of a law enforcement officer in uniform recorded on film begins. Robetta and Doretto were popular vaudeville actors who performed their act "Heap Fun Laundry" at the close of Tony Pastor's vaudeville production. They brought their act to Edison's "Black Maria" for filming during the week of November 26, 1894, along with many other vaudeville actors who also had their performances captured for Edison's Kinetoscope viewer. *Chinese Laundry* in its simplest form is a brief vaudeville slapstick comedy that was popular during these nascent days of first filmmaking; however, its limited narrative construct is worthy of moral and allegorical value. *Sherlock Holmes Baffled* (1900) is another early visual illustration of a law enforcement agent on film and is perhaps the first ever recorded detective film. Most likely recorded as an example of film trickery, the "stop trick" (stop motion) editing technique developed in 1896 by

Introduction

French director Georges Méliès, the film invites a multi-layered analysis of its representation of law enforcement. Another example is Wallace McCutcheon's *How They Rob Men in Chicago* (1900), a portrayal of a corrupt police officer. It this short film, a well-dressed senior man is on a sidewalk looking into the distance when a robber sneaks up behind the man and clubs him on the back of his head. The victim collapses on the sidewalk. As the robber flees, a uniformed police officer instantaneously enters the frame and finds the victim unconscious, as well as some of the victim's money that the thief has inadvertently left behind. The officer picks up the money, tucks it into his police duty-belt, and walks off, without any regard for the victim. Most, however, would agree that this view of police corruption is hardly a representation of decent law enforcement in early film, a topic that Chapter II explores further.

Chapter II further sharpens its historical focus to the short silent representations of law enforcement during the early silent film era. Films discussed in this chapter also include *A Gesture Fight in Hester Street* (1900), *How They Do Things on the Bowery* (1902), *The Moonshiners* (1904), *Life of an American Policeman* (1905), *The Kleptomaniac* (1905), *The Black Hand* (1906), *Fights of Nations* (1907), *A Corner in Wheat* (1909), *The Musketeers of Pig Alley* (1912), and *Suspense* (1913). The discussion of these films attempts to present a balance regarding representations. However, in the volumes of early cinema, most depictions of law enforcement are shown as incidental to their interactions with criminals or their portrayals as agents of the state. *The Great Train Robbery* (1903), arguably the first crime film, directed by Edwin S. Porter and produced by the Edison Manufacturing Company, is a prime example.[6] At only twelve minutes long, the film is action-packed with scenes of violence—innocent people are shot, a clerk is assaulted and tied up, a train employee is viciously bludgeoned with a rock and thrown from a moving train, a fleeing hostage is shot in the back—all while the camera focuses on the criminals in their aim to pillage and kill. The posse of citizens who eventually hunt and shoot down the robbers is a representation of law enforcement. While the film presents the viewer with a sense of justice—that crime cannot go unpunished, and those whose commit a crime will be held accountable—the short time for which these brave citizens appear at the end of *The Great Train Robbery* is very telling. It shows just how much emphasis in film narrative and plot was spent on the criminals and how early cinema was often sympathetic to the criminal's quest for upward mobility, especially when dealing with outlaws or urban gangsters.[7] This type of narrative also occurs because

Introduction

early filmmakers were aiming at their audience, the urban poor, and thus plots of this sort were popular.[8]

Moreover, each selected film in Chapter II depicts the appearance of law enforcement agents on film and how that appearance matters in context with the concurrent law enforcement climate in New York City while filmmakers and the police were simultaneously occupying the same public sphere. Chapter II highlights the Lexow Committee of 1894 that identified corrupt New York City police officials, such as then-captain William "Bill" Devery, a Tammany Hall collection man who illegally enriched himself with payoffs to acquire enough wealth to later become a co-owner of the Yankees baseball team; Inspector Alexander "Clubber" Williams, the archetypal figure of police brutality known for viciously clubbing thugs with or without provocation; and Detective Commander Thomas Byrnes, whose violent interrogations of criminals were contemporaneously represented in popular culture and from which the term third degree (a euphemism for torture) during interrogations is said to have originated as perhaps a pun on his name, third-degree "burns."[9] Chapter II, as well as every chapter in this book, is not encyclopedic, encompassing every film where law enforcement appears. However, the carefully chosen films offer a preponderance of correlations between the police, concurrent events, and their portrayals in early films.

Chapter III discusses longer feature films, such as *Traffic in Souls* (1913), *Easy Street* (1917), and *Cops* (1922), during the early silent film era. Although *Cops* is part of the late silent film era (1920–1927), it is included in this chapter because it succinctly dovetails the discussion of *Easy Street*, and other late silent era films such as *Underworld* (1927) fit appropriately elsewhere in Chapter IV. Each of these films provides representations of law enforcement, their roles in society, and, in general, how the public viewed them. Technological advancements in film led to feature films, which were much longer in length than previous works, and allowed for fuller developed narratives, characters, plots, and scenes. *Traffic in Souls* exposes "white slavery" (prostitution), and *Easy Street* centers on social anomie, police ineffectiveness, and police brutality, whereas *Cops* largely focuses on an unfair justice system, police brutality, and negative public sentiment toward law enforcement. All three films show how creative filmmakers used their works to create awareness, suggest reform, and placate viewers who craved storylines that exposed social issues they were contemporaneously enduring.

While the early imagery of policing on film largely represents a

Introduction

recklessly brutal and systemically corrupt force, the Reform era transitioned the police toward modern professionalization. During the 1910s Americans were intrigued with witty and brave police detectives, mostly in urban areas, following their criminal manhunts in the newspapers. Therefore, in the era when *Traffic in Souls*, *Easy Street* and *Cops* were filmed, the detective film serials were very popular. Ruth Mayer, a film scholar who concentrates on detective film serials of the late 1910s and 1920s, finds that the detective serial is "a dramatically under-researched format."[10] Detective serials were mainly low-budget mass entertainments that offered a wealth of information about law enforcement and societal perceptions and filmic representations. The detective serials grew from popular literary works of the late nineteenth century that started as weekly features in magazines, presenting characters such as Nick Carter, who began as a dime-novel detective in 1886. These stories of the famous fictional detective proliferated, and in 1891, Carter's adventures were serialized in the *Nick Carter Detective Library*. There are many points of comparison between early literary works and the early detective serials. And storylines involving detectives in procedurals in film noir abound in subsequent decades.

The film serial was designed to provide weekly entertainment to moviegoers who were treated to action and excitement, with a routine cliffhanger to entice viewers to return the following week. Edison Studio's *What Happened to Mary*, although not a detective serial concerning governmental or private investigators, did, however, provide the investigatory pursuits of its heroine, Mary Fuller, who sought to uncover her family background while mysterious forces complicated her efforts and attempted to gain control over her. Similar to the protagonists of many of the detective serials of the 1910s and 1920s, Fuller enacts the lay role of the investigator, thus resembling much later, yet similar, storylines. *What Happened to Mary* began America's fascination with the serial film and consisted of twelve one-reel silent episodes.[11] Collectively, the detective serials contributed to "discourses of criminality and detection that were tightly interlocked, and conversely, the figures of the detective and of the master criminal gained central importance in the mass-cultural narratives."[12] The serials were significant because they revealed representations of detectives conducting investigations. Serials also gave audiences an additional view of investigators as laypersons or detectives, which were also springing up at the time and who were independent of police departments. The private investigator would become a favorite film character in subsequent decades. However, there

Introduction

has been very little scholarly research on exactly how these films represent a relationship to law enforcement.

In contrast, studies that showcase the emergence of mass culture during the early silent film era provide a much better look into representations of law enforcement. Rob King's *The Fun Factory: The Keystone Film Company and the Emergence of Mass Culture* explains how Keystone "fashioned a style of film comedy from the roughhouse humor of cheap theater, [and pioneered] modes of representation that satirized film industry attempts at uplift."[13] King's work reveals how the Keystone Kops and their high-energy short films had a significant impact on society and, notably, how early law enforcement in the Keystone films characterized the police as being inept and worthy of lampoon. However, this depiction of the police was not, of course, necessarily always accurate in reality; one must consider that filmmakers were presenting these particular views of law enforcement to the masses because the urban poor preferred to see them.

When one thinks of the Keystone Kops, chances are they envision images of film scenes where the officers' faces convey a heightened sense of stupefaction. One hundred years after the popular film series, that comedic depiction of law enforcement still survives in our collective consciousness. For example, just over a decade ago, Senator Joseph Lieberman used the label of Keystone Kops to criticize the emergency personnel who worked under the Department of Homeland Security's (DHS) chief Michael Chertoff. Senator Lieberman claimed that the workers were running "around like Keystone Kops, uncertain about what they were supposed to do or uncertain how to do it."[14] Even more recently, *New Yorker* contributor John Cassidy criticized President Donald Trump and his White House by referring to them as the "Keystone Kops" in charge of the country.[15] The Keystone Kops provided the intertextual influence for Charles Chaplin's *Easy Street* (1917), a topic discussed in Chapter III.

An illustration of early societal views concerning law enforcement, Charlie Chaplin's *Easy Street* is an example par excellence. In the film, Chaplin's Tramp is appointed as a policeman in a troubled neighborhood. The film emphasizes how police are often on the front lines of societal change, tasked with the responsibility of fighting social issues and cultural blight, in addition to enforcing laws and caring for the community. Chapter III thus presents how the law enforcement realities in each of these films also affected the reception of the nation's rapidly-expanding police departments.

Introduction

Chapter IV focuses on the representations of policemen that populated film in the sound era (1926–1934), or the age of the "talkies." In the 1920s, America had also established a sizable number of organized suburban police departments, with forces composed of uniformed police officers that had replaced the old law enforcement of local constables or marshals. In the 1920s, Americans outside of the major cities were now familiar with the role of the law enforcement officer and no longer expected justice upheld by a few brave civilians or the victims themselves. Police now regularly arrested criminals and brought them before the court. Additionally, police agencies offered jobs to civilians, employing them to handle the extra paperwork associated with policing in the modern age.

These many changes in the world of policing during the first half of the twentieth century increased the public's fascination with the exploits of the new local and federal agencies. For example, national newspapers and radio programs covered the early FBI and their "G" Men as they hunted down outlaws and gangsters on lengthy manhunts that often spanned several states over the course of months. The narrative of the manhunt, or the pursuit of criminals, became a staple storyline in popular culture. American true crime readers and moviegoers raptly followed the work of detectives, who hunted down dangerous—and, occasionally, not so dangerous—criminals.

Films in the 1930s also tended to romanticize the criminal gangster, even more so than in previous and subsequent decades. As James O'Kane notes, "Rarely does the public honor the gangster of today, as it did some of those of the Prohibition era when the prestige of the gangster reached phenomenal proportions."[16] The move toward a more sympathetic criminal was a result of the 18th Amendment to the Constitution, which tremendously expanded organized crime, making lawbreakers out of ordinary Americans who created lucrative businesses bootlegging prohibited alcohol. The 18th Amendment banned the sale, production, and transportation of "intoxicating liquors" from January 17, 1920, to December 5, 1933. The National Prohibition Act, also known informally as the Volstead Act for its author Congressman Andrew Volstead, was created to enforce the 18th Amendment. During the Great Depression, the enterprise of selling alcohol made gangsters such as Alphonse Capone into Robin Hood–like characters. During the late 1920s and 1930s, Americans were enthralled with the upward mobility of the American outlaw and urban gangsters such as John H. Dillinger and Al Capone. Gangsters—unlike law-abiding citizens—had a chance

Introduction

of forging a better life for themselves, while also wreaking havoc on the very governing body that everyday people blamed for their own dire, poverty-stricken predicament.

The seminal film that marks the gangster era is Josef von Sternberg's silent film *Underworld* (1927). Its protagonist is the gangster kingpin Bull Weed (George Bancroft), a notorious criminal with a seeming heart of gold who helps out those who most need it. While fleeing from a robbery, Bull stops to help a person with quadriplegia begging for money, and he also cares for a hungry kitten. Clearly, by casting him in a favorable light, the film intends to have the audience sympathize with the criminal. During the late 1920s and early 1930s in the age of the "talkies," film narratives placed a heavy emphasis on protagonist criminals, mostly ignoring law enforcement officers as protagonists.

Films such as *Little Caesar* (1931), *The Public Enemy* (1931), and *Scarface* (1931) are each told from the view of a criminal protagonist, one who offers a romanticized view of the criminal underworld. Most of these romanticized criminals are sentimentally portrayed as victims of circumstance: through no fault of their own, it was the economy, poverty, unfair morality laws, or the government that kept them down. Oddly enough, many early crime films often depicted the police as just another gang. In these films, the police use similar extralegal methods as criminals did to pursue their professional objectives, while also often taking their fight on crime very personally. They are routinely depicted as locked in a rivalry with the criminals over turf while battling for the admiration of the public.

However, for the most part, due to the enforcement of film censorship by mid–1934, these roles reversed again when the Production Code Administration (PCA), led by Joseph I. Breen, began enforcing the rules of the Motion Picture Production Code (the Code) of 1930. The PCA was derived from an enforcement amendment to the Code requiring all films released after July 1, 1934, to obtain a seal of approval before being released.[17] The Code is also known informally as the Hays Code, named after the first chairman of the Motion Picture Producers and Distributors of America (MPPDA)—later known at the Motion Picture Association of American (MPAA)—William H. Hays. Under Hays's leadership, the Code was adopted in 1930 and strict adherence to the rules, such as criminals "should not be made heroes, even if they are historically," was in full effect by mid–1934.[18]

Therefore, actors who had previously played roles as villains were now starring as heroic lawmen in pursuit of despicable villains. For

Introduction

example, James Cagney transitioned from his notorious criminal characters in the early 1930s to a brave lawman in *"G" Men* (1935). Other films sympathetic to law enforcement, such as *Public Hero Number 1* (1935), *Whipsaw* (1935), *36 Hours to Kill* (1936), and *Midnight Taxi* (1937), made their way to the big screen. The remaking of law enforcement's image in the 1930s, in fact, opened the way for film noirs of the 1940s to include numerous roles for their intelligent, tough detectives and private investigators.

Accounts of representations of law enforcement in film during the 1930s and subsequent decades is found in several disciplines, including Gender Studies, and is often focused on the role of the detective and private investigator (P.I.)—either male or female—who were portrayed as agents of justice hunting down violent criminals, solving crimes and restoring order to the community. Philippa Gates's exhaustive work concentrates separately on men and women in detective roles in two works: *Detecting Women: Gender and the Hollywood Detective Film* and *Detecting Men: Masculinity and the Hollywood Detective Film*.[19] In *Detecting Women*, Gates argues that Hollywood's depiction of women as detectives appeared more as "peripheral products" in 1930s B films. In *Detecting Men*, Gates writes that much of the focus on the detective genre is highly concentrated on film noir; however, there is much to learn from the history of the character of the detective prior to this era. Gates argues that the character of the detective in film reflects changing social attitudes toward masculinity, as well as how these representations impacted ideals about muscularity, heroism, national identity, and law and order. Gates asserts that the detective genre film, which can be an outlet for both an expression of and remedy for problematic social issues, thus resolves social anxieties about constructs of masculinity and crime. Throughout the history of Hollywood detective films, the portrayals of the detective reveal American constructs of maleness and masculinity.

Continuing with the contrasts between filmic representations of the policeman and criminal, Chapter V analyzes portrayals of law enforcement in perhaps the wealthiest era in American film for this theme: film noir (early 1940s to late 1950s). A French term meaning "dark" or "black" film, film noir is essentially that—films that use night scenes, deep shadows, tight settings and camera angles, all designed to create a feeling of anxiety.[20] M. Ray Lott claims that in film noir, "the police and detective narratives, the night and the shadows were indicative of the characters in the films: women whose hearts were in total eclipse, and men

Introduction

who found themselves both prey to these women, and victims of a world where traditional moral values left them ill-prepared to survive."[21] An absence of Hollywood films in France from 1940 to 1946 caused French film critics, such as Nino Frank, to view them collectively when they finally arrived; it was Frank who, in 1946, observed a dark and gloomy pattern among American films of the war period.[22] This distinct style of film led Frank to first label them as film noir.[23] In film noir, private detectives were often those who solved the criminal mysteries, a move which only emphasized police ineptitude.[24]

By the 1940s, film noir had become a popular style of film; this extended into the 1950s. The types of narratives informing film noir were derived from the "hard-boiled" forms of American crime fiction in previous decades, such as the work of Raymond Chandler. As Paul Schrader observes,

> When the movies of the Forties turned to the American "tough" moral understrata, the "hard-boiled" school was waiting with preset conventions of heroes, minor characters, plots, dialogue and themes. Like German expatriates, the "hard-boiled" writers had a style made to order for the *film noir*, and in turn they influenced *noir* screenwriting as much as German film influenced *noir* cinematography.[25]

Many of the aesthetics of film noir were derived not only from German films but also from the German filmmakers who had fled Europe and were then working in Hollywood.[26] Raymonde Borde and Etienne Chaumeton, in their essay "The Source of Film Noir," find that "hard-boiled stories" are the "immediate source" of the film noir.[27] Originating in earlier decades, hard-boiled crime fiction appeared in the cheap pulp magazines that grew as an extension of the dime novel, with *Detective Story Magazine* being the first of its kind in the genre beginning in 1915. *Detective Story Magazine* was widely popular and ran until 1949, comprising 1,057 issues.[28] The *Black Mask* was the most significant hard-boiled magazine. It featured many of the best detective crime writers, including Raymond Chandler and Dashiell Hammett.

By the early 1940s American readers of detective crime fiction in prior decades were viewing these hard-boiled detectives on the big screen, beginning with *The Maltese Falcon* (1941)—then in its third version produced by Warner Bros.—the first "faithfully hard-boiled film" of the decade.[29] With this film, a significant shift in the portrayal of law enforcement in film is exemplified by the difference between the classical detective, whose role is to investigate from a distance while drawing attention to the socially disruptive crime, and the hard-boiled detective

Introduction

who was more immersed in the crime milieu "and is tested by it in a more physical and life-threatening manner."[30]

The most drastic shift in representations appearing in film noir of the 1940s is the role of the P.I.—the archetypal hard-boiled hero who presents an alternate view of law enforcement. Unlike detectives of the previous decades, the P.I. operates, as Frank Krutnik observes, as a "mediator between the criminal underworld and the world of respectable society."[31] The P.I. has a significant advantage over traditional detectives because they can "move freely between the two worlds, without really being a part of either."[32] They're tough, at times charming, and portrayed as highly intellectual and capable of outthinking criminals and the police. The P.I. is calm in the criminal's milieu, often capable of blurring his role as an investigator.

James Naremore's assessment of Borde and Chaumeton's seminal work, *A Panorama of American Film Noir, 1941–1953*, that sometimes treats film noir "as if it could be defined as an artistic style or a sociological phenomenon," argues that sometimes Borde and Chaumeton make "it seem like a loosely connected series than like an anti-genre representing the flip side of the average Hollywood feature."[33] Naremore supports his position by pointing out that Borde and Chaumeton use the example that unlike the police procedural of its time, "noir is usually told from the viewpoint of the criminal, who sometimes elicits our sympathy."[34]

Many noir films focus on the fight between good and evil by romanticizing the interplay between cops and criminals, while often obscuring the distinctions between them. The narratives of film noir usually follow the investigative process of the tough guy detective, or the uncontrollable private investigator, as they pursue criminals who are generally wanted for homicide. Representations of law enforcement during the period of film noir appear in many figures, such as private investigators in *The Maltese Falcon* (1941), *The Big Sleep* (1946), and *The Dark Corner* (1946), the police detective in *The Big Heat* (1953), or professional police officers working cases, such as in *The Naked City* (1948) and *Where the Sidewalk Ends* (1950).

The P.I. of the 1940s film noir is markedly different from the police investigator in earlier films. The noir private investigator moves freely between respectable society and the criminal underworld. Although a surrogate for law enforcement, he is often depicted as working on both sides of the law, being deceitful with police and committing his crimes while in pursuit of justice. While robust, the noir detective is most often

Introduction

a targeted victim of the femme fatale—the mysterious, highly attractive, and seductive female antagonist whose lustful attraction ensnares her lovers/suitors in difficulties that lead to dangerous, and often deadly, scenarios. Films such as *This Gun for Hire* (1942), *Double Indemnity* (1944), *The Woman in the Window* (1944), *The Postman Always Rings Twice* (1946), and *D.O.A.* (1949) accentuate the femme fatale. These films depict plots with a man on the lam because of his guilt, because of a crime committed by the femme fatale, or as an accomplice to a crime she has urged the seduced male into committing for her. Chapter V thus analyzes the ambiguous character of the private investigator in film noir as he works both with and against the police department.

In Otto Preminger's *Where the Sidewalk Ends* (1950), the police detective is a quintessential noir-era private detective. The film exhibits the old ways of interrogating suspects with the use of the third degree to coerce confessions during interrogations and the struggles of the police characters involved. It also displays how, in light of the Wickersham Commission, police departments were modernizing and distancing themselves from this method of brutal interrogations.[35] The protagonist, Detective Mark Dixon (Dana Andrews), accidentally kills a man in self-defense, covers it up, and dumps the man's body in the East River. He is eventually arrested on his admission, thus exemplifying the ambiguous character of the film noir detective as both a criminal and a law enforcement hero.

Film noirs hung around for a short while after the soldiers returned from the war in 1946, due to a slight recession and the many sacrifices during World War II. However, by the early 1950s, film noir had, in part, vanished due to many factors, including an improvement in the national mood after the war ended. During this time, the nation looked forward in a hopeful manner to the coming economic boom and away from the concerns of urban decay and the existential crisis that had previously been at the forefront of the American consciousness.

By 1953, America was celebrating its victory as the newly-crowned most powerful nation in the world and films reflected this optimism. America was at the beginning of a global postwar economic boom that would safeguard capitalism's future in the West. In tandem with America's strong exceptionalism during the 1950s ran a sign of respect for law and order. It was the time of American strength—the days when George Reeves, the "Man of Steel" in *The Adventures of Superman* television series, cleared the streets of crime and protected the planet. It was the time of the honest, trustworthy, wholesome paternal figures

Introduction

of *Dragnet* detectives, who worked within the boundaries of the law to fight crime and to defend the weak. Detectives in 1950s movies solved cases through their reliable, rational methods of deduction, rarely beat their suspects, and treated everyone with respect. It was the days of John Wayne, a symbol of a "real man," one who stood for nostalgic, warm, simple white authoritarian paternalism. It was the time of Gary Cooper in *High Noon* (1952), playing Marshall Will Kane, the local force who can civilize the world. The murkiness of the law and police representations in the noir-era yielded to the strong-willed defenders of the universe because, with America as the superpower of the world, there was now a whole world to defend.

The Coda offers a discussion of *High Noon* (1952) and how the movie illustrates where law enforcement was headed during the 1950s, thus providing a contrast to filmic representations of police in prior periods. The Coda additionally gestures toward future areas of inquiry and investigation of representations of law enforcement in film, suggesting that subsequent studies parse more completely law enforcement representations in film to build upon the findings of this study. Through the analyses of the selected films presented, this study provides an essential contribution to the understanding of portrayals of law enforcement in American film and their evolution from the early beginnings of American film to the middle of the twentieth century.

I

Early Twentieth-Century Law Enforcement and Cinema

The history of law enforcement, of course, begins much earlier than the advent of the cinema. However, what is commonly understood as modern law enforcement today began to evolve at the start of the twentieth century, just as aesthetic and technological advances in film provided a new medium of entertainment and representation. Taken together, these two entities, law enforcement and film, which although at first seem strikingly different, not only evolved closely in tandem, while continually improving, but also overlap in meaningful ways. What follows is how their tandem history provides an important context for an understanding of how both public perceptions and filmic refractions of law enforcement, as represented in early American film, influenced public views on law enforcement.

Most early law enforcers were not officially sworn-in officers as they are today, and they appear in many versions, characterized by forms such as kin policing in England during the Medieval period when family members were responsible for pursuing justice for acts against them (robbery, theft, assault, trespassing, etc.).[1] Family members who were unofficial agents of law enforcement were expected to hunt down criminals who harmed their relative(s), and to seek justice, in whatever ways they deemed sufficient. Thus, in antiquity, a punishment was highly varied in terms of severity. What one family felt was adequate punishment for theft, for example, another may have thought was not enough, so they would levy an even harsher sentence at the end of an ox-whip or club, or even through death.[2] The meaning of restorative justice, therefore, was highly interpretable.[3] Many of these views for meting out justice are still with us today, even though society has moved away from crimes committed against persons to crimes committed against the state. In other words, defendants who are brought before the criminal courts now stand in opposition to the state, not the victim. It is thus the state's responsibility to prove guilt beyond a reasonable doubt, and therefore the sense and meaning of justice for crime victims is sometimes blurred.

Cinema capitalized on the emotionally-driven force of kin policing early on. The closing minutes of George Loane Tucker's *Traffic in Souls* (1913), when an infuriated mob attacks Mr. William Trubus (William Turner), the wealthy social elitist who hides his misdeeds in the prostitution underworld by heading the International Purity and Reform League, is a prime example. Trubus is eventually exposed as a fraud and arrested. When he is released on bail and heads for a vehicle parked outside of the police precinct, an angry mob rushes him, causing the police to fight them back with batons. This scene presents a visual representation of the police on the frontline between order and disorder. It also shows the strong emotional reality of the citizenry taking justice into their own hands—a propensity that has existed for as long as humankind itself. And it is a reality that will continue, regardless of how crimes are challenged in a court of law. More contemporary examples include a parent attacking a defendant in court who had harmed their child or hunting the offenders down themselves to take justice into their own hands.[4]

Early examples of uniformed law enforcement are found in early Mesopotamia at a time when there was constant warfare between cities, although these representations are not indicative of any formally organized law enforcement entity. In these early representations, captured Nubian slaves were forced to wear different color clothing and function as "mercenary-like" forces that patrolled marketplaces and communities.[5] Ancient Greek cities also used African slaves to protect both marketplaces and royalty.[6] These slaves were chosen in particular because of their different appearance, which distinguished them from the citizenry; thus Greece's use of African slaves as protectors is arguably among the first attempts at making law enforcement personnel stand out.[7] However, their use of slaves was either short-lived or ended in outright failure.[8]

The Praetorian Guard created by Cesar Augustus, after the assassination of Julius Caesar, is an example of early versions of law enforcement that more closely resembles policing in recent centuries and is another attempt to make law enforcement personnel stand out.[9] The Praetorians were an elite unit of the Imperial Roman Army and served as special bodyguard forces for the Roman emperors. They identified and eliminated trouble among the citizenry, and as many as one-third of

I. Early Twentieth-Century Law Enforcement and Cinema

the guards worked undercover and conducted surveillance on citizens.[10] They were heavily involved in Roman politics, to the point of overthrowing emperors and choosing their successors, and were known for assassination plots. Constantine the Great eventually disbanded them in 312 AD, but their legacy continued, and the term "precinct" survived as a holdover from when Praetorians, operated in "precincts," or areas they were defined to protect.[11] Precincts are still familiar in many urban areas, including New York City.

During the Medieval period, law enforcement occurred in families or village groups, such as mentioned with kin policing in Britain that kept criminals and other outsiders out of their communities.[12] However, following the Norman invasion in 1066, English law instituted by King William formed a community-policing model where units, or "tithings," consisted of every male over twelve years old and enforced the law, such as those prohibiting murder and theft.[13] An area controlled by a constable called "hundreds" consisted of ten tithings. Ten hundreds were a "shire," which was overseen by a "shire-reeve."[14] The shire-reeve, or what we know today as the sheriff, was the top law enforcement official responsible for overseeing the apprehension of criminals, and who reported directly to the crown.[15] After the tithing system, a watch system was set up to combat the lawlessness that was a pervasive problem. The passage of the Statute of Winchester in 1285, comprised of six chapters, "sought to replace the weakened tithing system with the parish constable system."[16] This system required one man from each parish to serve unpaid duty as constable during the day and also to work with additional unpaid men at night to protect the community.[17] Although it "shifted the formal responsibilities for policing to the parish constables, in effect, every man continued to be responsible for policing his community."[18] This form of policing survived from the Norman Conquest to the Metropolitan Police Act of 1829, when an act of Parliament introduced by Sir Robert Peel established the Metropolitan Police of London—the first modern police force. The Metropolitan officers, called "bobbies" or "peelers" (both named after Peel), originated the slang term "coppers" from the copper badges worn on their uniforms.[19]

Across the ocean in colonial America, law enforcement functioned in two systems that operated simultaneously: (1) the French system, dating back to Holy Roman Emperor/King Charlemagne, where gendarmes (from the medieval French expression *gens d'armes* which translates to "armed men") were agents of the crown and (2) the English preference that involved volunteers and the constable arrangement.[20] Among the colonies, the volunteer and constable schemes were the preferred law enforcement methods.[21] Policing during this period was "both informal and communal," which is described as the "Watch," or private, and "The Big Stick," or for-profit policing.[22] The first watch system of community volunteers was created as a night watch in Boston in 1636 and mainly served to warn of approaching perils.[23] New York and Philadelphia followed suit in 1658 and 1700, respectively. The night watch was ineffective as a crime control design because many of these volunteer night watchmen joined with ulterior motives in mind, such as the avoidance of military service, or they were forced into service by their community or were performing the duties as a punishment.[24] A system of constables added to the watch systems, where official officers provided law enforcement services, such as executing warrants on a fee-based system and supervising the night watch volunteers in several cities.[25] Both the watch and constable systems operated simultaneously.

Before the American Civil War, the organizing of formal police departments continued with large agencies, such as that in New York City, which in 1845 became the first of its kind to operate in the form understood today as modern policing. For the first time, policing services operated around the clock in a standardized singular force. Albany and Chicago came next in 1851, Cincinnati and New Orleans in 1853, Boston in 1854, and Philadelphia and Newark, New Jersey, in 1855. After the Civil War, cities around the country began to incorporate police departments (and later municipalities in the early 1900s). In the early days of policing, many of the departments were ineffective because city political machines, such as Tammany Hall, used the departments for political expedience, thereby much compromising their effectiveness in terms of law enforcement. For example, political corruption involving the municipal police department in New York City was pervasive, and in 1857, legislators disbanded the force and created a new police department that included additional counties, placing the control of the department into the hands of five commissioners appointed by the governor and senate. New York City mayor Fernando Wood, a Tammany Hall political machine leader, refused to disband the police force, and a subsequent violent confrontation between the old and new policemen ensued on June 16, 1857, causing fifty-three injuries and the dispatch of the Seventh Regiment to intervene and quell the riot.[26]

The relationship between police and criminality and how they impacted one another in an historical context is also a massive part of the history of the late nineteenth century. To put it another way,

I. Early Twentieth-Century Law Enforcement and Cinema

throughout American cities the vice operations, especially gambling—since managers of this vice ranked higher on the scale of social acceptability—provided financial resources for politicians. Successful gambler and later politician (Democrat state senator and U.S. congressman) John Morrissey, leader of the New York gang the Dead Rabbits, is a significant example. Morrissey was backed by Tammany Hall and hired to stop William Poole, also known as Bill the Butcher, an enforcer for the Know-Nothing Party and leader of the Bowery Boys gang, from rigging political elections. Poole and his gang were infamous for stealing ballot boxes on Election Day. In exchange, Tammany Hall allowed Morrissey to operate a gambling house without interference from the police.

Law enforcement's close affiliation with politics and those in political power had survived like precincts had from the days of the Praetorians. For instance, since inception of a formal police department in New York City, the police officers were notoriously complicit with politicians in their corrupt efforts to enrich themselves. However, they were not equals. The politicians controlled the police and their enforcement duties. Political cartoonist S.D. Ehrhart's 1906 illustration "The Endless Game," which appeared as a centerfold in *Puck Magazine* on November 21, 1906, succulently captures this reality. Ehrhart's drawing depicts a game of chess between a hand labeled "Political Pull" showing a cufflink labeled "Brass Check" and a hand labeled "Reform." The chess board is labeled "[Depar]Tment of Police" and some of the squares are labeled "Race Track, Suburbs, White Lights, Gambling District, Goatville, Financial District, Tenderloin, Red Light District, Lonely Beat, [and] Hell's Kitchen." Ehrhart's chess pieces are police officers, some in plainclothes, and are labeled "Crooked Captain, Inspector, Sleuth, 'Fixed' Captain, Honest Captain, Grafting Captain, Honest Inspector, Plainclothes Man, [and] Sergeant." In other words, the police force—comprised of honest and corrupt officers—is externally controlled by hands not of their own (Figure 1). Although the Reform Movement contributed to the later professionalization of police departments, the flagrant truth is that since establishment of organized police forces, inherent corruption with political cronies is an undeniable matter of record.

This truth about police and political corruption helps, in part, to explain the attitude of early films and lower-class audiences. Sadly, there still exists today a deep involvement between politics and policing at all levels of law enforcement, and even more specifically, at the local level where politicians control municipal departments as well as in non-civil service departments that have a stronghold over hiring and promoting.[27]

Law Enforcement in American Cinema, 1894–1952

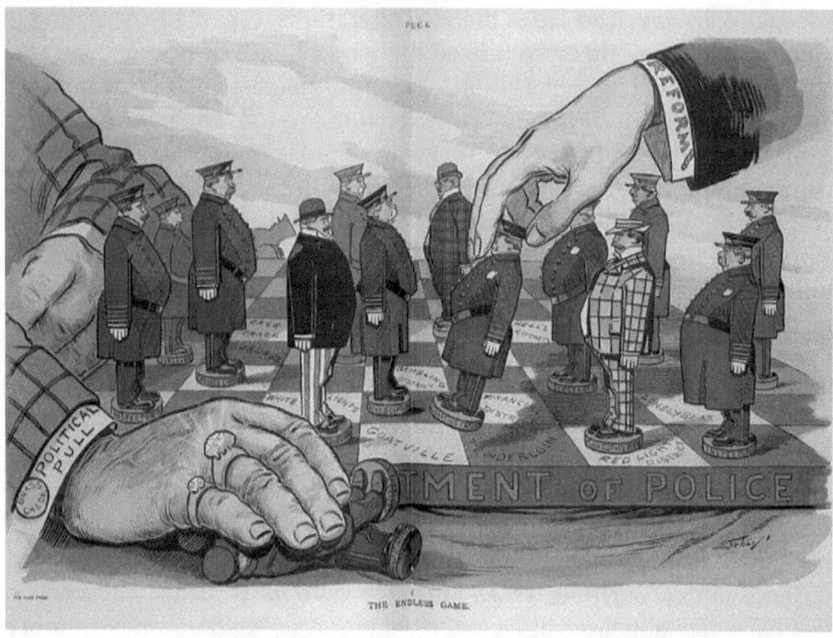

Figure 1. A political cartoon depicting a game of chess where external hands move police officers. 1906.

Though today politicians may go to great lengths to make it appear they are politically correct and divorced from the police departments, this could not be further from the truth. And since its inception, the American film industry has continually represented these harsh truths in its films.

Turning to the history of early film, film historian David Robinson notes the motion picture as we know it today was neither "invented," in a strict sense, nor developed over a "normal process of evolution."[28] It was instead derived from intermittent advances made over long periods of time, with each improvement emerging like a "piece of a puzzle" that when combined "perfected a device capable of producing and projecting animated photographs."[29] Robinson traces the first occurrence of antecedents to Venetian Giovanni da Fontana, who in 1420 "proposed the mischievous notion of painting demonic shapes on the horn window of an ordinary lantern in order to frighten people with grotesque shadows thereby cast upon a wall."[30] It would take another two and half centuries before this magic lantern "acquired the magic of precise representation" because "without a condenser to concentrate the lamplight

I. Early Twentieth-Century Law Enforcement and Cinema

or a lens to focus the image.... Giovanni's shadows must have been fairly vague."[31]

By the seventeenth century, the *laterna magica,* or magic lantern projector, had been invented by Christian Hugens, which he described in private correspondences exchanged in 1659.[32] At the time, Hugens found "little scientific value in the magic lantern and relegated it to entertainment purposes."[33] While the magic lantern is not a direct ancestor to the motion picture, in its advanced form it provided storytelling through a projection of images accomplished by the use of a light source onto a surface.[34] However, by the nineteenth century "the ambitions of the magic lantern clearly anticipated the cinema. The lantern was used to create narrative and spectacle; and from an early stage there was a dominant desire to make the screen image move."[35]

Before the invention of photography in 1839, "persistence of vision and the phi phenomenon were exploited for the purposed of optical entertainment."[36] Persistence of vision is when an "object does not cease for some time after the rays of light, proceeding from it, have ceased to enter the eye."[37] The phi phenomenon is an optical illusion that occurs when viewing still images in quick succession causes the appearance of motion. Hugo Münsterberg's theory of film derives from coupling persistence of vision and the phi phenomenon.[38] The Thaumatrope, a paper disc with strings attached to opposite points that could be twirled between fingers and thumbs to create the illusion of movement from different images imprinted on each face of the disc, was a favorite children's toy in the early nineteenth century.[39] The illusion of a moving picture occurred when spinning the disc: "the images seemed to merge into a single unified picture (a rider would mount a horse, a parrot entered its cage, etc.)."[40] After the Thaumatrope, the Phenakistoscope and the Zoetrope further advanced the illusion of moving images with the use of "some type of shutter device (usually a series of slots in the disc or cylinder itself) to produce the illusion of motion."[41]

The invention of still photography (Daguerreotype) in 1839 by Louis Jacques-Mande Daguerre allowed for the capturing of images that eventually led to the design of "series photography" by an Anglo-American photographer, Eadweard Muybridge.[42] In 1887, Muybridge used a series of twelve cameras electrically operated with a battery and wire stretched across a Sacramento horse racetrack to capture images of a horse galloping along the track. As the horse passed the wire, it tripped the shutters of the cameras.[43] Muybridge's technique captured the horse moving in successive stages and late in 1879 was demonstrated on a mechanism called the zoopraxiscope.[44] Although Muybridge recorded live-action continuously with the use of twelve separate cameras, "until the separate functions of these machines could be incorporated into a single instrument, the cinema could not be born."[45] In 1882 French physiologist Etienne-Jules Marey was the first to record series photographs in a single instrument with his invention of the portable "chronophotographic gun," which was shaped like a rifle and captured "twelve instantaneous photographs of movement per second and imprinted them on a rotating glass plate."[46]

The invention of celluloid was the next significant advance. Celluloid, or film stock, is the basis for any movie where the action is recorded by the camera on the film stock and then projected through a projector.[47] Early film stock consisted of glass plates or light-sensitive paper, but both of these materials were unable to accommodate motion pictures until 1889 when George Eastman developed flexible film.[48] In the same year, Thomas Edison and his assistant William K.L. Dickson invented a working moving picture camera.[49] Their first film, as aforementioned, only showed a man bowing, smiling, and leaving the frame.[50] Edison initially rejected projected film because he had a business interest in making his pay-per-view crank machines a success. He famously stated that "if we make this screen machine you are asking for, it will spoil everything. Let's not kill the goose that laid the golden egg."[51] With this statement, Edison made his first miscalculation about the cinema.[52] Soon, silent films captivated American audiences, as representations of law enforcement also appeared on the screen.[53]

At the start of the twentieth century, cinema rapidly advanced, moving from shorts flickering dimly at nickelodeons to full-length narrative movies.[54] Before film, the most accessible medium for entertainment was still largely vaudeville and theater, where live actors portrayed a storyline on stage, often with props.[55] Because performances were limited to one show at a time, the amount of money performers and production teams could earn from vaudeville was limited. Seats needed to be filled to pay the actors.[56] The advent of the motion picture, however, removed such limitations concerning potential profit earnings, as well as eliminated the need for live actors and their tours of different venues.

The first motion picture film studio is believed to have begun with the construction of Thomas Edison's "Black Maria," a "tar paper photographic shack" in West Orange, New Jersey.[57] Edison's studio was a single room structure measuring approximately 25 by 30 feet that had a large shutter that opened to allow sunlight in. Edison's studio resembled

I. Early Twentieth-Century Law Enforcement and Cinema

a "Black Maria" which at the time was slang for a police prisoner wagon (later known as a "paddy wagon") because of its wrapping with black protective tar strips.[58] Within a few years, Manhattan was the desired location for Edison, and his competitors Biograph and Vitagraph placed "rival stages atop Manhattan office buildings."[59] By 1898, independent studios were filming across the Hudson River in the shadows of New York City, in Fort Lee, New Jersey.[60] In 1910, D.W. Griffith's trip west to film *Old California* in Hollywood, California, marked the first movie made in Hollywood—which would soon thereafter become the motion picture capital of the American film industry.[61]

Early films were silent with no spoken dialogue or musical accompaniment. Many of these early American films during the silent era have been destroyed or simply deteriorated and are lost forever. In a 2003 study by the Library of Congress, the number of films lost is approximately 75 percent of all films produced before 1929.[62] Almost 11,000 films were produced during the silent era, yet only 2,749 remain, due to fires, purposeful destruction because of limited space in storage facilities, or through improper archiving that destroyed the films.[63] Early film stocks were manufactured using silver nitrate, which deteriorates quickly and is highly flammable; this directly caused massive fires that resulted in the loss of the irreplaceable films, and in some cases death. A major fire at the 20th Century–Fox film storage facility in Little Ferry, New Jersey, resulted in the loss of every film in the vault, and one person died. The hot July summer of 1937, coupled with inadequate ventilation, caused the nitrate film to spontaneously combust.

Censorship has been a large portion of the history of the film industry since inception. It is impossible to ignore because when researching early film history and the involvement of actual law enforcement, many patterns become apparent, particularly regarding censorship. Many scholarly studies on film censorship begin with discussions on *The John C. Rice-May Irwin Kiss* (1896), later known just as *The Kiss*, which was a man kissing a woman on film over and over again in a film loop. A simple kiss is not something considered provocative by today's standards; however, at the time, it was viewed as morally outrageous by some viewers, such as Herbert Stone, a Chicago journalist who claimed that the film was "absolutely disgusting" and called for police involvement.[64] *The Kiss* was, in fact, a re-enactment of the final scene of the stage musical *The Widow Jones*—a play Rice and Irwin were famous for. Viewers had not previously viewed a kiss in medium close-up angle, which at the time was considered improper in real life. The film thus lends itself

Law Enforcement in American Cinema, 1894–1952

to lengthy discussions of emerging censorship and narratives on a changing American moral consciousness, offering much insight into popular culture at the time. As the saying goes, "Any press is good press"; the national debates over *The Kiss*, and its seemingly indecent content, made it the first popular film produced by Thomas Edison's company.[65]

Also worthy of mention is that during the same year as *The Kiss*, Edison's company captured mounted uniformed police officers charging on film. Directed by James H. White with William Heise on camera, *Mounted Police Charge* is documentary footage of the New York State Police Department's mounted division.[66] In this twenty-four-second film shot on location in New York City's Central Park, a troop of mounted police officers, in full dress uniform, approach the audience at full gallop; suddenly halting within a few yards of the camera making each horse and rider appear full life-size. During these seminal days of film, the charging mounted division and their sudden halt could have plausibly caused viewers to jump aside from seeing the barreling of the cavalry approaching them. This reflexive response had been recorded prior on December 28, 1895, in France when the Lumière brothers rented a basement room in the Grand Café in Paris to show ten films for the first time to a paying audience, including *L'Arrivée d'un train en gare de La Ciotat* (*The Arrival of a Train at La Ciotat Station*) which showed a speeding locomotive approaching the audience. This film is said to have caused the audience to dodge aside at the sight.[67] Edison's *Mounted Police Charge* is similar with the cavalry thundering ahead like the locomotive and stopping before the camera. As movie making generated forward momentum in the years ahead, directors and producers replicated successful techniques and practices of competing filmmakers, including capitalist pursuits that used profitable themes, such as portrayals of corrupt police officers, intended for specific audiences.

It is no surprise the police are often targets of early filmmakers since they have been involved with the film industry since its origin, in terms of oversight, and their relationship was forceful regarding approved storytelling and imagery. In 1897 a Maine statute prohibited films that exhibited prizefighting.[68] The first film censorship ordinance was enacted in Chicago in 1907 through its licensing power to require the police department to regulate films shown to audiences in their jurisdictions.[69] This ordinance placed the power to issue a viewing permit in the hands of the Superintendent of Police; thus arguments of censorship and whether or not a film was morally appropriate played

I. Early Twentieth-Century Law Enforcement and Cinema

out in the confines of the Chicago Police Department and subsequently other jurisdictions throughout the country. The ordinance was challenged by James Block, who screened two Westerns that were denied viewing permits, *The James Boys in Missouri* (1908) and *Night Riders* (1908).[70] Block illegally screened the films in his chain of nickelodeons in the city.[71] He then challenged the legality of the ordinance, which eventually made it to the Illinois Supreme Court in *Block v. City of Chicago* (1909).[72] The court ruled in favor of the City of Chicago, thus "the industry took note of *Block* since it established a legal precedent legitimizing film censorship."[73]

In 1908, New York mayor George McClellan, Jr., used police power to close all movie theaters in the city. The forming of the National Board of Review of Motion Pictures (NB), a civic group, in 1909, attempted to take the oversight responsibility from the police. The NB made suggestions for objectionable material to cut before being viewed by the public. It concentrated on defining immorality and drawing the line between what is considered "suggestive behavior and heightened sensuality in the movies."[74] Scholar Jennifer Fronc examined the records of the NB, showing how they rejected control over censorship by government-appointed officials, such as police officers or others in authority whose influence can be manipulated, instead believing the only real guide rested among the opinions of the people.[75] In 1910 the International Association of Chiefs of Police (still an active organization today) adopted a resolution condemning the movie industry, its president arguing that in some films, "the police are made to appear ridiculous."[76] Later, in 1915, the Supreme Court ruling in *Mutual Film Corporation v. Industrial Commission of Ohio* found censorship did not infringe on either free speech or interstate commerce and therefore determined movies were not independent arguments worthy of First Amendment protection.[77] Movies were "mere representations of events, of ideas and sentiments ... vivid, useful, and entertaining, no doubt, but ... capable of evil," Associate Justice Joseph McKenna wrote in the court's decision. Jowett Garth and John Wertheimer are authoritative guides to understand this ruling and its impact on free speech and the film industry.[78] The ruling in *Mutual v. Ohio* was a victory for governmental oversight. It sparked drafting of censorship legislation throughout the country.[79] State by state, orders of censorship were given to films deemed immoral, thus the watering down of movies that, in some cases, destroyed the continuity of the film.[80] Take, for example, the showing of baby clothes was banned in Pennsylvania, while Kansas only allowed depictions of drinking (alcohol) if punishment was given to the drinker.[81] A reporter at the time noted, "A famous screenwriter who saw one of his movies in a Kansas theater after censoring failed to recognize it."[82] Thirty-seven years after *Mutual v. Ohio* the Supreme Court reversed itself.

Regarding the relation of mass culture to film, debates over the need for morality in the film industry quickly caught momentum. America was in a period of rapid social change. In the early twentieth century, women were attaining higher social status, mostly through their advances in industries that employed them in the workforce and enabled them to earn money and support dependents, as well as a move to the urban space wherein young women were subject to being corrupted, including by viewing films. Nevertheless, of course, women were earning very little at the time. Through the influence of women suffragettes and the many reform movements, women's voices in society were also increasing.

However, social narratives about America in moral decline continued to grow, along with the rapid technological advances in the film industry. In 1906, women's groups, such as the Women's Christian Temperance Union (WCTU), began to condemn the influence of movies, arguing that they negatively affected the health, well-being, and morals of America's youth, and further claiming that films were addictive and glorified war and violence. The WCTU also believed movies caused crime, juvenile delinquency, and immoral behavior and that the government should regulate them. These moral initiatives were taken into account by the film industry, and early films reflect a noticeable move toward incorporating moral narrative codes. Film historian Tom Gunning analyzes how moral narrative codes influenced early films, citing two films by Biograph as an example: *The Heathen Chinee and The Sunday School Teacher* (1904) and *A Drunkard's Reformation* (1909).[83] In the *Heathen Chinee*, there does not appear to be any condemnation of drug use, promiscuity, female missionaries, or racism, whereas *The Drunkard's Reformation* portrays a noticeable moral rhetoric about a drunkard, how the drink is ruining his life and family, and how turning to temperance provides him with a healthy and loving life.[84] Gunning argues that the cultural trend toward morality in the early silent era would not have allowed the content of the *Heathen Chinee* by the time *The Drunkard's Reformation* was released in 1909.[85] Gunning's work reveals early censorship by the film industry and how freedom of expression in early film quickly turned toward the social call for morality.

I. Early Twentieth-Century Law Enforcement and Cinema

Kathy Peiss's *Cheap Amusements: Working Women and Leisure in Turn-of-the-Century New York* illustrates this interplay between filmmakers and censorship and their eagerness to expand their audiences by producing films during the 1910s that "transcended Victorian morals and manners" and were deemed acceptable for middle-class viewers.[86] Peiss's work also demonstrates how the movies themselves altered women's public participation, as by 1910 women comprised of 40 percent of the working-class movie attendance.[87] Moreover, she makes the point that at the time the early silent film industry was transitioning into a business model that produced films for the audiences they were intended for.

By the 1920s, with the increasing threat of outside censorship, Hollywood found it more pragmatic to find common ground with the police. In the wake of Hollywood scandals that tarnished the industry—the trial of silent star Roscoe "Fatty" Arbuckle for rape and manslaughter, the federal tax investigations of movie icons such as Tom Mix, and numerous other improprieties involving stars and starlets—the industry began hiring moonlighting police officers to guard movie productions at "good salaries," forging interpersonal relationships with them to strengthen favor and influence.[88] Joe Domanick, an LAPD historian, writes that "cooperation between the movie business and police ensured discretion for carousing wild men like Errol Flynn and homosexual stars."[89] Hollywood and police departments thus eventually merged into a sort of unofficial partnership, where cooperation with police departments and officers—both active and retired—commenced, as later seen in the collaborations of actor Jack Webb and LAPD detective sergeant Marty Wynn and others. Webb had the feature role in *He Walked by Night* (1948) and worked with Wynn, who served as a technical assistant on the film. This partnership led to the widely popular radio and later television series *Dragnet* (1951–1959).

In 1927 self-regulating film censorship appeared in the Pre-Code era with the "Don'ts and Be Carefuls" adopted by the California Association for Guidance of Producers. This list of suggestions was an attempt for producers to adhere to moral guidelines, albeit it was loosely followed. For law enforcement representations on film, the "Don'ts and Be Carefuls" were promising because portrayals of sympathy for criminals were of concern for filmmakers as was their caution to be mindful of attitude toward "public characters and institutions," and scenes involving law enforcement or law-enforcement officers. The list is as follows:

Law Enforcement in American Cinema, 1894–1952

The Don'ts and Be Carefuls
Motion Picture Producers and Distributors of America, 1927

Resolved, That those things which are included in the following list shall not appear in pictures produced by the members of this Association, irrespective of the manner in which they are treated:

1. Pointed profanity—by either title or lip—this includes the words "God," "Lord," "Jesus," "Christ" (unless they be used reverently in connection with proper religious ceremonies), "hell," "damn," "Gawd," and every other profane and vulgar expression however it may be spelled;
2. Any licentious or suggestive nudity—in fact or in silhouette; and any lecherous or licentious notice thereof by other characters in the picture;
3. The illegal traffic in drugs;
4. Any inference of sex perversion;
5. White slavery;
6. Miscegenation (sex relationships between the white and black races);
7. Sex hygiene and venereal diseases;
8. Scenes of actual childbirth—in fact or in silhouette;
9. Children's sex organs;
10. Ridicule of the clergy;
11. Willful offense to any nation, race or creed;

And be it further resolved, That special care be exercised in the manner in which the following subjects are treated, to the end that vulgarity and suggestiveness may be eliminated and that good taste may be emphasized:

1. The use of the flag;
2. International relations (avoiding picturizing in an unfavorable light another country's religion, history, institutions, prominent people, and citizenry);
3. Arson;
4. The use of firearms;
5. Theft, robbery, safe-cracking, and dynamiting of trains, mines, buildings, etc. (having in mind the effect which a too-detailed description of these may have upon the moron);
6. Brutality and possible gruesomeness;
7. Technique of committing murder by whatever method;
8. Methods of smuggling;
9. Third-degree methods;
10. Actual hangings or electrocutions as legal punishment for crime;
11. Sympathy for criminals;
12. Attitude toward public characters and institutions;
13. Sedition;
14. Apparent cruelty to children and animals;
15. Branding of people or animals;
16. The sale of women, or of a woman selling her virtue;
17. Rape or attempted rape;
18. First-night scenes;
19. Man and woman in bed together;

I. Early Twentieth-Century Law Enforcement and Cinema

   20. Deliberate seduction of girls;
   21. The institution of marriage;
   22. Surgical operations;
   23. The use of drugs;
   24. Titles or scenes having to do with law enforcement or law-enforcing officers;
   25. Excessive or lustful kissing, particularly when one character or the other is a "heavy."[90]

Moreover, this form of self-regulating censorship was not as effective as the complete enforcement of the Motion Picture Production Code of 1930 when it went into full effect in 1934 with the adoption of the Production Code Administration (PCA); thus censorship advocates won a significant victory. After that, law enforcement perceptions appear to be more favorable. The PCA, which was instituted by the Hollywood industry to stave off outside censorship, was charged with the enforcement of a "prescriptive document of 'morally responsible' screen entertainment."[91] The application of the Code by the PCA affected the kind of stories the film studios could offer and their content, but "it was not a monolithic, inflexible organization that pasteurized all manner of potentialities into a bland gruel."[92] However, for the most part, it did what it was intended to do. Films appeared where "the requirements of the [Code] were thoroughly integrated with conventions of narrative, and in this sense censorship became more subtle and more pervasive."[93]

The "General Principles" and "Particular Applications" of the Code were "straightforward and seemingly comprehensive" and for this study provide the context in which law enforcement representations were, at times, scripted[94]:

General Principles

   1. No picture shall be produced which lower the moral standards of those who see it. Hence, the sympathy of the audience should never be thrown to the side of crime, wrongdoing or sin.
   2. Correct standards of life, subject only to the requirements of drama and entertainment, shall be presented.
   3. Law, natural and human, shall not be ridiculed, nor shall sympathy be created for its violation.

Particular Applications
I—Crimes against the law
These shall never be presented in such a way as to throw sympathy with the crime as against the law and justice or to inspire others with a desire for imitation.
   1. Murder
      a. The technique of murder must be presented in a way that will not inspire imitation.

b. Brutal killings are not to be presented in detail.
  c. Revenge in modern times shall not be justified.
 2. Methods of Crime should not be explicitly presented.
  a. Theft, robbery, safe-cracking, and dynamiting of trains, mines, buildings, etc., should not be detailed in method
  b. Arson must be subjected to the same safeguards.
  c. The use of firearms should be restricted to essentials.
  d. Methods of smuggling should not be presented.
 3. Illegal drug traffic must never be presented.
 4. The use of liquor in American life, when not required by the plot for proper characterization, will not be shown.[95]

In particular for this study, the enforcement of the Code, also known as the Hays Code, had an enormous impact on the representation of agents of the law in mid–1930s America: it specifically barred terrible representations of cops and good representations of criminals, thereby efficiently preventing any films like *Scarface* (1933) from being made between 1934 and the 1960s, when the Code finally waned.

However, by and large, representations of law enforcement in film during the early 1930s were secondary to those of the romanticized criminal, who, at the time, primarily played the starring role, albeit under a loose pretense that crime does not pay, and the law is to be respected and obeyed. Many of these films portrayed the gangster's lifestyles as ones of wealth, excess, power, and prestige, all of which resonated with many viewers who were enduring the difficulties of the Depression. However, by the mid–1930s when the Code went into full throttle, a considerable shift toward a desire for authority figures made it so many films displayed a "renewed respect" for law and order.[96] Villains on screen were now to be "hissed at," not rewarded.[97] Actors who formerly played bad guys were now in starring roles as heroic lawmen, such as James Cagney, who played the brave federal lawman James "Brick" Davis in *"G" Men* (1935), therefore supplanting the earlier criminal protagonist.

As this chapter has shown, the histories of both law enforcement and film extend in different forms far beyond the start of the twentieth century. Yet, what most Americans outside of the cities understand as widespread policing occurred in tandem with the development of the cinema. Therefore, the police have always been involved with the film industry since inception. Their involvement often dealt with issues of censorship, deciding whether or not films presented immorality. Since, as mentioned, local ordinances afforded the police a superior oversight of the film industry, debates over a film's content simultaneously played

I. Early Twentieth-Century Law Enforcement and Cinema

out in local jurisdictions throughout the county, as the film industry endeavored to take power away from the police with strict forms of self-regulation. In chapters that follow, the parallel histories of law enforcement and film and representations of law enforcement in film will be presented, further revealing how, in the early twentieth century, the intricacies of these relationships center on the debates over morality and censorship, a discourse of much public concern.

II

Just the Facts

The Police in Short Early Silent-Era Film

"There is more law in the end of a policeman's nightstick than in a decision of the Supreme Court."—Police Inspector Alexander S. Williams

From film's inception through the silent era, law enforcement depictions were often harsh and representative of their systemic corrupt and brutal ways. However, there were few positive representations regarding the work and risks officers take to protect the communities they serve. In early films, such as *Robetta and Doretto [No. 2]*, also known as *Chinese Laundry* (1894), *Sherlock Holmes Baffled* (1900), *How They Rob Men in Chicago* (1900), *A Gesture Fight in Hester Street* (1900), *How They Do Things on the Bowery* (1902), *The Moonshiners* (1904), *Life of an American Policeman* (1905), *The Kleptomaniac* (1905), *The Black Hand* (1906), *The Silver Wedding* (1906), *Fights of Nations* (1907), *A Corner in Wheat* (1909), *The Musketeers of Pig Alley* (1912), *Suspense* (1913), and many others, visual representations of law enforcement help reveal insights into the role of the police in society, as well as generally how the public viewed them, as films both reflected and refracted these views.

During the early days of film, brave muckraker journalists and newspaper political cartoonists exposed many of societal issues in need of reform. Their daring works filled newspapers and magazines with stories of governmental corruption, including those involving political machines and the police department. While the film industry was in its infant days, residents in cities like Manhattan had grown tired of the police oppression and offered a strong sentiment for reform.[1] Social reformers like Charles Henry Parkhurst stood up and pressured New York senators to probe corruption in the New York City Police Department. The New York State Senate responded with their Lexow

II. Just the Facts

Committee in 1894, which was so highly publicized in the newspapers that the scandal was largely the reason for Tammany Hall's political machine defeat in the mayoral election that year when William Lafayette Strong, a Republican, won the seat on the Fusion Party ticket of anti–Tammany Democrats. The irony of the Lexow investigation was that politicians, who were equally corrupt and in need of reform, were the ones who determined "it has been charged and maintained that the police department of the City of New York is corrupt."[2] Political cartoonist Louis Dalrymple captured this hypocrisy in an 1894 centerfold illustration in *Puck Magazine* called "Where is the Difference?" Dalrymple's drawing (Figure 2) shows a New York City police officer accepting money from a woman's hand extending from a window labeled "N.Y. Den" and a man labeled "U.S. Senate" accepting "Stock" from a hand extending from a window labeled "Trusts." Both men are corrupt agents of the government leaning on a solid pedestal labeled with a large "$" and the word "Protection."

While the earliest representation of a police officer in uniform on film appears in 1894 with Edison's capturing of a popular New York City

Figure 2. Illustration showing corrupt police officers and politicians in New York. 1894.

vaudeville act, *Robetta and Doretto [No. 2]* or *Chinese Laundry*, that same year the Lexow Committee, named for its chairman Senator Clarence Lexow, held numerous hearings in New York City. The committee amassed over 10,000 pages of testimony that uncovered police involvement in extortion, bribery, counterfeiting, voter intimidation, election fraud, brutality, and scams. It determined "some forty police officers, including an inspector and fourteen captains (nearly half of the department's total) faced indictments on Lexow-related charges of bribery, extortion, and neglect of duty."[3] The corrupt police conduct was the result of

> the spoils system of the municipal machine: the way the police were hired, fired, or promoted on the basis of pull and patronage rather than competence. This explained why the police enforced the law violently and selectively; it gave them leverage to extract bribes and favors.[4]

Simply put, the political party machines created a milieu where illegal conduct was socially accepted as a way to get ahead. Therefore, if the police officers had to pay bribes for professional advancement to politicians overseeing them, legitimate and illegitimate business owners would also have to pay the officers who oversaw them for their personal and professional gains. Nobody was getting ahead without paying those who turned a blind eye on their illegality or offered "protection" to make it happen. These reciprocal processes, although criminal, made many politicians and police officers very wealthy. Criminologists politely call this corrupt era of policing the "Political Era."[5]

As the Lexow Committee's proceedings were profoundly covered in the newspapers, Dalrymple captured another visual cartoon specifically emphasizing the police tenor of the times on the cover of *Puck Magazine* (October 3, 1894) with his drawing "THE POLICE VERSION OF IT: Let no guilty man (or woman) escape—widout dey put up de stuff!" Dalrymple's cover artwork (Figure 3) depicts a large police officer turning the crank on a giant press labeled "Blackmail," squeezing money out of a variety of merchants labeled "Boot Black, Gin Mill Keeper, Dive Keeper, Merchant, Green Goods, Contractor, Gambler, [and] Pawnbroker."[6] The Lexow findings determined among the most notoriously corrupt New York City police officials were departmental leaders, such as Superintendent William "Big Bill" Devery, Inspector Alexander S. "Clubber" Williams, and Detective Commander Thomas F. Byrnes. This reality in itself partly explains why New York City residents felt they had no recourse against the police who at times were worse than the criminals they also

II. Just the Facts

Figure 3. A large police officer turns the crank on a large press labeled "Blackmail," squeezing money out of a variety of merchants labeled "Boot Black, Gin Mill Keeper, Dive Keeper, Merchant, Green Goods, Contractor, Gambler, [and] Pawnbroker." 1894.

feared. Since the leadership of the police department was integrally corrupt, when residents reported crimes committed by officers, they often fell on deaf ears. This resulted in a police culture that was systemically crooked with many officers committing crimes with impunity. Early film narratives by and large represented these truths, as we will see shortly ahead in this study.

Of those identified in the Lexow report, it is of no astonishment that Police Superintendent Devery's criminal enterprises were a major part of the findings since Devery had operated in plain sight for several decades as an affiliate of the Tammany Hall political machine and was one of the most corrupt police administrators the department had ever seen. Devery's legacy is that of a Tammany Hall collection man, a notoriously corrupt police officer, and, interestingly, a co-owner of the Yankees baseball team.[7] On a policeman's salary alone it would have been impossible to become a co-owner of the Yankees baseball team, but Devery didn't let that stop him from enriching himself with wealth and opportunity.[8] As a police captain, Devery once informed his officers, "They tell me there's a lot of grafting going on in this precinct. They tell me that you fellows are the fiercest ever on graft. Now that's going to stop! If there's any grafting to be done, I'll do it. Leave it to me."[9] Although the Lexow Committee uncovered Superintendent Devery's corruption, he politically and professionally survived the blowback to later become the police department's first police chief in 1898.[10]

Whereas Devery is the quintessential example of police corruption, New York City police inspector Alexander S. "Clubber" Williams is an archetypical model of police brutality. Williams, also popularly known as the "Czar of the Tenderloin," was so brutal with his nightstick he also received the nickname "Clubber." Williams was known for his quickness to use his club to beat criminals and to use the symbolism of the nightstick to make statements. He was excessively brutal throughout his police career that began as a new patrolman in 1866 when he immediately sought to establish a reputation in the community for being the toughest and most fierce cop on the beat. Journalist Herbert Asbury recalls Williams' rookie days on the force:

> Williams was a huge and powerful man with a great bull vice which had been strengthened by many years at sea as a ship's carpenter. Two days after he had been assigned to the Houston Street area he selected the two toughest characters of the neighborhood, picked fights with them and knocked them unconscious with his club. He then hurled them one after the other through the plate glass window of the Florence Saloon, from which they had issued to attack him. Half a score of

II. Just the Facts

their comrades came to their rescue, but Williams stood his ground and mowed then down with his nightstick. Thereafter he averaged a fight a day for almost four years. His skill with the nightstick was extraordinary, and the fame of his powerful blows became so widespread that he was hailed as Clubber Williams, a sobriquet which he retained to the end of his career.[11]

Later, in 1876, Williams was transferred to Manhattan's 29th precinct, also known as the Tenderloin District, where he began a ruthless reign over the neighborhood. Williams was now in one of the most important precincts in Manhattan and policed Broadway's nightclubs, the gambling dens, and brothels. The informal name of the Tenderloin District is said to had originated from Williams himself who, when referring to the increased amount of bribes he would receive for police protection of both legitimate and illegitimate businesses there, remarked, "I've been having chuck steak ever since I've been on the force, and now I'm going to have a bit of tenderloin."[12] Williams's tenure in the Tenderloin District included he and fellow officers obsessively clubbing thugs with or without justification, making themselves resemble another violent street gang. This symbolism of the police as another street gang is discussed below in films such as *The Musketeers of Pig Alley* (1912). While in the Tenderloin assignment, eighteen charges of excessive force were made against Williams.[13] However, the Board of Police Commissioners consistently acquitted Williams on all charges.[14] When complaints were made about Williams using excessive force, he routinely justified his actions with his observation, "There is more law in the end of a policeman's nightstick than in a decision of the Supreme Court."[15]

Williams' brutal ways were well known in the city. His reputation as a corrupt officer willing to do illegal deeds for personal and professional enrichment was also known throughout the city. In 1887, cartoonist Eugene Zimmerman illustrated Williams's corruption and the complicit condoning of his behavior by city officials, specifically by then Mayor Abraham Hewitt. He is seen in the drawing "'The Finest' (Brutes) in the World Citizen (to Mayor Hewitt)—Protect me from my 'Protectors!'" Mayor Hewitt is holding a scroll reading: "Charges Against Police Captain Williams by Prominent Citizens." In this illustration Mayor Hewitt is shown offering cover for Williams whose corruption and brutality coupled with the complicit consent of the courts are emphasized by the adjoining images of brutal and corrupt police officers.

In the fallout from the Lexow Committee report it was speculated that Williams would be charged for his alleged crimes and brought before the court; however, he was ultimately allowed to retire after a meeting with the three police commissioners, which included Theodore Roosevelt. In retirement he was active in politics and defended his reputation and police record, most notably in 1912 when he lashed out against New York City mayor William Jay Gaynor who had derogatorily used his nickname "Clubber Williams." In a public statement, Williams defended his twenty-nine-year police career, saying, "Just ask the Mayor if he can point to a single person I ever clubbed that did not deserve it. He can't name one and he knows it."[16] Williams's leadership in the New York City Police Department created a culture where violence was not only permissible but also socially accepted as a means that justified the ends.

Thomas F. Byrnes, head of the New York City Police Department Detective Bureau from 1880 until 1895 and also identified by the Lexow Committee, is a prime example of the corrupt police culture since he led, instructed, and condoned his detectives to use brutal tactics to gain confessions. Byrnes may be behind the term giving a suspect the "third-degree," as it is perhaps a pun on his name "burns," for his violent interrogations.[17] Several series of novels written by Byrnes's friend Julian Hawthorne, son of novelist Nathaniel Hawthorne, including *The Great Bank Robbery* (1887), *An American Penman* (1887), *Another's Crime* (1888), *Section 558* or *The Fatal Letter* (1888), and *A Tragic Mystery* (1888) popularized Byrnes's techniques which were a combination of physical and psychological torture.[18] In 1895, like Williams, Byrnes too was pressured to retire from the police force by Theodore Roosevelt who sought to rid the department of rabid and systemic corruption and the divide between the police and the community they served. As discussed ahead, *Life of an American Policeman* shot in 1905 attempted to soothe this harsh truth with a much-needed narrative that showed the heroism and dedicated work of the New York City police officers. However, as we see here in this chapter, the actuality of police officers acting appropriately and ethically on film is merely a speck when analyzing the surviving films where police are depicted. Therefore, it is correct to assert that from film's inception through the silent era, law enforcement depictions are often discordant and representative of their systemic corrupt and brutal ways, like aforementioned with the insalubrious examples of Devery, Williams, and Byrnes whose careers were simultaneously occurring in the same city and same time as the film industry was developing. Furthermore, films offering positive representations of the work and risks officers took to protect the communities they serve were underrepresented, as early filmmakers capitalized on sensationalism of police corruption and brutality.

II. Just the Facts

As we move ahead in this chapter the stated early silent films, and many others, present early visual representations of law enforcement and help to reveal insights into the role of the police in society, as well as generally how the public viewed them, as films both reflected and refracted these views.

Robetta and Doretto [No. 2], Also Known as *Chinese Laundry* (1894)

Edison's 1894 *Robetta and Doretto [No. 2]* or *Chinese Laundry* is where the first visual representation of a police officer in uniform recorded on film begins. *Chinese Laundry*'s characters Robetta and Doretto were admired vaudeville actors who performed their act "Heap Fun Laundry" at the close of Tony Pastor's vaudeville production. They brought their act to Edison's "Black Maria" for filming during the week of November 26, 1894.[19] As aforementioned, during this week many vaudeville actors came to Edison's studio to have their performances captured for Edison's Kinetoscope viewer.[20]

Chinese Laundry in its purest form is a quick vaudeville slapstick comedy that was favored during these primitive days of first filmmaking. Tom Gunning termed this era the "cinema of attractions" because filmmakers were mostly fascinated by other potentials, such as uniting different approaches like the trick film and actuality film to bring different views to the spectator audience.[21] It's important to note that during these early years of exhibition, the cinema itself was an attraction.[22] "Early audiences went to exhibitions to see machines demonstrated, as they did for other technological wonders such as the widely exhibited x-rays or the phonograph, rather than to view films," Gunning notes. "It was the Cinematograph, the Biograph, or the Vitascope that were advertised on the variety bills for which they appeared," not the films these technological devices featured.[23]

Chinese Laundry features acrobatic vaudeville performers Robetta and Doretto as "Hop Lee," a Chinese laundry employee and an irate uniformed policeman. It is unknown which character played each role. In this moving picture, the scene opens with the police officer standing in front of Hop Lee with his arms crossed as to signal a conversation that quickly escalated since Lee is holding a wash-bucket over his head that he smashes on the head of the officer, knocking off his policeman's hat. Lee then enters a door in a scene that is made to resemble a storefront with an overhead sign "Heap Fun Laundry." The officer pursues Lee, who acrobatically pulls himself above the signage sitting on the top of the set when the officer exits the door confused as to Lee's whereabouts. Lee quickly locates a presumably wooden board and throws it down on the officer, striking him in the left shoulder, temporarily stunning the officer and thereby allowing Lee to jump down and escape through the center door of the laundry storefront.

Currently, there is limited scholarship offering delineated versions of this narrative, mostly because these primitive films in content and form were limited to narrative construction.[24] Film historian David Cook noted, "The 50-foot maximum format (approximately sixteen seconds at a speed of 40 fps; 60 at the later standard rate of 16) was not conducive to the construction of narrative, but was eminently suitable for recording quick vaudeville turns, slapstick comedy skits, and other kinds of performances."[25] Many of these early films of stage acts, when "dancers, contortionists, acrobats, and novelty acts also continued to visit the 'Black Maria' from September of 1894 through the following spring"[26] offer little or no narrative forms. For example, other filmed vaudeville acts, such as Sandow—the modern Hercules—captured earlier in 1894 at Edison's "Black Maria" is a memorialization of strong man Eugene Sandow flexing his muscles, with limited narrative construction. Equally, another vaudeville actor who visited Edison's laboratory, Professor Ivan Tschernoff with his performing dogs, would show Kinescope users an act of highly trained dogs performing without a story telling narrative.

Although *Chinese Laundry* is a film mostly to show the audience something rather than tell a story, we must ask why these twenty-one seconds of film featured this specific portion of Robetta and Doretto's popular vaudeville act. The film's scene and characters themselves offer a wealth of information and, although limited, have a narrative construct worthy of moral and allegorical value. *Chinese Laundry* was filmed contemporaneously with the highly publicized Lexow Committee investigations of police corruption and brutality, and though what effect this had on their act is unknown, it's plausible that Robetta and Doretto were pacifying their audience's desires to see the police as the enemy of the citizenry endeavoring to pull themselves up while the government held them down. *Chinese Laundry* is also an early glimpse into what later filmmakers would realize that the film-making medium could be used for storytelling. From the opening the police officer in *Chinese Laundry* is attacked; whereas viewers of Sandow would marvel over

II. Just the Facts

his herculean-built body, viewers of *Chinese Laundry* would ask why and what caused the laundry store employee to attack a police officer, thereby constructing a narrative. What initiated the dispute? Could it be anger from paying "protection" money to the police? The film continues with the irate officer pursuing Lee, albeit never succeeding to capture him, thus showing the superiority of the laundry store employee or common man's greater ability and intelligence. When the officer is assaulted for a second time—when Lee threw presumably a wooden board from the top of the set down on the officer striking him in the left shoulder, this arguably solidifies the narrative that the police, at least in this film, are inept, ineffective, and worthy of lampooning—a hallmark of slapstick comedy where the police are the focus of mockery.[27] *Chinese Laundry*'s visual portrayal of the popular vaudeville act and seminal construction of narrative filmmaking is worthy of more detailed research and analysis from film historians endeavoring to connect the later works of narrative filmmaking with its origins. To simply dismiss *Chinese Laundry* as worthy of solely spectatorship categorization along with Sandow's display of athletic prowess or Professor Tschernoff's dog show is misplaced.

Sherlock Holmes Baffled (1900)

Six years after *Chinese Laundry*, another film that recorded the appearance of a police officer is *Sherlock Holmes Baffled* (1900), which shows a detective or plain-clothes policeman. This film is arguably the first recorded detective film.[28] It was recorded as an example of film trickery and editing by using the *stop trick* (stop motion) developed in 1896 by French director Georges Méliès.[29] Arthur Marvin for American Mutoscope and Biograph Company directed this short thirty-second film that was lost for many years until rediscovered as a paper print in the Library of Congress in 1968.[30] It was originally shown in the Mutoscope machine, which was similar to Edison's Kinetoscope; however, it was a cheaper and simpler viewing machine that also did not project onto a screen and provided viewing to only one person, bringing dominant commercial success to the American Mutoscope company in the coin-in-the slot "peep show" arcade business.[31]

The main character in the film is author Arthur Conan Doyle's detective, Sherlock Holmes, a widely popular character of the time. The film begins with Holmes entering his parlor to find a burglar filling a sack with his tableware. Holmes, with a cigar pressed between his lips, taps the burglar on his shoulder. The thief instantaneously disappears, surprising Holmes who attempts to ignore the event, sitting at his table and lighting his cigar when the thief's reappearance startles him. Holmes tries to reclaim his stolen goods, reflexively drawing his pistol from his dressing gown pocket and firing it at the intruder, who again vanishes leaving behind the sack filled with Holmes's property. Holmes recovers the sack and is seen walking toward the door to exit his parlor when the sack suddenly vanishes from his hand, reappearing instantly in the thief's hand, who presumably disappears through an open window. At this point the film ends abruptly with Holmes looking "baffled."

This film, though made to show the example of film trickery, gives viewers a glimpse into societal attitudes of the police at that time. One must ask why the advantageous usage of the film trick was not afforded to Holmes to capture the thief—to present the superiority of law enforcement. Why was the criminal selected to appear advantageous as opposed to Holmes—a well-established law enforcement character whose notoriety was the reason for his casting in the film? Perhaps the criminal's plight, although abhorrent on the surface, was what intended audiences (working-class and urban poor) preferred to see.[32]

Although *Sherlock Holmes Baffled* further complicates early law enforcement perceptions by showcasing law enforcement's ineptness, and the criminal's superior ability to evade and escape detection, the most flagrant portion of the film comes when Holmes draws a pistol from his coat and fires at the thief. In other words, using deadly force in defense of property. At no point is the thief attempting to assault or confront Holmes; however, as with other films of this period, the inference of the police's quick to use unwarranted force is once again a narrative staple that is reflective of coexistent events. Take for example a real-life example of unwarranted force that happened in 1900 in New York City when *Sherlock Holmes Baffled* was filmed. The tensions between the police and the racial communities in the city that summer had boiled to the point that a race riot erupted on August 15 and 16 in the Tenderloin section of Manhattan—a predominately Irish community. The spark that ignited the riot began days earlier on August 12, when plain-clothes Patrolman Robert Thorpe had attempted to arrest a black female named May Enoch for soliciting. Enoch's boyfriend, Arthur Harris, allegedly (different accounts of the incident exist) had mistaken the identity of the plain-clothes officer for an attacker.[33] A scuffle ensued

II. Just the Facts

and Harris stabbed Officer Thorpe two times in the stomach and then fled to his mother's house in Washington, D.C.[34] Thorpe's death the following day ignited an angry mob of hundreds of whites who assaulted African American community members, which was later confirmed by approximately eighty affidavits from African Americans who affirmed not only that citizens attacked them but police complicity in the violence as well.[35]

A cartoon appearing on August 19, 1900, in the *New York Tribune* succinctly captures the reality of police brutality while showing a rare sympathy for African Americans. In this cartoon, "He's on the Police Force Now," a tiger is dressed as a police officer with a belt that reads "Tammany." The tiger officer is gleefully twirling a nightstick while an African American man sits on the ground clutching his chest from a beating levied by the police officer. The cartoon is a response to how New York City Mayor Robert Van Wyck and Police Chief William Devery sent 700 police officers into the riot to quell the violence; however, blacks were disproportionately arrested and many were severely beaten while in police custody. The premise of the drawing is Tammany packed the police force with political supporters who were presumably Irish Catholics and who were brutal against black citizens during the riot.

In the riot's aftermath, many leaders of both racial communities condemned the violence but differed on whom to blame for the aggression.[36]

> Republicans and the Good Government Society polarized the racial violence and traced the police brutality to Tammany Hall. Black religious leaders focused their attention on both the white hordes and the police. A citizens protective league formed to bring suits against the city on behalf of the victims beaten by the authorities.[37]

The commonality in all these responses demonstrate that unwarranted force was an issue largely on the minds of the urban residents, and these realities, not surprisingly, are represented in early films such as *Sherlock Holmes Baffled*.

How They Rob Men in Chicago (1900)

Another observable example of the disconnection between society and law enforcement is found in a film that was also released in 1900, *How They Rob Men in Chicago*. Directed by Wallace McCutcheon for

Law Enforcement in American Cinema, 1894–1952

American Mutoscope & Biograph Production Company, the film was shot on location in New York City. At a length of only twenty-six seconds, a well-dressed elderly man is standing in front of a store looking out toward the street when a young robber hidden behind a wooden barrel jumps out behind the man and clubs him in the back of his head. The man collapses on the sidewalk. The robber is then seen searching through the man's pockets as he lies unconscious. Hurrying to steal the money, the thief inadvertently leaves some of the man's money behind. A uniformed police officer appears, walking casually with a club in hand, and finds the man's body on the sidewalk. Looking down, he notices some of the man's money, picks it up, tucks it in his duty-belt, and walks off, while indicating no concern for the victim or for the crime that was just committed.

This early representation of law enforcement is brief, and, of course, intended as a comedy of sorts, but it speaks loudly about the view of the uniformed officer working in the city. The story is simple: if one gets clubbed over the head and robbed, the police will do nothing to help and are only concerned with personal gain while neglecting their duties to pursue a robber or to render aid. The casual way in which the officer arrived indicated he had no intention of pursuing and arresting the robber. Moreover, it portrays the police as immoral and not an effective entity for crime victims to rely upon to pursue justice.

The criticism of the Chicago police in *How They Rob Men in Chicago* is consequential from decades of Chicago Police corruption familiar to Americans as newspapers routinely covered the former prairie town where cowboys, Indians, and traders had conducted business, before it turned to a hotbed for organized crime. Although there were some ethical and professional officers, Chicago's reputation for crooked cops came from decades of criminality. For example, during the mid-nineteenth century, Chicago's Superintendent of Police Michael Cassius McDonald was a fierce organizer of Chicago's criminals. In the period between the end of the Civil War and the turn of the century, McDonald built a massive criminal base comprised of politicians and police who stole everything in sight.[38] McDonald opened and ran a brothel, saloon, and gambling den. He eventually moved into politics, organizing his party: Mike's Democrats. McDonald's rise in political prowess afforded him the power to control the city and the police, and he and his associates became very wealthy from public projects. McDonald eventually purchased the *Chicago Globe* newspaper, and by the time Al Capone arrived in Chicago, McDonald's heirs were respectable citizens of Chicago.

II. Just the Facts

However, there is no denying that Chicago's Police force of the late nineteenth and early twentieth centuries was largely characterized at being married with organized crime syndicates and in many ways appear as criminals in uniforms with guns and badges. *How They Rob Men in Chicago* exposes these truisms.

A Gesture Fight in Hester Street (1900) and *Fights of Nations,* Part Two: "Our Hebrew Friends" (1907)

Another surviving film depicting a law enforcement officer as a character was shot by cinematographer Arthur Marvin for American Mutoscope & Biograph Company approximately two months after *How They Rob Men in Chicago*. Marvin's work *A Gesture Fight in Hester Street* (1900) is a short film of twenty-four seconds that opens on a street scene. The main character is a bearded, street peddler who hawks his goods on a sidewalk with a storefront in the backdrop. A young woman walks past disinterested with the peddler, and this causes him to angrily gesture at her. Behind him another bearded peddler enters the frame and inadvertently bumps into the peddler with his cart. An argument between the street peddlers erupts into a physical altercation where a uniformed police officer enters the scene clubbing the men on their backs.

The film is intended as a comical of sorts aimed at ethnic humor of the day. Although a ghastly attempt, it depicts two Hebrew men on Hester Street in Manhattan's Lower East Side, where many immigrant Jews lived during the later nineteeth and early twentieth centuries. As films of the day were designed for specific audiences, in this case Jewish residents living in the poor neighborhood of New York City, it shows how the "gesture fight" is apparently humorous to those living contemporaneously in the city, where they easily understood the fight began with waving fingers and poking each other, followed by knocking off each other's hat and wrestling, rather than a more direct street fight of swinging fists to knock out an adversary. The paradox here is that the men are exaggerative in their fight; however, that exaggeration turns soberingly real with the entrance of the policeman swinging and hitting the men with his club. The actuality of both men's backs being turned to the officer and that he immediately raises his nightstick and begins clubbing the men in an attempt to break up the fight is an affirmation of officers

Law Enforcement in American Cinema, 1894–1952

like Inspector Alexander "Clubber" Williams and Detective Commander Thomas Byrnes who were brutal with city residents. This scene also exposes how officers were quick to use force, to gain compliance. As discussed previously, many reports uncover the injustice of police brutality and the suffering the victims sustained at the hands of officers criminally swinging their clubs. Moreover, the placement of a police officer to break up the "gesture fight" is telling. The neighborhood at the time is filled with poor Jewish settlers, and the policeman is the symbol of government: corrupt, heavy-fisted, and brutal in their approach with the vulnerable population. Police officers are often described as the first line of visible government the residents have access to. Their displeasure with their government is often taken out on the police as we see represented over and over throughout the history of narrative filmmaking.

Contemporaneous viewers of *A Gesture Fight in Hester Street* would have found the gesture fight itself comical and the beating of the police officer rather more representative of the police's (and the government's) corruption and misunderstanding of a community where clearly a beating with a night stick was over-charged to break the men up. Moreover, the men were quarrelling with each other and neither presented a direct attack on the police officer, thereby not warranting an elevated usage of mechanical force. The uniformed officer portrayed in *A Gesture Fight in Hester Street* is yet another example of police quickness to use excessive force to gain compliance, an unfortunate reality that viewers of this short film were intimately familiar with.

Another evidentiary film appearing several years later called *Fights of Nations* (1907) is analogous to *A Gesture Fight in Hester Street* because the second part "Our Hebrew Friends" is a similar attempt at ethnic humor with a narrative involving the police worthy of analysis. *Fights of Nations* exposes police corruption, specifically by portraying the paying off of a uniformed police officer. The film opens with two Hebrew men arguing (one is a street peddler holding goods) on the street. The men are seen quarreling in an obvious embellished fashion to accentuate the ethnic mannerisms of the Hebrew men. A third man arrives and the dispute endures with now three men arguing. The dispute persisted with the men kicking each other in the buttocks, while circling in what appears to be a giddy dance, when a uniformed policeman with club in hand arrives to break up the fight. As the policeman threatens one of the men with his club, the man scuttles the officer aside to tell him he will pay him off with a bribe. The police officer accepts the bribe and is seen standing with his back to the man who places the money in the officer's back pants pocket. The bribe money is attached to a string so when the officer walks away, joyfully swinging his club obviously pleased with the payoff, the man pulls the string and retrieves his money. Upon tricking the corrupt policeman, the three men join together and happily dance.

As stated earlier, police corruption was rampant during these early days of law enforcement and many films reflected this reality. Equally, the uniting of the fighting men after tricking the police officer shows film viewers would understand the police are not on their side, and although they may have differences that turn to a physical altercation, the police are far worse adversaries to their urban ethnic community, and they were better off sticking together—an unfortunate but undeniable presumption of reality.

How They Do Things on the Bowery (1902)

How They Do Things on the Bowery (1902) is an excellent film to illustrate both the social environments of the urban ghetto during this period and the shift by filmmakers to produce films with their intended audience in mind. This Edison film directed by Edwin S. Porter, who at the time was the head of Edison's New York Studio directing the actors, operating the camera, and assembling the final print, appears seven months after Edison lost his patent suit that formerly allowed him a virtual monopoly on the filmmaking industry from July of 1901 through March of 1902.[39] Edison's defendant, the American Mutoscope & Biograph Company, appealed the ruling to a higher court and won, thus opening up the industry for competition through creativity, and dramatically altering Edison's company's commercial standings.[40] Porter immediately began working on a series of short narrative films, including *Appointment by Telephone* (April 1902), *Jack and the Beanstalk* (July 1902), and *How They Do Things on the Bowery* (October 1902). Porter's capitalistic purpose was to expound upon prior years of documentary filmmaking and visual newspapers styles, with which he was heavily involved, to make narrative films that provide viewers (the urban working class and poor) with movies they would pay to watch.

How They Do Things on the Bowery is as much of an attempt to entice audiences as it is a visual representation of the times. The Bowery district of New York City at this time was a ghetto where denizens gathered and immorality flourished. It was a skid row of brothels and flophouses, complete with saloon owners and gangs who preyed on hapless visitors.[41] "The Bowery," a song written by Charles H. Hoyt and Percy Gaunt for the play *A Trip to Chinatown* (1892), offers a vivid description of the Bowery in six verses. Take verse six as an example:

> I struck a place that they called a "dive,"
> I was in luck to get out alive;
> When the policeman heard of my woes,
> Saw my black eye and my batter'd nose,
> "You've been held up!" said the copper fly.
> "No, sir! But I've been knock'd down," said I;
> Then he laugh'd, tho' I could not see why!
> I'll never go there anymore![42]

Although images of the Bowery were memorialized playfully in Hoyt and Gaunt's song, with verse six's jovial depiction of a police officer laughing at the ignorance of the victim, life at the Bowery was much harsher. It was the place where Stephen Foster (the father of American music who wrote such hits as "Oh Susanna" and "Camptown Races") drank himself to death.[43] It is where "prostitutes killed themselves with carbolic acid at McGurk's Suicide Hall, and where the 'Bowery Boys' attacked the homeless."[44] The conditions on the Bowery were so dire that sources estimate that by 1907 approximately 25,000 men lived in flophouses.[45] The police, who at this time were a national target of reform, are often synchronously represented in films that offer "gleeful accounts of urban criminality alongside a world-weary cynicism about the corruption of police"[46] *How They Do Things on the Bowery* is indicative of this realism.

How They Do Things on the Bowery opens with a street scene with the action unfolding on the sidewalk with storefronts and people in view. A well-dressed woman, possibly a prostitute, walks toward an opposing countryman, conceivably a farmer based by the way he is dressed, and the type of suitcase he is holding, which also signals his heterogeneity. The woman, an early view of a femme fatale (an attractive woman who ultimately brings misfortune to a man who becomes involved with her), drops her handkerchief as a ruse. The hapless farmer "rube" picks up the handkerchief and politely hands it to the woman who, judging by gestures, invites the farmer inside the restaurant for a drink. The woman and the farmer enter the restaurant and the next scene shows them conversing at a table where the woman lights a cigarette and a waiter pours them each a drink. The farmer turns to the waiter to pay him while the woman slips "knock out drops," also known

II. Just the Facts

as a "Mick Finn," to incapacitate the farmer. The waiter is in direct view of the woman dripping the drug in the farmer's glass yet remains disinterested, indicating, perhaps, a complicit consent of the criminality where tavern owners themselves partook in crimes. This was the case at Chicago's Lone Star Saloon and Palm Garden Restaurant that operated from 1896 to 1903 with owner Mickey Finn (for whom the term to describe the knockout drug "Mick Fin" originated), drugging wealthy customers and rendering them unconscious. When the saloon closed, he and his staff dragged the victim into a backroom, dubbed an "operating room," where they stole the victim's money and valuables, then tossed him outside into the alley.[47] The drug, possible chloral hydrate, renders the victim unable to recall what happened while they were under its influence.

The Bowery scene in the restaurant continues with the woman and farmer toasting, and shortly thereafter the farmer is slouched in his chair, incapacitated. The woman speedily rummages through the farmer's coat pockets, locates his wallet and timepiece, and exits the restaurant. The waiter enters the frame angry with the farmer, waking him by startling and shouting, and then physically heaving the farmer out onto the street, tossing his suitcase outside with him. The next scene shows a horse-drawn police "paddy wagon" with a large uniformed officer hopping off the rear bumper, clutching the farmer off the sidewalk, hauling him into the back of the paddy wagon, and leaving the area. The last image is of the waiter throwing the farmer's suitcase into the street.

The police officers' involvement in the narrative is purposeful. The farmer who did not commit a crime was arrested and hauled off by the police, thereby reinforcing the popular belief that the police, criminal shopkeepers, and the Bowery underworld were correspondingly involved in criminality where unsuspecting outsiders were routinely and permissibly victimized. As the verse mentioned above in Hoyt and Gaunt's song "the Bowery" ring true, the police were keenly aware of the criminality of the Bowery and saw much of the victim's as "rubes" whose ignorance facilitated their victimization. Porter understood viewers craved film narratives that vicariously showcased their lives, stories that juxtaposed the affluent high society with the lowly urban poor, narratives that offered a sympathetic view of criminals, with police officers who co-conspired with criminals and who were inherently biased and corrupt. These approaches worked well for capitalist filmmakers of the period, replicating these realities over and over in these early years before full-blown censorship.

Law Enforcement in American Cinema, 1894–1952

The Moonshiners (1904) *and Suspense* (1913)

The Moonshiners and *Suspense* are two films that show depictions of law enforcement shooting at fleeing suspects to effectuate an arrest. They have very different storylines; however, the representations of the police in both films are unsavory. The major difference between the films is how they treat the criminal. *The Moonshiners* offers a sympathetic view of the criminals, whereas *Suspense* clearly shows no sympathy for the criminal. Nonetheless, *Suspense* is discussed as ancillary to *The Moonshiners*, where an early view of police shooting to make an arrest is presented.

The Moonshiners, which features law enforcement as federal revenue officers endeavoring to detect an illegal moonshining distillery and arrest the criminals, exemplifies an early "amoral" film. Directed by Wallace McCutcheon and filmed in Scarsdale, New York, *The Moonshiners* is an early Mutoscope & Biograph film that complicates a favorable view of law enforcement and is challenged by its sympathetic treatment of the moonshiners, a seemingly respectable husband and wife team, while showing the agents as rough in their approach in seeking to shut the distillery down. *The Moonshiners* is thus an early film that is sympathetic to the criminal, while also showing the graphic killing of the officers.

The Moonshiners opens at the moonshiners' mountain home where they are shown loading illegal jugs of moonshine onto a horse-drawn vehicle. The moonshiners (a husband and wife) and another woman seated in the back of the wagon drive off to trade the moonshine for corn. Unbeknownst to them, a spy on horseback for the federal revenue officers sees their trade and gallops back to the headquarters of the federal officers, who immediately arm themselves with firearms and begin to hunt for the surreptitious still. The still is hidden in the mountains, and the scene of the men making moonshine looks much like a documentary film. The officers overpower a lookout for the moonshiners, tie his hands, and then one officer with a rifle remains guard on the lookout while the other officers continue to approach the still with their guns in hand. The officers surprise the moonshiners and a shootout begins. One of the moonshiners is shot and killed, as well as one of the officers. The husband and wife flee as the officers pursue them. Although the intertitle reads "The Law Vindicated," to show that the officers are justified in their actions, the following scene shows the husband running down the road in a serpentine pattern so as not to get shot in the back by the officer. The wife is running ahead of the officer but falls to the ground.

II. Just the Facts

The officer advances past her, stops, plants his feet, aims and fires several times, shooting the man in the back. This presents the viewer with an early view of officers shooting at fleeing suspects to render an arrest. From the ground, the wife steadies herself on her knees, draws a pistol and shoots the officer in the back, killing him.

The Moonshiners ends with the wife racing to her husband and holding him in her arms. When the husband dies melodramatically, the wife collapses on top of him. *The Moonshiners* is not concerned with the rightness or wrongness of the husband and wife's actions, nor is the film concerned with having shown the explicit killing of officers in the movie. Thus this film presents significant challenges regarding early representations of law enforcement in cinema. By displaying the officer who pursues the husband as a corrupt coward, willing to kill a man by shooting him in the back while he is unarmed and running away, indicates to the audience that the law is not to be trusted. The wife also shoots the officer in the back; however, she does so sympathetically, in defense of her husband against the evilness of the law. The film thus depicts the criminals as the victims and the law as an adversary to a family just doing what needs to be done to survive.

Another film selected to provide ancillary support of scenes with officers shooting at a fleeing suspect to perform an arrest is later found in *Suspense* (1913), directed by Phillips Smalley and Lois Weber. Weber wrote the screenplay and stars in the film as the mother who is left alone at home with her baby after a servant quits without notice. The police in *Suspense* are more central figures, although they are also portrayed as aggressive.[48] The films narrative begins with a criminal "Tramp" seeing the servant leaving the home key under the doormat and entering the home. The mother (Lois Weber) phones her husband who rushes home from work, stealing a car to get there faster. The vehicle's owner and the police pursue the husband, nearly catching him along the way. This film thus presents one of the first examples of a police car chase; creating suspense as the vehicles are speeding down the roadway. Meanwhile, the mother barricades herself in her bedroom. The Tramp breaks through the door with a large knife and enters the room. Her husband arrives with police in hot pursuit.

As the husband is running up the grass to rescue his wife, both officers are seen firing their pistols at him, thus illustrating the "shoot first, ask questions later" mentality when attempting to arrest a fleeing felon. The scene further shows the police as heavy-handed in their approach by shooting a man fleeing for a perceived vehicle theft, which does not warrant being killed by the officers. The film remedies the police's aggressiveness by showing how they pat the husband on the back for doing what he did to rescue his wife. The representation of the police who are quick to fire their weapons appears over and over again, as discussed ahead.

Life of an American Policeman (1905)

The anti-law enforcement sentiment is a dominant narrative in early films; however, there are also early movies that render law enforcement in a positive light, most notably *Life of an American Policeman* (1905).[49] Directed by Edwin S. Porter and Wallace McCutcheon for the Edison Manufacturing Company, it was filmed in the fall of 1905 with the cooperation of the New York City Police Department.[50] Of all the Porter films, this one is the closest to nineteenth-century demands for realism.[51]

While *Life of an American Policeman* is one initiative the New York City Police Department took to improve their image in 1905, several newspaper accounts indicate the department was also actively seeking to purge the agency of corrupt officers to clean up their poor reputation. For example, also in 1905, at the direction of Police Commissioner William McAdoo, they began to investigate Police Officer Frank McLaughlin for brutally clubbing a well-known newspaper journalist, James P. Robbins. McLaughlin was said to have been a brutal clubber on the streets and had eighteen prior complainants against him. According to Robbins, on December 20, 1904, at 2:04 a.m., he was standing on the sidewalk waiting for a streetcar when without warning he nearly fell from a nightstick blow across his back by Officer McLaughlin.[52] Robbins told how he was subsequently clubbed numerous more times that resulted in a fractured wrist and lower portion of his arm being paralyzed, followed by Officer McLaughlin standing over him with his revolver aiming at him. Robbins reported that McLaughlin had squeezed the trigger but the gun jammed, and he was able to run away. Commissioner McAdoo immediately responded to the press, stating, "The man has had eighteen complaints against him since 1896 and has been fined sixty-eight and one-half days' pay. If all that is told of this case is true, it is an outrage. It is a mystery to me how such brutes as this man can get on the force."[53] Another police official, Captain Cooney, stated:

II. Just the Facts

> A policeman who attacks a citizen with his club as McLaughlin is alleged to have done is a disgrace to the force and brings decent policemen into disrepute. When such a man is found out the courts should make an example of him. The police should be more anxious to be rid of him than anyone else.[54]

McLaughlin was charged with felonious assault for clubbing Robbins, and upon review of his tenure as a police officer, it was found that he gave a similar account to his usage of deadly force earlier in May of 1904 when he shot and killed John W. Patterson outside a black dancehall. In that incident, accounts indicate that McLaughlin dispersed a crowd outside the dancehall and left the area. When he returned five minutes later, he found the crowd still in the area, which included Patterson, who he clubbed. He claimed that Patterson had a brick that he was going to attack him with, so he shot and killed him in self-defense. The account was very similar to the Robbins incident and ultimately led to McLaughlin being charged with murder. However, McLaughlin was granted a retrial that dragged out for several years and was eventually dismissed because it failed to meet the standard of a speedy trial.[55] Irrespective of the dismissal, McLaughlin was still released from the force, proof the department was proactively seeking to clean up its poor image after notoriously corrupt officials like the aforementioned Devery, Williams, and Byrnes, retired. Also, the above statements issued by Commissioner McAdoo and Captain Cooney demonstrate a police agency aware of their insalubrious reputation and a willingness to do something to correct it.

Life of an American Policeman is filled with counter narratives that the police are ethical, moral, and decent in their approach with the citizenry, specifically their aid to vulnerable demographics. The first scene shows the film's protagonist police officer having breakfast at home with his family at their dining table. After the meal, the wife helps her husband put on his policeman's coat; he kisses the family goodbye, and they watch and wave to him from the window as he heads off to the police precinct. This scene importantly shows the policeman as a person of traditional wholesome family values, a symbol of male paternalism. It gives viewers an inside look beyond the uniform to show how officers are also citizens who live modest and respectable lives. The uniform, weaponry, and paramilitary structure can make police agencies appear like occupying forces; therefore, the imagery presented in this scene helps to humanize the officers.

The next scene takes a harder approach by showing uniformed officers impeccably dressed and professional as they exit the precinct to begin their duties. The appearance of police officers sharply dressed, regimented, and walking out of the police station demonstrates how the police are a professional agency ready, willing, and capable to protect and serve the residents of New York City. It further portrays their authority by showing many tall and strong officers standing proud, chests out, and walking with a commanding presence. The officers exhibit their paramilitary structure by saluting, their military-like uniforms, and their obedience to superiors. The scene also shows the police forces strength in numbers, sending a clear message to the criminal gangs and would-be criminals that the police are powerful, well equipped, and prepared to combat lawlessness and those who prey upon the weak.

Life of an American Policeman continues with the film's protagonist policeman walking on his beat where he finds a lost child who he carries to a market and purchases food for the child with his own money. The officer is then shown helping a mother and child cross a busy city street. These images show the kind nature of the police officer and his benefit to the community, illustrating the police as a force for good. The film's main focus throughout is a chronicle of the compassionate and heroic activities officers perform to protect the weak and vulnerable. This scene showing an officer helping a child was purposeful as it displays the work officers do every day to assist this susceptible demographic. This counter narrative was sorely needed at a time when negative sentiment toward the police was palpable. Although the media's constant bombardment of negative perceptions were justified in many incidents, surely all officers were not corrupt, and many were good, decent, men who performed a dangerous job to protect the weak and vulnerable and arrest the criminals who preyed upon the citizenry. Showing the compassion of an officer to help a defenseless child affirms the need for the police force in a rapidly-changing urban environment.

Life of an American Policeman builds suspense by portraying the courageousness and chivalry of the police officers rescuing a would-be suicidal woman from the river. The rescuing police officer jumps in the water, and responding officers make a human chain to pull her from the river. It shows the intelligence of the officers to adapt in stressful situations to overcome challenges and save lives. This perilous act of heroism displays compassion and reinforces that the police are a force for the greater good of the community, are effective at rescuing residents during perilous times, and are willing to risk their lives while serving others. Moreover, it shows first-aid procedures to render help before the

II. Just the Facts

arrival of a physician; officers help transfer the woman to gurney and to the awaiting horse-and-carriage (ambulance) that rushes the victim off to presumably a local hospital. Porter and McCutcheon continues to move the narrative at a high-speed, cutting from the river rescue to a police officer on horseback racing to aid a frantic woman mounted on a runaway horse. The mounted officer gallops at full speed pursuing the runway horse, successfully gains control of it, dismounts in time to catch the victim as she falls from her horse, and saves the woman. This rescue is another demonstration of how officers help the vulnerable during grave incidents.

The film presents additional portrayals of heroic police officers. A later scene, which was apparently lost and was sold separately as the *Desperate Encounter Between Burglar and Police* (1905), reenacts the murder of an officer as he attempts to make an arrest.[56] This scene was based on the actual instance of NYPD patrolman Hugh J. Enright attempting to apprehend burglary suspects.[57] Upon consideration, it makes sense to sell the later scene as a separate film because the other scenes in the movie present a positive tone, and to offer the killing of a police officer at the end would drastically shift the film to a somber ending, hardly the film's intention.

Life of an American Policeman is a clearly a response to boost the police department's image and to show that although there are bad officers, as covered heavily in the press, there are many on the force who are decent men risking their lives for the safety of others. With the help of directors Porter and McCutcheon, the New York City Police Department was able to address their poor reputation and offer a counter narrative at a time when they sorely needed it. However, as we will see ahead, it takes many decades to ultimately reach a level of professional policing where the tarnished reputation of the early days of policing somewhat subsides.

The Black Hand (1906) and *The Musketeers of Pig Alley* (1912)

The Black Hand (1906) and *The Musketeers of Pig Alley* (1912) are films that illustrate the dangers of police work in combating organized crime in New York City. At the time these were filmed, organized crime was flourishing in American cities that were expanding rapidly with influxes of immigrants and shifts by Americans to occupy urban spaces.

Law Enforcement in American Cinema, 1894–1952

This created a social environment ripe for the advancement of organized crime during the mid to late nineteenth century when police departments were simultaneously formalizing and being conflicted by their associations with corrupt politicians and organized crime syndicates.

However, by the end of the nineteenth century, a divide in the relationship between the police and organized crime is noticeable with the assassination of New Orleans police chief David C. Hennessy on October 16, 1890. It is believed Hennessy was killed to silence him for his upcoming testimony against the Provenzano organized crime faction operating in New Orleans. After a sensational trial, a group of not guilty verdicts sent shockwaves across the nation. The day after the acquittal, an angry mob forced open the prison and lynched 11 of the 19 Italian men who had been indicted for Hennessy's murder. It was from this highly publicized event that the word "Mafia" came about in popular usage due to newspapers' usage as Hennessy's murder was the first widely publicized Mafia incident in the United States.

Historians concentrating on organized crime during this period generally agree:

> Organized crime is an urban phenomenon, rising from and with the evolving structures of local politics and industrial labor characteristics of post–Civil War American cities. Organized crime's particular ethnic bases were just a function of the changing population of certain American cities from the 1880s through the early 1920s.[58]

Although this is correct, organized crime originated in the United States long before the first shot of the Civil War was fired at Fort Sumter in 1861. It began in the New World with colonial pirates. These former naval mercenaries working for England during the war against Spain were an organized faction of international trade. "The pirates, it is clear, were the racketeers of their day, bribing officials, corrupting entire governments and looting to maintain a vast underworld market in forbidden goods."[59]

Another example of organized crime prior to the massive influx of Italian immigrants is observed in the early 1820s when Rosanna Peers and her Forty Thieves partook in organized crime in New York. Attorney and historian August Bequai, writing extensively on organized crime, provides details:

> Rosanna's vegetable market in the early 1820s became the center of activity for Edward Coleman's gang (the Forty Thieves), which engaged in robbery, murder, and theft. Rosanna's place also gave rise to a second gang, the Kerryonians, which

II. Just the Facts

recruited many of its members from New York's Irish community, most of whom had been born in County Kerry.[60]

The Black Hand is a fictional up-close look into organized crime in the Italian ethnic community of New York City. It is an early surviving film about the Mafia. Its name represents the criminal syndicates of Italian-Americans in cities across the country in the late nineteenth to the early twentieth century. *The Black Hand* plot has gangsters threatening a local butcher, telling him that if he does not pay, they will kidnap his daughter. When the butcher does not pay, the Mafia kidnaps his daughter. The butcher summons police detectives, who hide in the meat locker in his shop. When an armed man enters the shop and threatens the butcher, the detectives spring from the meat locker and wrestle with the gunman, effectively arresting him. This scene shows the bravery and strength of the police. In the end, the police rescue the butcher's daughter from the gangster's den by surprising and overpowering them. The cops are heralded as superior to the criminals and not afraid to bring them to justice, as well as useful at combatting the power of the criminal underworld.

Law enforcement additionally receives a favorable portrayal in *The Silver Wedding* (1906) produced by F.A. Dobson for American Mutoscope & Biograph. In both *The Black Hand* and *The Silver Wedding*, the police are seen in procedural roles, but the plots they appear in are representative of a society intimately aware of criminality. *The Silver Wedding* is noteworthy because the plot is basically wealthy people being robbed of their valuables at a wedding by the underclass—career organized-crime thieves from the ghettos who dress up as wealthy wedding guests to gain access inside the venue to hatch their trap. The police in this film are limited in their appearance to the closing scenes, but nonetheless are seen as effective and strong. They chase down the criminals, struggling with them as they successfully arrest them and haul them off to jail. However, considering the film portrays wealthy people being robbed and the reality that the audience was not one of them, the audience very well may have not cared who won. As aforementioned, films during this period were made and shown in cities where the working class and the poor frequented their screening—the wealthy saw these venues as subpar and underclass gatherings not worthy of their participation.

Another film involving the police and the underworld is D.W. Griffith's *The Musketeers of Pig Alley* (1912). This film was shot in Fort Lee,

New Jersey, which doubled as a location for New York City in many early pictures. *The Musketeers of Pig Alley* is an early surviving gangster film where the police partake in a minor role and their effectiveness to combat organized crime is challenged. The main takeaway is that justice is in the hands of the victim, and the police are not to be counted on to pursue it. The scenes show police officers working in the ghetto where organized crime succeeds. Written by Griffith and screenwriter Anita Loos, the primary focus of the film is on an impoverished married couple living in New York City and a criminal syndicate occupying the same public sphere. After returning from traveling as a musician, the husband's wallet (his earnings from the trip) is stolen by a gangster named Snapper Kid. The husband endeavors to get his earnings back himself, while his wife "The Little Lady" (played by Lillian Gish) attends a ball where there is an attempt to drug her, but coincidently she is saved by the Snapper Kid. This act creates a rivalry between two gangs, and a shootout ensues outside. The husband is caught in the shooting and recognizes Snapper Kid as the thief who stole his wallet. The husband sneaks his wallet back from Snapper Kid.

During the shootout, a group of uniformed police officers arrives and join in the fray, thus symbolizing the police as the third gang involved. The Snapper Kid is able to stun a cop who tries to detain him and runs away, thereby demonstrating the superiority of the criminal. The husband and wife return safely to their apartment. The police pursue the Snapper Kid, who is now also at the couple's apartment. The Snapper Kid tells the wife how he saved her from a man who was going to drug her. The husband and wife deceive the policeman by giving a false alibi. The moral is that the public handles and pursues justice themselves, and they can deceive the police if it better suits them. Clearly, the police, although strong, are meant to be treated with suspicion.

A Corner in Wheat (1909)

As with many early films, D.W. Griffith's *A Corner in Wheat* does not portray police officers in a favorable light. They are instead seen beating the poor and firing their pistols against a public upset over a lack of bread, when the reason for the deficit was the direct result of a greedy tycoon who corners the world market on wheat, thus making bread no longer affordable. *A Corner in Wheat* displays genius with its

II. Just the Facts

juxtaposition of wealthy society and the poor, accomplished by crosscutting between scenes of the poor on a bread line with the rich dining in excess. D.W. Griffith, although not the inventor of the crosscutting technique, is considered the vanguard for employing it.[61]

The popular theme of the rich versus the poor and the ill-treatment they receive in an unfair justice system is also found in an earlier Edison Manufacturing Company film, *The Kleptomaniac* (1905) directed by Edwin S. Porter. In *The Kleptomaniac* a wealthy woman shoplifts from a department store, is arrested, and gets off on the charges, while the justice system punishes a poor woman who steals a loaf of bread to feed her hungry family. The role of the uniformed police officers in *The Kleptomaniac* is purely procedural, but they are agents of a compromised justice system where the poor are maltreated, as opposed to the rich who can commit crimes without penalty.[62]

Americans, especially those living in poor urban communities, had known of a corrupt government that figuratively held them down, denying them access to the American dream, while the rich got more prosperous and they got hungrier and were often beaten for stealing a loaf of bread to feed their starving family. Filmmakers understood this theme well. Like *A Corner in Wheat*, the imagery of a father stealing a loaf of bread to feed his hungry family is found earlier in political cartoonist Thomas Nast's 1871 illustration "Wholesale and Retail" (Figure 4). In Nast's illustration, the top cartoon shows Boss Tweed exiting the New York City Treasury with his corrupt cohorts; their pockets are stuffed with cash while two police officers with their clubs down salute the men, showing how the politicians control the government and the police are complicit in their crimes. The bottom drawing shows two police officers beating a poor man who stole a loaf of bread to feed his family while his wife and child are show cowering behind the wall of the bakery. This accessible rich versus the poor theme was designed for the viewers in urban America who resented the rich and their gluttonous ways while they struggled to make ends meet. *A Corner in Wheat* is an excellent film that addressed this reality.

D.W. Griffith and Fran E. Woods adapted *A Corner in Wheat* from the novel *The Pit* and from the short story *A Deal in Wheat* by Frank Norris. The main takeaway from the portrayal of law enforcement in the film is that they are agents of the government and are not on the side of the people, even when the lives of the poor are ruined because of the greed of the rich. In the scene involving two large officers in the bakery, both are equipped with long clubs and beat a hungry family of

Figure 4. A political cartoon illustrating the thievery of police officers and politicians while a poor family is beaten for stealing a loaf of bread. 1871.

II. Just the Facts

men, women, and children. The film shows the officers swinging their clubs and pointing their pistols, and one officer fires a warning shot into the ceiling of the bakery while the good-natured people cower to the law and appear helpless—their only crime hunger (Figure 5). Since the officers are not on the side of the people, the film's message about law enforcement is clear: be wary of trusting the police because they are not on the public's side and will beat and kill innocent, hungry people who are victims of a society where the wealthy are concerned only with massive profits, even if that means destroying the lives of the poor. *A Corner in Wheat* is a problematic film representation for a profession that was expanding during this period. This stark contrast between the rich and poor was a prevalent social issue during the Progressive era when many demanded reform.

Since the cinema industry and early law enforcement emerged contemporaneously during the early days of cinema, films such as *Robetta and Doretto [No. 2]* or *Chinese Laundry* (1894), *Sherlock Holmes Baffled* (1900), *How They Rob Men in Chicago* (1900), *A Gesture Fight in Hester Street* (1900), *How They Do Things on the Bowery* (1902), *The*

Figure 5. Two sizeable uniformed police are beating hungry people for arguing with the baker because they can no longer afford bread. 1909.

Law Enforcement in American Cinema, 1894–1952

Moonshiners (1904), *Life of an American Policeman* (1905), *The Kleptomaniac* (1905), *The Black Hand* (1906), *Fights of Nations* (1907), *A Corner in Wheat* (1909), *The Musketeers of Pig Alley* (1912), *Suspense* (1913), and others depicted in this chapter help to uncover emerging attitudes toward police officers and their work. Although not encyclopedic, the chosen films in this chapter demonstrate the push and pull between positive and negative law enforcement representation in this early period of censorship. Undeniably the lion's share of police portrayals in early films are deleterious, arguably because concurrent incidents involving police forces, especially, in New York City where the movie industry was budding, were similarly abhorrent. Since the police were a primary target of reform, it is not surprising that negative visual representations of officers appeared en masse on film, since film both reflects and refracts how the police's role in society was viewed and generally how the public considered them. As we move ahead to Chapter III, we see the further development of police portrayals on film during the Progressive era, when filmmakers had the advantage of offering longer movies with many scenes and additional storytelling abilities.

III

Cops in Silent-Era Feature Film

Traffic in Souls (1913), *Easy Street* (1917) and *Cops* (1922)

> If there is one human type more than any other that the whole wide world has it in for, it is the policeman type. Of course, the policeman isn't really to blame for the public prejudice against his uniform—it's just the natural human revulsion against any sort of authority—but just the same everybody loves to see the "copper" get it where the chicken got the axe.[1]—Charlie Chaplin, 1917

Since feature films such as *Traffic in Souls*, *Easy Street*, and *Cops* appeared in the United States during the Progressive era—a period rife with social reform initiatives that were at the forefront of American consciousness—it is no surprise filmmakers drew upon the sensationalism involving social unrest and street crime, as well as "white slavery" (forced prostitution) and other crimes, since all were pervasive concerns. By the 1910s, the population had largely shifted to urban spaces, and massive, rapid influxes of immigrants filled the expanding cities, while poverty and social inequality created a ripe climate for organized crime and police corruption. Progressive reformists worked to eliminate corruption from municipal governments, for the abolition of child labor, and for the right for women to vote, as well as other social-issue reforms including temperance and birth control for women. Included in this list were improvements to the police, who were considered to be too often "uneducated, corrupt and brutal."[2]

Feature filmmakers during this period understood the power of incorporating scandalous topics in their films. They played to the worries and public perceptions of the viewership because both gave their viewers the narratives they enjoyed and, in turn, was profitable for the budding film industry, thus emphasizing the film industry's venture as being capitalistic. Major productions include Italy's *Cabiria* (1913), which saw a lavish set and large cast, thus influencing D.W. Griffith's *Birth of a Nation* (1915)—America's first film that established cinema. There is a wealth of information for interpretation originating from this era, where historical research of film and American culture is still emerging. Take, for example, *The Birth of a Nation*, a highly successful film that is among the most discussed because of its massive production and the immensely controversial aspects, such as its positive portrayal of the Ku Klux Klan and its interpretation of black men as unintelligent and highly sexually aggressive toward white women. Therefore, it appropriately has been the focus of many academic works.[3]

Traffic in Souls (1913), *Easy Street* (1917), and *Cops* (1922) were capitalistically motivated films that harnessed the power of interwoven sensationalism storylines. The focus of *Traffic in Souls* was "white slavery," a primary concern at that time. *Easy Street* concentrated on social anomie and cultural blight in the urban ghettos where drug addiction, poverty, domestic violence, assault, prostitution, gang violence, and police brutality were rampant. *Cops* emphasized an unfair justice system, police brutality, and negative public sentiment toward law enforcement. These three films were selected for this chapter because they demonstrate how films reflect popular cultural perceptions of law enforcement at the time of production and how historians can locate these representations through analysis of the films.

In terms of law enforcement representation, *Traffic in Souls* provides a more sympathetic attitude toward the police, while also calling attention to their flaws. *Easy Street* and *Cops* demonstrate how the police of the 1910s and 1920s were considered to be heavy-handed individuals, viewed as inept and deserving of satire. However, *Easy Street* poked lighter fun at the police, who were still portrayed on the side of good but who were also overpowered and unable to address the crimes overrunning the community. *Cops*, as stated, was much more direct in its approach in showing open contempt for the police and the justice system. *Easy Street* and *Cops* are derivatives of shorter slapstick comedies such as the earlier mentioned Keystone Kops, which for the most part are negative depictions of police as blubbering idiots unable to solve a crime, even if the crime evidence falls at their feet. They are shown as agents of chaos, disconnected from the laws they are supposed to uphold. Unfortunately, over 100 years later, these unfavorable

III. Cops in Silent-Era Feature Film

representations of law enforcement are still part of popular culture—the "Keystone Kops" snub is still used to insult police agencies across the country perceived as incompetent. This label, while admittedly at times earned, is mostly not justified. (Today, the overwhelming majority of law enforcement agencies are professional departments that exist for the greater good of society and the protection of the citizens they serve; therefore, the idea that the law enforcement profession closely resembles the Keystone Kops of yesteryear is a fallacy of copious proportions, an unfortunate snub.)

Traffic in Souls, *Easy Street*, and *Cops* also demonstrate how local censorship during the early silent film era was a reality, as previously discussed; however, writers and actors like Chaplin and Keaton were able to convey disparaging representations of law enforcement in their films through using the cloak of comedy. In *Traffic of Souls*, George Loane Tucker also covertly portrays prostitution in the light of reformist advocacy to fend off censors. *Traffic in Souls* is for the most part a positive portrayal of police; however, it shows the reality that vice was rampant under their watch, nevertheless exposing police corruption. *Easy Street* and *Cops* further depict police brutality coupled with a sense of the ineffectiveness of the police and the mistrust by the communities they serve. As we saw in the previous chapter, much of this mistrust had come from decades of systemic police corruption and brutality, so by the time of the 1910s, the public was demanding the police abandon their old ways and revolutionize their treatment and service to the public. Public outcry over wildly egregious incidents involving police corruption, including police-involvement in murder, birthed several investigative bodies, like the previously mentioned Lexow Committee. The public demanded investigations, and therefore, committees assembled to examine alleged police-involved audacities. Scholar Robert Fogelson, writing in 1977, succinctly summarizes these probes across the country:

> In 1909, Mayor Arthur Harper, Chief Edward Kern, and a prominent pimp formed a syndicate that attempted to monopolize prostitution in Los Angeles by instructing the police department to enforce the law and harass the prostitutes everywhere except in the vicinity of a few houses recently purchased by the syndicate. Three years later several gunmen, who were allegedly acting for Lieutenant Charles Becker, head of one of the New York City Police Department's vice squads, shot and killed Herman Rosenthal, a professional gambler who had just charged the force with protecting gambling and was scheduled to appear before the district attorney to substantiate his charges. A major scandal broke out in San Francisco in 1913 when the press reported that Frank Esola, Louis Droulette, and nearly a dozen other detectives had recruited a gang of swindlers and, in return for 15 percent of

the estimated gross of $300,000 a year, protected its members from the rest of the police department. An even worse scandal erupted in Chicago a year or so later when several members of the underworld who operated out of the Twenty-Second Street Levee tried to cripple Mayor Metellus L.C. Funkhouser's moral squad by threatening his deputy's life, stabbing one officer, and shooting another.[4]

Although law enforcement during the 1910s was drastically advancing, there were many incidents like the above mentioned that fed continued intense narratives of distrust and resentment. In New York City, the press and public outrages over the alleged murder commissioned by police lieutenant Charles Becker led to his arrest, conviction, and sentencing to death by execution in Sing Sing's electric chair. Becker is the only New York City police officer to be executed for murder.[5] Becker maintained his innocence in the murder plot, and on the day before he was executed, he's said to have told the prison warden, "Sure, I told them to put Rosenthal out of the way, but I didn't mean they should kill him. I wanted them to get him out of town so he wouldn't blab. Killing him was Rose's idea and the others. They wanted to save their own skins."[6] In other words, Becker admittedly condoned beating up the complainant to keep him quiet. In a world-weary of police brutality, Becker's confession, in part, shows how force to achieve objectives was inconsequential to corrupt officers who were, in many ways, criminals in uniform operating in plain sight. *Easy Street* and *Cops* holds no punches while exposing this reality.

As we move ahead, this chapter aims to discuss police representations on film through the specific lens of *Traffic in Souls*, *Easy Street*, and *Cops*—films concentrating on sensationalistic topics that play to the public consciousness of the viewers. Because the film industry targeted their audiences as being primarily comprised of working-class viewers, these films refract the views of these communities and their mistrust of the police. They tell the larger story at a time when societal change was rapid, and police reform was befitting.

Traffic in Souls (1913)

Traffic in Souls is an early feature-length film that addresses a moral panic at the time about "white slavery" or forced sex trafficking and prostitution of young white women. In particular, newly arriving young female immigrants were being preyed upon by seemingly respectable men, who, after gaining the young women's trust, forced them into

III. Cops in Silent-Era Feature Film

prostitution. Eventually, this form of sex trafficking would also include American women—white American maidenhood—being forced into the sex industry.[7] Director George Loane Tucker treats this criminal activity by juxtaposing two examples of women forced into white slavery: a pair of newly arrived naïve Swedish immigrants and an American woman, whose father is an inventor, and her sister, who is the girlfriend of a police officer. The officer appears in different scenes, depicted as both in police uniform and as a plainclothes detective.[8]

While shopping the screenplay, Tucker pitched it as a way to show how pimps were stalking and abducting young women and forcing them into prostitution and how awareness and advocacy through the film's narrative could prevent other unsuspecting women from becoming victims. Although a social indictment as well as a documentary of sorts, the film is also an early melodrama. Additional movies of the 1910s that dealt with social issues such as drug abuse, child marriage, juvenile delinquency, and abortion began to appear, such as Lois Weber's *Where Are My Children* (1916), which condemned abortion and advocated for birth control for working-class women. *The Inside of the White Slave Traffic* (1913) also dealt with the issues of prostitution and immorality. Shorter than *Traffic in Souls*, the film still manages to adequately portray the methods by which young women were being kidnapped and forced into prostitution.

To provide some context about why "white slavery" was such a dominant issue of the 1910s, Reginald Wright Kaufmann's novel about white slavery, *The House of Bondage*, was so popular that after its release in August of 1910 it underwent twelve subsequent printings by July of 1911. The book shocked the public. Kauffman wrote in the book's opening that the story was intended for "those who have to bring up children, for those who have to bring up themselves, and for those who, in order that they may think of bettering the weaker, are, on their own part strong enough to begin that task by bearing a knowledge of truth."[9] Kauffman goes on to tell how white slavery is pervasive in the life of the underworld in every large city and how he has "written only what I myself seen and myself heard."

Traffic in Souls provides historical images of the 1910s, allowing windows into the past through scenes shot in Fort Lee, New Jersey, on the streets of New York City, and at Battery Park in lower Manhattan, where real immigrants recently arriving from Ellis Island are seen in the background.[10] Other images of the 1910s social milieu include trolley cars, automobiles, horse and carriages, attire of the day, and city populations, including tenement houses. Before this period, still photographs, paintings, or literary accounts memorialized images. *Traffic in Souls* also portrays images of the brothels of the day, including the pimps who committed violence against their abductees, the African American madams, and the prostitutes themselves. The film also dramatizes how young women, such as the newly arrived Swedish girls—dressed in stereotypical Swedish costumes with long-braided wigs—are taken advantage of by men whom, at first, appear respectable but soon force the young women into prostitution.[11] The film presents the grim reality that immigrants, who have fled their home country in search of a better life, do not always find that better life, and in some cases even find their new home far worse than the one they fled. It also demonstrates a popular film narrative about class bias, as seen in the fictional portrayals of social elitist and philanthropist William Trubus—a member of the ruling class who controls public vice in the underworld—and how the rich profit from the poor.[12]

For the purpose of this study, *Traffic in Souls* importantly provides a wealth of representations of law enforcement and their interactions with the criminals they pursue; for instance, in scenes such as where NYPD police officer Larry Burke first detects a brothel and single-handedly frees the women and arrests the criminals. This scene, however unrealistic in suggesting that one officer could fight off numerous offenders while rescuing a group of women and bringing them all into the stationhouse, nevertheless represents police as defenders of morality, capable of capturing criminals with the drawing of their pistol. For example, when Burke draws his police pistol, and the criminals throw their hands in the air to comply with his orders, there are moments when they can overpower him. However, most attention in the film is focused on the criminals and their victims, while the police are shown merely as agents who end the problem of white slavery. Nevertheless, the film also leaves the audience with a sense of how police corruption could allow the brothels to thrive right under their noses, such as when the criminals casually attempt to pay off Officer Burke in a way that indicates it is considered socially acceptable among officers to accept bribes. Burke declines the bribe, but the film still leaves the audience with the understanding that paying off the police is at least possible.

Several scenes involving the police also importantly show the wizardry of intelligence-led policing. Isaac Barton, the wheel-chair-stricken inventor, who is the father of kidnapped Lorna Barton, invented a recording microphone device that allows the police to eavesdrop, an

III. Cops in Silent-Era Feature Film

Figure 6. Police officers depicted as brave defenders of the victim. 1913.

early representation of what would later become known as a phone bug. Although the technology was not possible at the time, and neither was the tablet used by the criminals where the daily earnings magically appeared in Trubus's office (arguably a prescient version of email as we know it today), the film nevertheless expresses how technology was an essential aspect of both early law enforcement and the criminal milieu. In the end, this technology is used by the police to support the case against Trubus.

Traffic in Souls winds up with the police as the defenders of the weak, as they rescue the victim (Figure 6). In this scene, Officer Burke saves the kidnapped Lorna Barton and shows the police as the brave defenders of the weak and protectors against the criminal underworld. As shown in the above figure, the officer holding Barton shows compassion for the victim.

The film ends with the arrest of Trubus, as the intertitle informs us, at "the proudest moment of Trubus's life. While his daughter's betrothal was being arranged," thus showing how the police were able to move easily within the milieu of the working-class and are at times even superior to the ruling class. *Traffic in Souls* ends with the moral lesson that crime does not go unpunished. The final scene also depicts Trubus's wife seemingly committing suicide to "escape her husband's shame." Trubus's distraught daughter blames her father for her mother's death. The film closes with Trubus crying out in anguish at his wife's deathbed, as he falls to the floor.

Although the police in *Traffic in Souls* are depicted as heroes, as the agents fighting the good fight against white slavery and its immorality, the contrasting reality that prostitution, in fact, existed openly on their watch en masse speaks to both their ineffectiveness and corruption at the time. As aforementioned, the example of NYPD's first chief of police William Devery's corruption and grafting from the vice of the criminal underworld exemplifies how actual police corruption was a palpable reality, as *Traffic in Souls* reveals. During the same year that *Traffic in Souls* was released, another film, *The Bangville Police*, a comedy featuring the Keystone Kops, uses slapstick to illustrate this point. The plot of *The Bangville Police* is mostly that the police are not to be trusted and are in many cases unintelligent, unethical, and are not the solution to the problems of the times. These particular constructs of police identity were widely popular and continued in film throughout the decade.

Easy Street (1917)

Easy Street is the best early example of police working to handle social anomie in the community while being portrayed as having been defeated in their efforts against rampant violence and crime. At the time of this Chaplin film in 1917, drug use, poverty, domestic violence, assault, prostitution, gang violence, and other social anomies were running amok in the inner cities. The only lines between the destruction of the community and a chance at peace were the police and the church; however, the police were considered to be much less useful as well as worthy of lampoon in the eyes of the working-class that mostly comprised the film viewership of the day. Publishing his reflections on the film in a 1917 issue of *Reel Life*, Chaplin remarked that

> if there is one human type more than any other that the whole wide world has it in for, it is the policeman type. Of course, the policeman isn't really to blame for the public prejudice against his uniform—it's just the natural human revulsion against any sort of authority—but just the same everybody loves to see the "copper" get it where the chicken got the axe.[13]

Chaplin continued, pointing out that

III. Cops in Silent-Era Feature Film

> I make myself solid by letting my friends understand that I am not a real policeman except in the sense that I've been put on for a special job—that of manhandling a big bully. Of course, I have my work cut out tackling a contract like that, and the sympathy of the audience is with me, but I have also the element of suspense, which is invaluable in a motion picture plot. The natural supposition is that the policeman is going to get the worst of it and there is an intense interest in how I am to come out of my apparently unequal combat with "Bully" Campbell.[14]

Chaplin had worked at Mack Sennett's Keystone Studios, acting in the slapstick film series Keystone Kops, from which *Easy Street* was drawing upon for representations of law enforcement. However, the film does not depict the police as being as considerably inept as their portrayal in the Keystone Kop films. *Easy Street* opens with Charlie Chaplin (the derelict also known as the Tramp) lying against the stairway of a church, while mass services are commencing. The Tramp enters the church, and from his mannerisms, it is apparent that he is not familiar with the church edict or social norms. The Tramp is an outsider from the faith, and therefore this is an allusion to his immorality and his present circumstances in life. However, through a brief encounter with the minister and his daughter, an awakening occurs, illustrating how the church is a force for good in society and how a "new beginning" or transformation can take place if one only seeks the moral guidance of the church. Their kindness so compels the Tramp he returns the collection box, which he had been hiding in his pants, thus signaling a transformation had occurred not only in thought but also in action.

The Tramp leaves the church and walks out onto Easy Street, where a rough and tumble scene of violence is taking place. A big thug Bully towers over three police officers who lay at his feet, while he gives them a hard beating. In their initial appearance, the police are depicted as inferior to criminals and their strength. In the following scene, the "Police return from Easy Street," the officers are shown to be punch-drunk and injured from the brutality of the Bully, so much so that it suggests that they have lost all control of the streets and at present are ineffective in solving the problems that are destroying the morality of the neighborhood. A subsequent scene shows the uniformed police officers being beaten up severely by the Bully who again displays a blatant disrespect for authority by tossing them onto the street like rag dolls.

Thus the film presents a direct representation of the public's mistrust of police during the 1910s, especially, as stated, since at that time films were predominately made with working-class viewers in mind. Today, although perhaps not quite as flagrant as the 1910s, there are

Law Enforcement in American Cinema, 1894–1952

Figure 7. The Tramp (Charlie Chaplin) stands outside the police station with a sign posted "Police Wanted at Once." 1917.

still many communities that do not trust the police. Recent explosive riots in cities such as Ferguson, Missouri, in 2014, in the aftermath of a police-involved shooting, show a story of resentment that is palpable. In such communities, communication barriers between the police and the community created volatile situations over the course of many years.

The narrative of police and community mistrust continues in the following scene where the Tramp is seen walking along Easy Street, where he finds a sign posted outside the police station: "Police Wanted at Once" (Figure 7). The Tramp paces back and forth, continuing to read the sign, while internally struggling: could a man of the street, who only moments prior attempted to steal from the church, serve as a police officer?

The Tramp enters the stationhouse and is initially mocked by the precinct inspector, who implies he is not strong enough to perform the police job. In actuality, police officers at the time were first examined for their appearance, stature, and display of strength, with many departments requiring minimum height requirements for employment. The

III. Cops in Silent-Era Feature Film

traditional officer had to meet these height and athletic prowess requirements, and the Tramp did not, with his short stature and thin appearance, but the joke in the film is that the police are so desperate that they will even take the little Tramp to help fill the ranks.[15] Again, as both a person from the streets and one who is not the typical size of police officers, the Tramp is marked as an outsider. As a test of will, the precinct commander slaps the Tramp, who, in turn, reflexively slaps him back, thus impressing the commander. This scene, used to show someone who is willing to fight at a time when the police are being beaten badly on Easy Street, also signals a world where police brutality was accepted as a means to justify an end and when a display of force was necessary to overcome chaos. This scene also ridicules the police by showing the viewers that anyone can become a police officer, even a criminal, and therefore does not provide a favorable light in which working-class viewers would see the police. Of course, the film is a comedy; however, the context of the scenes and actions nevertheless are reflective of negative sentiments of law enforcement at that time, as evidenced by Chaplin's aforementioned statement that "everybody loves to see the 'copper' get it where the chicken got the axe" and the police slated as targets of reform during the Progressive era.[16]

The Tramp, now dressed in police uniform, meets a resident on the street who mocks him because of his not looking like a typical police officer. In response, the Tramp hits the man over the head with his nightstick, again reaffirming the belief that the police are willing to use violence whenever their authority is challenged. The following scene reasserts this challenging of authority by depicting the Bully wearing a policeman's hat (cadged from one of the officers he had beaten up) while walking on Easy Street, thus suggesting that the criminals rule the street. The Bully and the Tramp meet, with another juxtaposition of the authority of the offender and the weakness of the police; however, the Tramp outsmarts the Bully—a man of brute strength who even bends a gas lamp pole. Thinking quickly, the Tramp gets the Bully's head inside the lamp, turns the gas on full force, thus rendering the Bully unconscious. When the residents of Easy Street reappear, they see the Tramp standing over the Bully and are immediately scared of the Tramp, hence signaling a shift in power—they are confronted with the reality that restoring law and order is possible; however, it takes a police outsider (or a community insider) to accomplish it.

The Tramp now assumes the role once held by the Bully as the enforcer of the street. Seven officers arrive on the scene to find the

Tramp sitting on the Bully, clearly indicating his superiority over the criminal and the authority of the police. The seven officers represent the police establishment, in both their ineptness and inability to police the streets, through their being scared of a child licking a lollipop. The story next takes a twist as the Bully is led off to the police precinct, and the Tramp uncovers a woman stealing a ham. When the Tramp learns she is poor, in a Robin Hood–like manner, he helps her steal more food. The message to the audience is the reality that the police can be compassionate and also serve as protectors of the poor; however, it would again take an outsider, or a new way of thinking, for this to happen. The minister's daughter soon appears and observes the Tramp's kind nature, also reassuring the viewer that the Tramp kept his promise to reform his old ways. However, this scene is also a powerful illustration of a society where police mistrust is a severe issue. Even while he is a hero, a woman who apparently despises his presence tosses a flowerpot from a window at the Tramp.

Easy Street continues to address social issues of overcrowding and poverty in the inner cities, as well as families having many children. The Tramp is brought to an apartment of a family with a lot of children, so many that he is, in fact, perplexed about how many children the family has. (At the time working-class families were large due to a high mortality rate, religious beliefs, less awareness and use of birth control, more hands needed to work, and also to assure a better chance of family survival as parents aged.) Meanwhile, there is a crosscut to the Bully who regains consciousness, breaks the handcuffs, and begins to beat the police officers again, tossing them around like rag dolls. Another crosscut takes viewers back to the Tramp and the poor family. The Tramp places his badge on the father and then returns to feed the family, sprinkling grain like chicken feed on the ground for the children in Chaplin's comedic way to show the problem with overpopulation and poverty.[17] The Tramp's temporarily taking off of his badge and placing it on the father's jacket shows that he is consciously aware the police are servants of the people, therefore highlighting the concerns with police corruption and the need for reform.

The seriousness of domestic violence confronts viewers next. The Bully is now slugging it out with his wife in their bedroom. The Tramp responds, and a fight ensues between the Tramp and the Bully. The other criminals of Easy Street also attempt to assault the Tramp. However, the Tramp again outsmarts the Bully by pushing a stove out of a second-floor window directly onto the Bully. The stove is a symbol of

III. Cops in Silent-Era Feature Film

family nourishment and is weaponized to escalate the violence.[18] The minister's daughter appears again and attempts to rush to the Tramp's aid; however, she is kidnapped by the street thugs and placed in a cellar with a drug fiend who attempts to rape her. The imagery of the drug fiend injecting drugs shows how drugs, as a dangerous social issue, was a considerable problem affecting the urban space. It also suggests that drug use and sexual assaults are related.

The thugs of *Easy Street* soon overpower the Tramp, coincidentally tossing him through a utility hole that leads to a cellar where the drug fiend and the minister's daughter are confined. The drug fiend is again attempting to rape the minister's daughter, but the Tramp fights him off as well as dozens of thugs, rescues the minister's daughter, and restores order to Easy Street. The final scene shows a bright and clean Easy Street as the Tramp and churchgoers head for Sunday Mass. They nod and display respect to the Tramp, including the Bully, who has learned the errors of his criminal ways and is now a seemingly moral citizen with respect for authority. The scene fades out with the Tramp and the minister's daughter walking arm-in-arm toward the church. The power of the church is also used to illustrate how through religion a return to morality is possible, even for cities and their citizens who are overrun with immorality and crime. Moreover, the church and an outsider's mindset to the methods of the police are the way to accomplish this. *Easy Street's* main takeaway, however, is that the police are in need of reform as are the social issues of the inner cities.

Cops (1922)

Likely inspired by the negative sentiments he had for law enforcement during the third trial of his friend and mentor Roscoe "Fatty" Arbuckle, who was charged with rape and manslaughter in which both trials resulted in hung juries, Buster Keaton's *Cops* (co-written with Edward F. Cline) has an interesting similarity to the accusations and subsequent trials of Arbuckle.[19] Arbuckle was charged with raping and murdering young movie starlet Virginia Rappe in a hotel room in San Francisco after a Labor Day weekend party in 1921. Although Prohibition was in full effect, the party was a secret "gin party," and ultimately Rappe died of a ruptured bladder aggravated by alcohol.[20] Why Rappe's bladder ruptured is a mystery that played out in the press, including a myth that Arbuckle had sexually penetrated Rappe with a champagne bottle.[21] The prosecution also offered that Arbuckle's overweight body on top of the slim Rappe during the sexual assault contributed to the rupturing of her bladder. Ultimately this theory was not proven beyond a reasonable doubt.[22]

Arbuckle had brought Keaton, "The Great Stone Face," into the film business, and the two remained friends, working on several projects together.[23] *Cops*' main character (Keaton) is also accused and pursued for crimes he did not commit. The plot shows how the entire situation for which the police pursue Keaton is a misunderstanding—however, he is nevertheless continually pursued. Keaton reaffirms the idea of an innocent man being hunted and ultimately destroyed, as evidenced in the final scene where Keaton is pulled into the stationhouse by a huge group of cops. The last image the viewers see is a tombstone with "The End" engraved on it, and Keaton's porkpie hat hanging from the edge, thus sending the message that Keaton is dead, killed for a crime he did not commit. Similarly, even after Arbuckle's third acquittal, his career was destroyed. However, he found work directing films under a pseudonym, William B. Goodrich. Keaton suggested he should call himself "Will B. Good," an obvious pun against the perceived injustices against him. Arbuckle opted for the former since it was, in fact, his father's name.[24]

Cops opens with Keaton standing behind a sizeable iron-wrought gate, one that initially looks as if he is in prison—an essential symbol for what the lead character embodies. Keaton is speaking to the mayor's daughter, who states (through an intertitle), "I won't marry you until you become a big businessman." From the start, Keaton depicts how a man is perceived as imprisoned both in a visual sense and also metaphorically, because he is not accepted for who he is. Keaton thus sets out to find success as a businessman. When walking down the street, he finds a wallet a large man dropped from his pocket. Moments later we find out the big man is a police officer; his sheer size indicates his authority, and Keaton—a much smaller man—shows his ability to outfox the policeman, thus illustrating again how the police are perceived to be incompetent, clumsy, and quick to be hard-fisted. Keaton leaves with the policeman's money, believing it is a start for him to reach his goal. This scene is, of course, the most problematic for Keaton's overall premise; however, it was a petty theft and therefore not worthy of the massive police response that comes his way, nor was it deserving of capital punishment.

The following scene shows how a con artist who saw Keaton with

III. Cops in Silent-Era Feature Film

the handful of money fools Keaton into believing the furniture a family was gathering outside their home was his for sale so that he could feed his children. Keaton falls for the con and pays the man, who quickly makes off with the money. Keaton believes the furniture is a way for him to jumpstart a business. Not surprisingly, the owner of the furniture (the father) just so happens to be another giant policeman.

The scene continues with more misunderstandings. Keaton walks across the street toward a horse and carriage with a for sale sign that indicates the cost for the pair is five dollars; however, the sign is really for a suit jacket outside a men's store. A man is in front of the horse and carriage; Keaton mistakes him as the owner and pays him the five dollars. The man, too, misinterprets Keaton's intention to purchase the horse and carriage, takes the money, and pays the owner of the store for the suit jacket, walking off in his new coat. Keaton escorts the horse and wagon across the street; the family mistakenly believes Keaton is the hired hand to transport their furniture. They begin to load the wagon, while Keaton, stunned, sits and watches them. These mistakes of identity and multiple misunderstandings are all designed to show how the police and the law are not infallible; sometimes, the wrong person is arrested for a crime they did not knowingly, or intentionally, commit. It is also a demonstration of police precipitateness.

Keaton begins his travel in the carriage, and when he signals a turn with his left hand, a dog on the back of a truck misreads his intentions and bites his hand. Thinking quickly, Keaton uses an accordion-style coat rack, on which he affixes a boxing glove at its end to make a turn signal. He then travels past a cop in the middle of the street directing traffic, when the boxing glove unintentionally springs from the carriage and knocks the cop to the ground. The scene shows how the police, and the authority they represent in uniform, are vulnerable to attack. Even though assaulted under a comedic charade, a cop is the target, and not a baker, carpenter, or anyone else, therefore signaling that law enforcement is the central issue. This assault by chance, in fact, occurs twice, leaving the cop punch-drunk in the street.

The film continues with mocking the police with the intertitle "Once a year the citizens of every city know where they can find a policeman." This is an ironic remark, since, on the one hand, the policemen will be at the yearly parade; however, on the other hand, every other day of the year they are in hiding or cannot be found when needed. The scene of what appears to be several thousand police officers in parade dress uniform marching militantly is exaggerated, since this was not a realistic number of police officers employed at that time by the Los Angeles Police Department. During the parade, Keaton has trouble with his horse and mistakenly turns into the parade route. Attempting to look calm, Keaton lights a cigarette, while an anarchist bomber from a rooftop tosses a lit bomb onto his carriage, which he uses to light his cigarette, and after realizing it is, in fact, a bomb, he reflexively throws it into the parade of cops, unintentionally blowing them up.[25] The police now pursue Keaton en masse. Keaton crashes and escapes by outsmarting the dimwitted police. A captain says to the mayor in an intertitle, "Get some cops to protect our policemen." Here is the most precise sense that Keaton portrays law enforcement as both incompetent and hopeless. The pursuit continues, with Keaton continuing to outwit the police and evade capture. Using the cloak of comedy, *Cops* has two uniformed officers swinging clubs at Keaton, who is seemingly just standing there, thus symbolizing police brutality and their eagerness to beat a man who is not attacking them. Keaton steps aside, and the officers hit each other and fall to the ground (Figure 8).

Keaton eventually defeats all of the police who pursue him, finally corralling them inside the police precinct and locking them in, throwing away the key in a garbage can, suggesting that law enforcement itself is in need of detainment. Not coincidentally, the old, "lock 'em up and throw away the key" happened to be the type of "yellow journalism" Arbuckle was facing by the media.[26] The mayor's daughter approaches Keaton on the street and sees him dressed in a policeman's uniform. She shows disdain for the uniform and the profession. Being a policeman was not a noble profession worthy of her marriage. Keaton thus removes the key from the garbage can, unlocks the precinct doors, and surrenders. The final image of a tombstone, as mentioned earlier, engraved with "The End" and with Keaton's porkpie hat hanging from it, puts forth the final message that Keaton was an innocent man killed for crimes he did not commit.

Traffic in Souls, *Easy Street*, and *Cops* demonstrate how filmmakers concentrated on scandalous topics on the American consciousness at a time when social reform initiatives were highly regarded and routinely covered in the press. The film industry had developed more into an art form, and this developing medium was used to push narratives of injustice: prostitution in *Traffic in Souls*, social anomie in *Easy Street*, and the corrupt justice system in *Cops*. Tucker's exposing of prostitution, Chaplin's feature on societal blight and police ineffectiveness, joined with Keaton's usage of the film as a metaphor for his believed legal injustices

III. Cops in Silent-Era Feature Film

Figure 8. Two Los Angeles police officers are swinging clubs at Buster Keaton, as he appears to simply stand there. 1922.

against his friend Arbuckle, show how creative filmmakers used their work to create awareness and suggest reform. The audiences who predominately viewed these films craved storylines that exposed societal issues, and therefore filmmakers produced films to placate their desires and, in turn, achieved financial success and notoriety.

In the decades to come, crime films were increasingly brutal and pushed the boundaries about how far an attack on the police could go; consequently, reformist and religious groups again called for stricter film censorship and a remaking of the image of law enforcement in film. The following chapter examines what effects film censorship had on representations of law enforcement in cinema, turning portrayals of the police from those of being unprofessional, dimwitted, and worthy of ridicule into images of the law enforcement as having a respectable and professional status worthy of praise and admiration.

IV

Enforcing the Law in the "Talkies"

> Colorful. What color is a crawling louse? Say listen, that's the attitude of too many morons in this country. They think these big hoodlums are some sort of demigods. What do they do about a guy like Camonte. They sentimentalize, romance, make jokes about him. They had some excuse to glorify our old Western bad men. They met in the middle of the street at high noon and waited for each other to draw. But these things sneak up and shoot a guy in the back and then run away.—Chief of Detectives in *Little Caesar* (1931)

In 1926, a watershed moment in the film industry occurred when Warner Bros. and Western Electric (the manufacturing subsidiary of American Telephone and Telegraph) allied. They named this venture Vitaphone.[1] Vitaphone's first film, *Don Juan* (1926), although not technically the first "talkie," included the new sound-on-disc technology that added a music score and sound effects to the film but no spoken dialogue.[2] In the film's prologue, Will Hays, the industry's official censor, speaks; thus his was the first voice many viewers heard in the cinema.[3] Warner Bros. continued to seek a feature film with spoken dialogue, and by October of 1927, they premiered the *Jazz Singer* (1927)—a silent feature "except for its musical sequences and brief segments of apparently improvised dialogue that issued from the mouth of star Al Johnson."[4] The film played to record crowds in cities across the nation, impressing audiences with Al Johnson's singing and speaking.[5] Three months later, Warner Bros. released the first film where all the dialogue was recorded, *My Wife's Gone Away*, a ten-minute comedy based on a vaudeville playlet by William Demarest that critics and audiences adored.[6] The transition from silent film to "the talkies" was underway.

Let's put this period into perspective. The end of the Victorian age

IV. Enforcing the Law in the "Talkies"

had given way to an America consumer culture. Mass-produced goods such as clothing and electronic appliances were widely available. Stores were selling washing machines, refrigerators, irons, and many of the appliances that make our life convenient today. Radios were mass produced, with many Americans listening to daily programming. In 1934, a twenty-two-year-old Ronald Reagan had already graduated from college and was working his way to becoming a top sports broadcaster.[35] Betty White, age eleven, was aspiring to one day become an actress. Television was introduced in 1933 and displayed to the public at the Century of Progress Exhibition by the Hudson-Essex Corporation.[36] Movie theaters were air-conditioned, and movie stars and starlets were hustling for the big production houses, affirming a culture of celebrity fanatics.

Airplane, bus, train, and boat routes were all well established. Traversing the country and abroad was no longer a challenge. Airplane travel in the continental United States was growing popular as fare prices declined by nearly half since they spiked in 1929.[37] By the summer of 1933, airplane routes cost 6.1 cents per mile.[38] Automobiles were reliable and mass produced. Americans lived further from their jobs and extended families.

Organized suburban police forces had already replaced the constable or marshal with uniformed police officers. Justice was no longer levied on the shoulders of a few brave civilians or the victim. Cops would arrest criminals and bring them before a court, which was set up to address the alleged act as a crime against the state. American true crime readers and moviegoers shadowed detectives hunting and tracking down criminals. Just like today's detective films or novels, true crime readers and moviegoers of the 1930s had similar experiences.

By the time films had sound, the outlaws of the Old West had already been enshrined in popular culture and were now being replaced with modern outlaws.[7] The legendary outlaws Jesse James and "Billy the Kid" were known to most Americans, who grew up reading about their exploits. Therefore, not surprisingly, these outlaws were featured characters in early films, such as *The James Boys of Missouri* (1908) and *Billy the Kid* (1911).[8] The 1930s saw reincarnations of these outlaws drawn from other real-life outlaws, such as John Dillinger, Bonnie and Clyde, and "Baby Face" Nelson. The appeal of outlaws would become a mainstay of popular culture with the appearance of new urban gangsters, such as Al Capone, Vito Genovese, Benjamin "Bugsy" Siegel, and Hyme Weiss. The film industry, as well as literature and the music industry, successfully turned these criminals into sympathetic victims of circumstance:

they were common folk who stood up against immoral laws or who only wanted to improve their financial situation at a time when there were few other routes for upward mobility available.

The popularity of the figure of the outlaw was so prominent that when these notorious public enemies died, throngs of spectators endeavored just to get a glimpse of their bodies, such as when massive crowds lined up outside the Cook County morgue when Dillinger was killed.[9] Dillinger's celebrity was so widespread that in 1934 Lake County prosecutor Robert Estill struck a friendly pose with him at the jail at Crown Point, Indiana.[10] This photograph was a potent image because it showed that Estill, a representative of the law, respected the celebrity of Dillinger, a notorious criminal.[11] Dillinger was certain to be memorialized in the annals of American folklore for centuries ahead as the "common man"—one who sought to change his circumstances that were allegedly of no responsibility of his own. A useful guide by William Beverly helps to understand why Dillinger rose to become a prominent figure in popular culture. Beverly explains his argument through analysis of Dillinger as a fugitive. In his work *On the Lam: Narratives of Flight in J. Edgar Hoover's America* (2003), Beverly shows how Americans are fascinated with the storytelling of a manhunt and how that in itself creates a platform to propel a criminal into the public consciousness.

In the late 1920s into the early 1930s, American audiences saw films that regularly featured the character of the sympathetic criminal during a time when many of these viewers were being challenged in ways never before experienced in their lifetime. Although there were impressive technological advancements, the national economy had collapsed, and the real chance of moving ahead was hindered as joblessness and homelessness brought many to near starvation. Dust storms, caused by overused farmland, ravaged the land destroying crops and farms. To make matters worse, the government was not set up to help the people during the Depression. And while most were suffering, others, such as the American outlaw or the urban gangster, were moving upward, their criminality providing a chance of forging a better life for themselves while challenging the very government they held responsible for the dreadful national economic condition. Newspapers, novels, magazines, and films championed the cause of the American urban gangster and rural outlaw, successfully telling deprived citizens that there was unequal access to the American Dream.[12] According to sociologists Ian Taylor, Paul Walton, and Jock Young, "The American Dream which urges all citizens to succeed whilst distributing the opportunity

IV. Enforcing the Law in the "Talkies"

to succeed unequally: The result of this social and moral climate, inevitably, is innovation by the citizenry—the adoption of illegitimate means to pursue and obtain success."[13] This ability to improvise success based on illegal activities played out again and again in film, radio, music, and literature.

In the film *Little Caesar* (1931), dialogue between detectives at their bureau reveals the power of the criminal in popular culture. The chief detective suggests Tony Camonte, the gangster protagonist, is a colorful character the public adores:

> Colorful. What color is a crawling louse? Say listen, that's the attitude of too many morons in this country. They think these big hoodlums are some sort of demigods. What do they do about a guy like Camonte. They sentimentalize, romance, make jokes about him. They had some excuse to glorify our old Western bad men. They met in the middle of the street at high noon and waited for each other to draw. But these things sneak up and shoot a guy in the back and then run away. Colorful. Did you read what happened the other day? Three kiddies playing hopscotch on the sidewalk got lead poured into their little bellies. When I think what goes on in the minds of these lice, I want to vomit.

This speech illustrates law enforcement's battle over image where the gangsters were winning in popular culture, and were seen as good guys in a sense, effectively making law enforcement an adversary to the common man or agents of the government existing to keep the people down. This also illustrates the seriousness of organized crime and how volatile the situation was in the inner cities where real-life citizens were being heinously victimized as the popular culture whitewashed this reality. It also offers a glimpse into how the film industry placed a heavy emphasis on criminal protagonists during the late 1920s and early 1930s, mainly ignoring law enforcement as protagonists, until the mid–1930s when *"G" Men* (1935) inspired a cycle of other films sympathetic to law enforcement, such as *Public Hero Number 1* (1935), *Whipsaw* (1935), *36 Hours to Kill* (1936), and *Midnight Taxi* (1937).

In *Bullets or Ballots* (1936), Edward G. Robinson plays Detective Johnny Blake, a lawman who infiltrates the gangster underworld; thus Robinson plays both lawman and gangster. In the end, as the lawman, he busts the rackets wide open. Clare Bond Potter's *War on Crime: Bandits, "G" Men, and the Politics of Mass Culture* argues that America's popular obsession with stories of "G" Men and gangsters provides insight into how Americans understood their country, as well as its transformation through political and social change. Potter notes that the "war on crime" was fought on many fronts, including through legislation and

Law Enforcement in American Cinema, 1894–1952

governmental hearings, as well as through moral messages in movies. Representations of organized crime in film during the 1930s, as well urban gangsters, are plentiful. Along with the criminals, there are just as many representations of law enforcement on screen, all working to complicate the criminals' efforts of their pursuit of wealth, status, and power.

In real life, the gangster of the 1930s that the film industry portrayed had been a decade in the making, courtesy of the 18th Amendment of the U.S. Constitution that established Prohibition beginning on January 17, 1920, lasting until its repeal on December 5, 1933. Prohibition did more to advance the organized criminal underworld than any legislation enacted to stop it. Prohibition itself expanded the massive criminal underworld, and in essence, made "criminals" out of ordinary Americans who chose to indulge in the banned libations. The desire for alcohol propelled gangsters and mob bosses into the roles of pseudo-Robin Hood figures in the popular imagination. Al Capone—a notoriously hardened gangster who was responsible for the deaths of many—understood the power of public relations and gaining sympathy from the ordinary citizens. On Thanksgiving Day 1931, he fed over 5,000 men, women, and children from his soup kitchen in Chicago. Americans knew he was a crime boss, but at the time he was seen as just an ordinary man providing what the government was not. Some saw him as a good guy who did bad things, as opposed to a bad guy who did good things. For many Chicago's residents, his contrived generosity was both sorely desired and much appreciated.

Perhaps Capone and other gangsters of this time had come to understand the power of empathy through portrayals of gangsters in films, such as the gangster kingpin Bull Weed (George Bancroft) in Josef von Sternberg's *Underworld* (1927), who, while a notorious criminal, was depicted to have a heart of gold. The character of Bull Weed helped people out who needed care, such as when he was fleeing from a robbery and stopped to help a quadriplegic begging for money or how he cared for a kitten by dipping his finger in milk to feed it. *Underworld* (the seminal film that started the gangster film genre) represented the criminal in a sympathetic and favorable light. The message was clear: even hardened criminal gangsters who would kill on a moment's notice have redeeming qualities and are, at times, no different than the everyday man doing what he needs to do to survive in an unforgiving world.

The celebrity of Al Capone was tremendous. Crowds cheered for

IV. Enforcing the Law in the "Talkies"

him when he appeared at baseball games. He made donations to many charities, thus furthering his status as the Robin Hood of his time. As Fred Pasley wrote of Capone in 1930, "The hoodlum of 1920 had become page-one news, copy for the magazines, material for the talkie plots and vaudeville gags. Jack Dempsey had shaken hands with him. McCutcheon had cartooned him.... Al had grown from local to national stature."[14] Capone was publicly visible and embraced his celebrity status, and many saw him as just an opportunist, or ordinary man, who began as the son of poor Italian immigrants and became a successful business entrepreneur, albeit a criminal mastermind, who enjoyed celebrity status up until his death and beyond.[15]

Meanwhile, Prohibition had overburdened the newly-emerging criminal justice system, and law enforcement struggled to keep up with the workload. Police consumed with other police duties often turned a blind eye to incidents involving illegal alcohol. In a small town in New Jersey, the police ledger of 1930 tells of incidents when police ignored the law. In one example, a resident phoned the police to report a disturbed man on her front lawn. The police officer responded and found the man to be "high on illegal booze" yet didn't investigate further. The officer's report indicated a casual response to the crime—no mention of where the alcohol was purchased, etc. This plays out over and over in the police ledgers.[16]

Prohibition was a hopeless endeavor, since politicians, lawmakers, respected community figures, and even the police themselves, often indulged in illegal spirits at speakeasies and other hidden venues across the United States. Bar owners, bartenders, waitresses, helpers, janitors, rumrunners, distillers, bottlers, gang members, and others all received the bounty of working illegally with the prohibited alcohol. As Prohibition was repealed and the Depression worsened, desperation grew, with some who turned to petty crime to feed their families ending up in prison. This practice allowed Americans to empathize with the common criminal and to see them as victims of an intolerant justice system. Although petty thefts and such were a violation of law, it is plausible to assume many Americans, as they have had in previous generations, understood a parent stealing a ham or loaf of bread to feed their hungry dependents was not a crime worthy the attention of the justice system.[17]

Drastic changes in American law, the economy, and national psyche during the period of Prohibition drove the country in a direction never before experienced. Americans, especially newly arriving immigrants, found that crime was an accessible way to pull oneself and their families up from poverty and into higher social class. Honest work, if one could find it, was not going to bring needy families quickly into a higher class. Illicit profits from criminal enterprise offered a faster and obtainable alternative. James O'Kane's research presents a substantial historical and sociological foundation, detailing the clashes of ethnic newcomers and those of the traditional American society. O'Kane details how these newcomers began at the bottom and through criminal enterprise pulled themselves up by their bootstraps. He shows further how the children of these unlawful newcomers often enjoyed relatively middle-class lifestyles, opting to become lawyers, doctors, business professionals, and so on, while condescendingly frowning upon the illegal activity of their forbearers.[18] In this manner the newcomers are assimilated into the larger society, handing the proverbial opportunistic criminal torch to newly incoming ethnic groups.[19] "G" Men's protagonist James "Brick" Davis (played by James Cagney) illustrates O'Kane's thesis. Davis is a man of the streets, who is taken in by a powerful crime boss, "Mac" McKay. McKay pays Davis's way through law school while guiding him away from a life of organized crime. In contrast to McKay, Davis leads a life of respectability and frowns upon crime and eventually becomes an FBI agent who vows to bring criminals to justice.[20] The character of Davis exemplifies Edwin Sutherland's theory of *differential association*, which would argue that McKay had set Davis on this path early on when he first found him on the streets suffering from anomie.[21] McKay could have instead steered Davis toward a life of crime through his participation with McKay's gang with "an excess of definitions favorable to violations of law over definitions unfavorable to violations of law."[22] Sutherland's theory, however, is evidenced in the film with the interactions of the antagonist gangsters who show that participating in criminal behavior is learned in intimate personal groups, and thus with increased frequency of learned criminal behavior, the scales tip and an individual differentially associates to become a delinquent.

Although the film industry capitalized on the popularity of organized crime with characters that were shown as fighting the system during the Prohibition period, organized crime was, of course, not new.[23] To further expound on the previous discussion in Chapter II, there is much historical evidence that organized crime existed in antiquity. In the fifth century AD Roman Empire, the Bucellarii protected Roman notables from brigands and barbarians for retainers.[24] These

IV. Enforcing the Law in the "Talkies"

private armies also committed acts of banditry to supplement their income.[25] The Huns, who were considered brigands and barbarians by the Romans, were a group of nomadic people led by tribal chieftains (before Attila) and often raided the Roman Empire, forcing the Romans to pay tributes in return for peace.[26] After Attila's death, the Huns vanished into history. However, for several centuries they "preyed on their neighbors and lived on tribute."[27] In the American colonial period, organized crime was visible with the common practice of bribing legislators to obtain land grants. In essence, for as long as humankind has been assembled in groups and goods or money were personal objectives, some forms of organized crime has been present; however, organized crime in its most violent forms blossomed into a significant force in American society during Prohibition, which "acted as a catalyst for the mobilization of criminal elements in an unprecedented manner."[28] It also changed the relationship between criminals and politicians during this period, unleashing "competitive violence and serve to reverse the power order between criminal gangs and politicians."[29]

Filmic narratives of organized crime played well since, for generations, Americans understood the power of criminals in society. At the time when early films about the mob were released, volumes of novels and magazines had already been written from the criminal's perspective, a new view for those consuming popular media. However, after the Production Code (1930), film production companies sought to convey the message that crime does not pay. *Doorway to Hell* (1930), *Little Caesar* (1931), *Scarface* (1932), and *The Public Enemy* (1931) all depict their criminal protagonist dying at the end, essentially paying for their violence and misdeeds. In *"G" Men*, the criminal antagonist dies in a hail of bullets at the end.

As a representation of authority, *Underworld* presents the police not as characters by name but as a demonstration of authority in minor roles. The film focuses instead on the plights of the gangsters, where the protagonist is complicated by a love triangle involving his girlfriend and his friend and not the pursuit of the police as in *Scarface, Little Caesar,* and *"G" Men*. The first appearance of the police in *Underworld* shows them responding to a burglary involving Bull Weed, with both officers firing at Weed's fleeing car, seemingly emptying their pistols, indicating that the police are a force that shoots first and asks questions later. Interestingly, in the diner scene in *Little Caesar*, when Rico is discussing his willingness to become a criminal mob boss, he mentions how when he gets in a tight spot, he "shoots first, argue[s] afterwards." This contrast between the police and gangsters shows the police are similarly a gang of sorts and are willing to use extralegal methods to accomplish their objectives, a recurrent theme in gangster films.

The police in *Underworld* are thus basically absent from the narrative until the end, when a massive showdown ensues in a classic ending that pits good versus evil, where the good guys overcome the bad and order is restored to society. This complies with the Motion Picture Producers and Distributors of America "Don'ts and Be Carefuls" (1927) specifically illustrating a proper "attitude toward public characters and institutions," by showing sensitivity involving "scenes having to do with law enforcement or law-enforcing officers."[30] Later films such as *Little Caesar*, *Scarface*, and *"G" Men* all have such endings because of the Production Code, specifically abiding by the Code's requirements that "law, natural and human, shall not be ridiculed, nor shall sympathy be created for its violation," thus the police overcome the criminals, who are punished for their crimes.[31] Therefore, after the enforcement of the Production Code the police in film supersede.

Another similarity in these gangster films is the anguished declaration of love by women, such as those who appear in *Underworld*: Feathers McCoy and her love for character Rolls Royce, *Scarface*'s Poppy and her love for Tony Camonte and *Little Caesar*'s Olga Stassoff declaring her love for gangster-turned-good-guy Joe Massara. Another sameness is the number of the men who are after the crime boss's girlfriend, as seen in *Underworld* and *Scarface*, wherein both films include narratives of love triangles by women with resulting unresolved sexual tensions. Since *Underworld*, popular storylines and narratives developed and came to define the genre of the gangster film.

The films of the late 1920s and early 1930s present a major shift from what viewers of the 1910s and early 1920s had seen on the big screen in terms of portrayals of law enforcement. In many early twentieth-century crime films, the police are, as aforementioned, shown almost like another gang, using similar extralegal methods in pursuit of their professional objectives. They take their fight on crime very personally and are locked into competition with the criminals over turf, as well as with vying for the esteem of the public. These competitive similarities in film appear to change by the mid–1930s, thus contributing to the changing public perceptions of law enforcement. By the mid–1930s, the criminal was now to be thrashed, while the police and the law were to be championed. The films discussed below, *Little Caesar*, *Scarface*, and *"G" Men*, exemplify this remarkable narrative transition.

IV. Enforcing the Law in the "Talkies"

Little Caesar (1931)

Little Caesar is a crime film in which the protagonist is a gangster. The police appear in minor roles, until the ending when they are portrayed as the good guys winning against evil. Written in 1929 and filmed in 1930, the film was written from the criminal's perspective. Many subsequent gangster sagas in cinema and novels imitated the movie's plot. It was a plot that worked so well by pitting the criminal versus the powerful man that it influenced the mythology of the American gangster, thus violating the rules of the Code that criminals are neither to be held in high regard nor elicit sympathy from the viewers. Take, for example, how the movie's poster clearly emphases a romanticism of the gangsters.

Caesar Enrico "Rico" Bandello (Edward G. Robinson) is a common man who seeks notoriety and upward mobility through criminality. He is seen as someone who cannot make it to the top of society without resorting to crime. The character of Caesar is a prime example of anomie theory, which was built from a concept that originated with French sociologist Emile Durkheim in the nineteenth century.[32] Later, in the United States, Robert Merton provided a social and cultural explanation for Rico's deviant behavior, specifically his preoccupation with economic success that Merton terms pathological materialism. Rico is a symbol of American society at the time, where

> the pressure of prestige-bearing success tends to eliminate the effective social constraint over means employed to this end. The-end-justifies-the-means' doctrine becomes a guiding tenet for action when the cultural structure unduly exalts the end and the social organization unduly limits possible recourse to approved means.[33]

Therefore, anomie results when complications between goals and means "become estranged from a society that promises them in principle what they are deprived of in reality."[34]

Little Caesar provides sufficient evidence of anomie theory in Rico's early discussion in the diner with his friend, Joe Massara (Douglas Fairbanks, Jr.). Rico reads a newspaper article with the headline "Underworld Pays Respect to Diamond Pete Montana." Rico tells Massara, "Diamond Pete Montana. He don't have to waste his time on cheap gas stations. He's somebody. He's in the big town doing things in a big way. And look at us, just a couple of nobodies, nothing." Rico explains how he can do the same things Montana does, but he never got his chance in life.[35] He wants to be somebody of notoriety. For Rico, the path to this social success is criminality.[36] This scene is evidence that honest methods working within the boundaries of the law obstruct the common man's ability to reach the American Dream; therefore toiling outside of the law through criminal enterprise provided conceivable and efficient access to the American Dream.

Throughout the film, law enforcement is portrayed as unable to capture the elusive gangsters, who are seemingly controlling the town. The first appearance of law enforcement begins with the scene involving Police Commissioner Alvin McClure (Landers Stevens), whose presence at a nightclub during a robbery is coincidental. As McClure and his associates are walking out of the nightclub, they come face-to-face with the gangster Rico, who reflexively shoots McClure. This scene presents the police as vulnerable to the gangsters who are brave enough to attack them. It further shows the viewer how much power the gangs possess. McClure's guest, who apparently saw Rico shoot the commissioner (as well as other guests) could have easily identified Rico; however, the film continues with Rico living undetected for this shooting. This fear to become involved with identifying a gangster illustrates how much control the gangs have over the community, where even those who are known to the police (McClure's friend) are afraid to provide statements that implicate the criminal. This reality is an early version of the "snitches get stitches" adage. This is demonstrated over and over throughout the film, until the ending where the girlfriend of Rico's longtime friend calls the police with the information that leads to the police seeking to arrest him.

Shortly after the shooting of Police Commissioner McClure, three plain-clothes police visit the criminals at the crime boss Sam Vettori's (Stanley Fields) café. Before the detective's arrival, Vettori paces, concerned that the gang is now going to get trouble from the police. When the police arrive, Rico leaves the room before they see him. Sgt. Flaherty (Thomas E. Jackson) questions Vettori and his men about a crashed vehicle down the block. This scene shows the police and the criminals as equally tough, as if they are competing gangs of sorts. It portrays the offenders as legitimate businessmen in the mob-run café where the police have been brave enough to confront the gangsters on their turf. The scene also pits the police against the strong criminal, thus showing how there is an imbalance between good and evil, where evil has the upper hand. The cops are ineffective to stop them, and can only sarcastically wish the gangsters "merry Christmas."

When Rico is being celebrated at a banquet in his honor on his turf,

IV. Enforcing the Law in the "Talkies"

the police again appear. Sergeant Flaherty and his men enter the room, and Rico confronts the officers:

> RICO: Who invited you here?
> SGT. FLAHERTY: You're getting up in the world, aren't you, Rico?
> RICO: The downstairs is open to anybody, even cops. But the upstairs is private.
> SGT. FLAHERTY: But I like to keep my eye on you, Rico. You see, I am your friend. I like to see a young fellow getting up in the world, that's all. So long.

Here again, the police are presented as brave, strong, and willing to barge into the private party of a gangster and challenge him in front of his friends; however, again the police lack any evidence to arrest the criminal(s) and are thus also ineffective—the best they can offer is sarcasm. The police are just another competing gang on the streets of Chicago—their tone suggests their being equal with the gangsters, their contempt is apparent, and their willingness to make these interactions personal is a sign that they are locked in fierce competition.

When Rico is wounded in a drive-by shooting, Sgt. Flaherty again confronts him, and in a compelling exchange:

> SGT. FLAHERTY: *[after Rico is shot]* So somebody finally put one in you.
> RICO BANDELLO: Yeah, but they just grazed me, though.
> SGT. FLAHERTY: The old man will be glad to hear it. He takes such an interest in you.
> RICO BANDELLO: Are you telling me the cops couldn't get me no other way, so they hired a couple of gunmen?
> SGT. FLAHERTY: If I wasn't on the force, I'd have done the job cheap.

Sgt. Flaherty telling Rico that if he were not on the force, he would have done the job cheaply, meaning he would have been the hired gun to kill Rico, is a distorted view of the role of the police in society. It suggests that, yes, the police are the ones tasked with bringing criminals to justice, yet Sgt. Flaherty openly admits that he is willing to kill another man he deems immoral, had it not been for his being a cop, and he was the type of person who would do that. This interchange also suggests the reality that policing is personal. However, again, the police are made to be unsuccessful in their legal pursuits against crime, and thus are willing to operate more like gangsters to achieve their objectives.

Toward the end of the film, the police are finally able to hunt for Rico with the help of his best friend Jose Massara's girlfriend, Olga Stassoff (Glenda Farrell), cooperating with the police. This cooperation gives the cops a much-needed break to finally pursue and arrest Rico. The police begin to chase Rico, who shoots a cop chasing him. The shooting of the officer is suggested out of frame, an explicit convention of the

Production Code that "the technique of murder must be presented in a way that will not inspire imitation" and "brutal killings are not to be presented in detail."[37] Therefore, this scene evidences the film producers' unwillingness at the time to graphically show an officer shot in close up. This unwillingness is a significant departure from *Underworld*, which four years earlier showed a police officer rushing up the stairs to Bull Weed's apartment when he is apparently shot dead by Weed and falls down the stairs. Stronger calls for censorship at the time of the filming of *Little Caesar*, and the resulting successful attempts to control the narrative of the film, are at work here.

Rico successfully eludes the police; months pass where he is living in a flophouse. Other men in the flophouse happen to read an article in the newspaper that quotes the now–Lieutenant Flaherty calling Rico a coward, mocking him: "his rise from the gutter, it was inevitable that he should return there." The men in the flophouse apparently do not know Rico and talk about him being a coward. Their gossiping prompts Rico to spring from his bed, grab the newspaper, and leave the flophouse in anger. This scene portrays Rico as an ordinary man, who, although a notorious deviant, has values just like any ideal paternalistic man of the time.

In the closing minutes when the gangster Rico phones the police station to yell at the cop who challenged his masculinity in the newspapers, viewers observe the criminal (Rico's) perspective, and how the lawmen have the upper hand. Tracing his phone call, they subsequently execute him as he lies in wait (gun in hand) behind a billboard near an old flophouse. The scene shows how the police can ensnare a criminal in a trap, backing him into a corner with no chance of escape. The cops are calm and relaxed, while the criminal, Rico, is full of anxiety, therefore indicating a significant shift in dominance. The film ends with Flaherty standing over a dying Rico, symbolizing how law enforcement wins at the end of the day, and that ultimately "crime doesn't pay." This attempt in the Pre-Code era to whitewash the violence and criminal actions of the protagonist, and abide loosely by the Code with an appropriate ending, was not amiss—the film was widely popular, and subsequent films appeared in its likeness, such as *The Public Enemy*.

Scarface (1932)

Scarface was adapted from the 1929 novel *Armitage Trail* and loosely based on the life of Al Capone (whose nickname was Scarface);

IV. Enforcing the Law in the "Talkies"

this gangster movie violates the PCA's rule that law-breakers should not be rewarded, valorized, or held in superior regard to law enforcement. The film depicts gang warfare and police intervention in a world of gangs fighting for control over the city of Chicago. Maurice Coon, who spent a lot of time immersed in the Chicago gangland's underworld befriending Sicilian gangsters, wrote the book with censorship in mind. There were numerous passages where he placates censorship, to balance criticism that the book aimed to glorify the gangster. However, censorship did not stop Al Capone from liking the movie so much he owned a print of it.[38] *Scarface* was one of the most violent films of the 1930s. It was the first film where the gangster used a machine gun.[39] The movie was filmed in 1930 but was not released until 1932 because the Hays Office called for the cutting of violent scenes, such as the St. Valentine's Day Massacre, and also a title change to *Scarface: The Shame of a Nation*. As much as the Hays Office endeavored to battle the glamorization of gangsters and mobs, J. Edgar Hoover, director since 1924 of the Bureau of Investigation (renamed the Federal Bureau of Investigation in 1935), also insisted on condemnation of criminals deemed moral rogues who destroyed honest and wholesome American society. Co-producer Howard Hughes eventually yielded to the pressure of the Hays Office, adding a prologue and scenes that would counter romantic images of the gangster with pictures of the condemnation and thrashing of gangland evil. Therefore, the revisions to the movie *Scarface* show how the aligning of the perspectives of law enforcement with the movie-making process influenced what viewers consumed, although this film preceded the full enforcement of the PCA in 1934, and had it been produced later on, it would have faced even more censorship.

The criminals in *Scarface* are the primary focus of the film, with the police shown again as ineffective to stop them, until the ending. Censorship is made apparent from the beginning as the following three sentences appear in consecutive frames:

> This picture is an indictment of gang rule in America and of the callous indifference of the government to this constantly increasing menace to our safety and liberty. Every incident in this picture is the reproduction of an actual occurrence, and the purpose of this picture is to demand of the government: What are you going to do about it? The government is your government. What are YOU going to do about it?

Scarface was widely famous for its portrayal of the criminal underworld and the drama associated with it. The entire movie, however, was not a reproduction of actual occurrences. Al Capone did not die in a hail of police bullets. He died much later in 1947.[40]

The first appearance of the police in the film is in the barbershop when the lead character, Antonio "Tony" Camonte (Paul Muni), is sitting in the barber chair with his face covered in towels. The police's presence is picked up on by Camonte's henchman, Rinaldo (George Raft), who alerts Camonte. Rinaldo then tosses his handgun into a basket of towels. Camonte casually hands the barber his pistol, which the barber also throws into the basket and covers with towels. The significant insight here is that organized criminals are a part of the community, where the citizens are complicit in their actions. The sight of a firearm in the barbershop aroused no suspicion in the barber. He is just someone supporting the criminals and their deception. Detective Guarino (C. Henry Gordon) enters the barbershop. Detective Guarino tells Camonte he will bring him in to the police headquarters. Laying back in the barber's chair, Camonte said, "What's your hurry? I am getting a massage too." "We'll finish that in headquarters. Put your coat on," Detective Guarino counters, a pun on police brutality, especially during interrogations. The scene continues with posturing between Camonte and Det. Guarino showing how the police and the criminals were opposing forces. Camonte is calm and sarcastic, casually striking a match off the detective's badge—a symbol or his authority as a law enforcement officer. Detective Guarino punches Camonte in the face knocking him to the ground, while Rinaldo reflexively clenches a fist, as does Camonte, but neither attack the detective. This scene is an example of a power struggle between the police and the criminals, where the police are willing to assault an offender if he challenges their authority. It is thus a depiction of police brutality cloaked in the sense that violent criminals will not respect authority without first experiencing violence against them. It also portrays the police as a rival gang. The police escort Camonte to their stationhouse, where the chief of detectives (Edwin Maxwell) questions him about the recent murder of a crime boss.

In this interaction, we see representations of the police as permissibly heavy-handed with their approach to fighting crime. They are questioning Camonte, when Guarino, who is sitting in an elevated position over Camonte's right shoulder to signal his superior authority, asks the chief, "Should I smack it out of him?" The chief responds, "I'll let you hit him in a little while." The takeaway here is that brutality is married with police interrogations, and the police will go to great lengths to get confessions. (The third degree—a euphemism for torture employed by the

IV. Enforcing the Law in the "Talkies"

police as a tactic during police interrogations—is discussed at length in Chapter V in relation to the film *Where the Sidewalk Ends*.) The questioning by the chief is unproductive. Camonte snaps, exclaiming that when he knows something he doesn't tell the police. The chief signals to his detective to take Camonte out for a beating. While walking out the door, a message (a writ of habeas corpus) to release Camonte is handed to the chief by Camonte's attorney. A writ of habeas corpus is a redress in law where the release of a person in police custody is ordered with the demand to appear before the court to determine if the police have lawfully detained the person. In this instance, the writ of habeas corpus is used to show how even criminals have cunning lawyers who can get them out of trouble. (This taking advantage of legal technicalities by dishonest attorneys to aid criminals is also illustrated in *"G" Men* when Davis refuses to partake in the corruption of the law). In a final interaction, the chief, Camonte, and Detective Guarino verbally spar with each other:

> CHIEF OF DETECTIVES: I spent my life mixing with your breed, and I don't like it, get me? You can hide behind a lot of red tape, crooked lawyers, and politicians with the give-me's, writs of habeas corpus, witness that don't remember overnight, but we'll get through to you just like we got through to all the rest.
> CAMONTE: Maybe me, I am different.
> DETECTIVE GUARINO: No, you're not. Take your gun away, and you get into a tough spot, you'll squeal just like all the other rats.
> CAMONTE: You're gonna get me, eh?
> DETECTIVE GUARINO: In your particular case. I'd give up a month's pay for the job.

This scene evidences the power battle between the police working inside of the law as opposed to meeting outside of it, while the criminals find loopholes and technicalities in the law giving them the upper hand and making the police's jobs less effective. It also shows how the police are willing to move outside of the law if it gets them to the conclusion they are seeking. In other words the police believe the end justifies the means because gangsters are a detriment to society and any wrong committed through stopping the gangsters is excused because of the favorable outcome. Camonte is led out the station by his attorney where they discuss the writ of habeas corpus again, demonstrating how the laws sometimes work against the police and in favor of the criminal and how the police are ineffective to stop organized crime through their use of crooked lawyers.

Law Enforcement in American Cinema, 1894–1952

Law enforcement is noticeably absent for a significant portion of the film, until they reappear again briefly to reinforce the criminals' power over the use of habeas corpus, as well as the police's ineffectiveness to arrest the criminals, all the while massive violence is destroying the community. Shortly after that the police are discussing the machine gun, and how the laws are also against them in their fight to end the violence. This scene is another example of how the police, through no fault of their own, are ineffective in stopping the criminal pursuits of the gangsters, who are outperforming them on every front. It is an interesting dynamic at play here, where everyone is a victim of circumstance (again, to no fault of their own). Criminals are portrayed as just ordinary men who are trying to get ahead in a dire economy and are fighting against an immoral law, whereas the police are well-intentioned, yet ineffective, because well-meaning laws are rife with technicalities that are perverted by crooked lawyers.

While the violence escalates, and the police are still unable to capture the criminals, the moral dynamics of the police ebb and flow as the story unfolds—however, the police are mainly depicted as the good guys, the ones who are fighting the good fight, while the criminals are now seen as hurting the public. However, the scene with detectives discussing the romanticization of criminals, as aforementioned, also shows how the criminals and their plight for upward mobility, and even their use of violence, remains romanticized and accepted by society. The film portrays the detective chief as being right with his assessment that the public needs to understand what is going on in gangland Chicago, where bodies are piling up from gang war over the distribution of illegal alcohol and gangs encroaching upon each other's turf. It is a bloody battle derived from the massive profits Prohibition afforded organized criminals, a reality presented in the film.

The police reappear at the end of the film when they are dispatched en masse to pick up Camonte for the murder of Rinaldo. They show up at Camonte's home with a massive display of force, indicating that they are superior to the criminal; however, their shooting from the vehicles as they arrive is hyperbolic and again reinforces the notion that police officers, like the gangsters, are a force that shoots first and asks questions later. The ending culminates with the policing using a smoke canister to flush Camonte from his home and away from his gun. In the end, *Scarface* abides by the Code, portraying Camonte as a coward who is alone, shaking, crying, and begging. Camonte attempts to flee and is struck down in a hail of police bullets. The film's ending depicts the

IV. Enforcing the Law in the "Talkies"

Figure 9. Police officers stand over dead gangster Tony Camonte. 1932.

police as moral and righteous, while the criminal is decidedly immoral and pays for his misdeeds with his life; thus "crime doesn't pay," and the law is superior to the criminals (Figure 9). This engineered ending thus conciliates to the demands of censorship.

"G" Men (1935)

As a result of the Production Code Administration insisting upon the upholding of law and morality in film, the gangster film genre was severely compromised by the mid–1930s. Films that overly depicted violence or portrayed law enforcement in a negative light (as did many gangster films, such as *Little Caesar*, *Scarface*, *The Public Enemy*, and others) were all candidates for censorship, thus presenting a significant problem for the genre. How could they continue to offer gangster films with such moral oversight in mind? Warner Bros.' *"G" Men* (1935) was the answer. The movie is full of gangsters set as antagonists, with the protagonist (James "Brick" Davis) as an honest lawyer who associated with the gangsters but is on the right side of the law. James Cagney, who previously stared in notorious gangster roles, now played Davis—the good cop fighting the gangsters. Therefore, the demand for crime films was still met, just on new terms.

Celebrating the FBI as the elite authority among American law enforcement agencies, *"G" Men* opens with a look into the future. It shows how the FBI stems the tide of gang violence and restores America back to a decent society. This image-making in the 1930s lent the FBI a favorable representation as the premier law enforcement agency in the nation for decades to come. *"G" Men* also helped to make the FBI's image as a legitimate law enforcement agency, comprised of honest, brave, and educated lawmen—a different breed from the portrayals of the beat cop or gritty detective willing to move outside the law when deemed appropriate. This image-making is evident in the lead character, Davis's first appearance as an honest lawyer, where a gangster comes into his law office and asks him to represent criminals. Davis refuses, and thus the intended perception is that of a man of morals and conviction. From this interaction, the viewer learns of Davis's association with the crime boss, "Mac" McKay (William Harrington), who brought Davis up from the streets and into respectability, with no strings attached, to live on the right side of the law.

McKay's character lends to the gangster image of benevolence and other redeeming qualities, such as seen in *Underworld*'s gangster kingpin, Bull Weed. Moreover, when Davis is challenged as being a shyster for McKay, Davis punches the man, throwing him out of his office, thus reinforcing his intolerance for unethical behavior. Davis's former law school roommate turned FBI agent, Eddie Buchanan (Regis Toomey), enters, and from this interaction, law enforcement is cast in a favorable light. The message is that through law enforcement one can live a self-fulfilling life of honor, truth, and justice. This narrative is a radical departure from prior gangster films, where respectability was achieved instead through illicit criminal activity. Shortly after that, Agent Edward Buchanan is murdered by the gangster, Danny Leggett (Edward Pawley), thus sending Davis on the trail of redemption in the name of justice as a law enforcement officer, again reiterating that a noble life is possible in the law enforcement profession and that not all cops are corrupt.

The film celebrates the FBI as an advanced law enforcement agency through its use of modern technology, such as detecting criminals through microscopic images of bullets' "rifling," fingerprints, and the broadcasting of messages on closed airwaves exclusive to law enforcement agencies. It is no surprise that Davis is a highly skilled marksman

IV. Enforcing the Law in the "Talkies"

and an intelligent tough guy, who becomes a top agent at the FBI, because these are the attributes the FBI sought in their agents. The film; however, also presents Davis as a friend of former mob boss McKay, thus as an organized crime insider, which shows that in this newly-emerging federal force, an insider is what is needed to solve the organized crime problem.

A film of only mild violence between cops and organized criminals, *"G" Men* has shootouts and murders that are not overly graphic, such as those seen in *Scarface*. For the most part, the film is an advertorial of the FBI and how they developed and transformed from an agency where agents could not carry firearms and were eventually designated as being able to supersede laws that were challenged by state lines and other technicalities of the law. Therefore, federal crimes for bank robbery, kidnapping, the murder of a government agent, witness tampering, and fleeing across state lines became federal laws enforceable by the FBI. This legislation gave the FBI much-needed prowess to fight crime.

The ending of *"G" Men* is predictable: the FBI wins the battle between good versus evil. Although law enforcement is seen as quick to shoot criminals, *"G" Men* makes sure to show that the officers' actions are justifiable in officer-involved shootings, whereas in previous movies these actions were questionable. When compared to the earlier gangster films, representations of law enforcement experience a significant shift with *"G" Men*. They are now the focus of the narrative, instead of ancillary to it, and are presented as superior to the pathetic criminal who should be condemned. Movies such as *"G" Men* make clear that for wholesome American values to blossom during this difficult period, gangland evil must be eliminated. It also illustrates that the police are on the side of justice and are equally as courageous as the romanticized criminal in their willingness to stand face to face with and stare down evil, bring offenders to justice, to restore the safety and security of the community.

Law enforcement representations in the cinema thus underwent a major evolution in the 1930s. Early in the decade the criminal in film was set as the sympathetic protagonist, albeit one who committed major crimes, including multiple murder. He was adored, romanticized, and mythologized. He was portrayed as a victim of circumstance, through no fault of his own. It was the economy, poverty, unfair moral laws, or the government keeping him down. He was no different than that of the struggling neighbor next-door, endeavoring to put food on his table to feed a hungry family. He was easily relatable. Most of these images

Law Enforcement in American Cinema, 1894–1952

on film were a result of Prohibition, which created the romance of the urban gangster in the massive underworld of crime as never before seen. The failure of the economy, destruction of farmlands, and poverty during the Depression reignited the romance of the rural outlaw, such as Dillinger, "Baby Face" Nelson, Bonnie and Clyde, and urban gangsters, such as Al Capone, Benjamin "Bugsy" Siegel, and Hyme Weiss. The film industry took advantage of these popular cultural narratives, and thus these films were very successful. However, in the mid–1930s with movies like *"G" Men*, a shift in the representation of law enforcement began in response to censorship and calls from activists to produce films that placed law enforcement in higher regard. Therefore, the remaking of the law enforcement officer into the brave, intelligent, tough guy paved the way for the following decade of the courageous, yet shadowy, detective and P.I.s routinely featured in 1940s film noir.

V

Shadows of Law Enforcement in Film Noir

> I'm reducing your rank, Dixon. You're going back to second grade. Any more complaints against you for cruelty or roughhouse and you'll be back in uniform pounding a beat. It's no fun telling you this. You're a good man with a good brain, but you're no good to the department unless you learn to control yourself.—Police Inspector Nicholas Foley in *Where the Sidewalk Ends* (1950)

> Against a hardened criminal, I never hesitated. I've forced confessions—with fist, black-jack, and hose—from men who would have continued to rob and to kill if I had not made them talk. The hardened criminals know only one language and laughs at the detective who tries any other. Remember this is war after all! I am convinced that my tactics saves many lives.[1]—New York City police captain Cornelius William Willemse (1931)

A popular film style in the 1940s, American film noir extended into the early 1950s. The characteristic look of film noir appears during the 1940s because of "an influx of foreign directors, a world at war, horrors and death on a scale never before witnessed by any generation, and men in battle wondering what their wives and sweethearts were doing back home."[2] This new style of film that came to be known as film noir, from the French word meaning "dark or black,"[3] was different in style, setting, and tone than prior films because of their use of "deep shadows, night shooting, claustrophobic settings and unusual camera angles to accent anxiety or subversion."[4] Films noir also focus on the struggle between good and evil by romanticizing the interplay between cops and criminals, often blurring the differences between them. Many noir films follow the investigative process of tough-guy detectives or the rebellious private investigator hunting down criminals mostly wanted for homicide. By the early 1950s, film noir, in part, disappeared because the national mood improved. However, it lingers for a little while after soldiers returned from the war in 1946, when there was still a slight recession and a few reasons yet to be glum. By 1953, however, America was flush with victory, having been newly-crowned the most powerful nation in the world, one that was at the forefront of a global postwar bloom that would secure capitalism's future in the West for some time to come.

In addition to film style, major shifts in filmic representations of law enforcement also occur in the 1940s. For example, the P.I. of the 1940s moves freely between respectable society and the criminal underworld, sometimes confusing his role as a surrogate agent of law enforcement. He's tough, brash, cocky, and at times deceitful, especially when dealing with the police. He is a targeted victim of the femme fatale—the mysterious female character routinely depicted as both seductive and highly attractive, whose charm traps her lovers/suitors in predicaments that more often than not lead to dangerous, or even lethal, situations. The femme fatale usually possesses "a keen intelligence and are shrewd and cunning."[5] They lack morals and are "bent on satisfying their own lustful, mercenary, or violent desires, utterly aware of their unique feminine tools, and willing to capitalize on them whenever necessary."[6] The beauty and mystery of these seductive women hook the P.I. or the police detective's heart, and as a result, compromises his role as a representative of law enforcement. Also widely popular during this period was the subgenre of film noir that depicts the man on the run, or on the lam, because of some guilt or loose co-conspiracy involving a crime committed by the femme fatale, or her contriving to do so. Films such as *This Gun for Hire* (1942), *Double Indemnity* (1944), *The Woman in the Window* (1944), *The Postman Always Rings Twice* (1946), and *D.O.A.* (1949) all have similar narratives involving the highly-seductive, attractive femme fatale who complicates the lives of the male characters. In film noir, the femme fatale is just as important or, at times, even more so, than the P.I. She's a complicated, romanticized criminal who moves stealthily, keeping a sizeable distance from the law.[7]

The P.I. of film noir, like the femme fatale, is, in many ways, similar to the gangsters of the previous decade. Living by his laws, he follows his own moral code where he decides when to abide by the law, and when to disobey it. Similar to the P.I., the law in film noir is generally treated in an ambiguous manner. While the films routinely end with a sense of legal justice, the detectives typically move outside of the law to reach

V. Shadows of Law Enforcement in Film Noir

this conclusion. This illegality ultimately confuses the roles of the police and criminals, and, in many cases, emphasizes the narrative that while justice is doled out, laws need to be bent or broken for a compromised justice system to work.

Film noir accounts of law enforcement appear in many varieties, such a private investigator in *The Maltese Falcon* (1941), *The Big Sleep* (1946), *The Dark Corner* (1946), the police detective in *The Big Heat* (1953), or professional police officers working cases such as in *The Naked City* (1948) and *Where the Sidewalk Ends* (1950). In *The Maltese Falcon*, the P.I. is an example of a law enforcement surrogate who is in direct competition with the police, is adversarial or deceptive at times, and yet still begrudgingly works with the police when it suits him during his investigation. *The Big Sleep* is another example of the P.I. as a lone investigator, but his relationship with the police is more professional, and he is seen more as an extension of the detective services of the police—their objectives aligned with less conflict—as if he were a detective working for the police department. *Where the Sidewalk Ends* combines the roles of the P.I. and the police detective. While there are no P.I. characters in the film, the police detective, in many ways, displays many of the established traits of the P.I. The protagonist, Mark Dixon (Dana Andrews), is an NYPD police detective who is tough, often disregards the law by working outside of it to solve cases, and who is routinely in conflict with his supervisors. When he gets into a scuffle with a criminal he was questioning, he punches the man and accidentally kills him. Fearing sanctioning from his superiors, he attempts to hide the death of a criminal whom he has accidentally killed, and for which the situation was easily explainable had he told the truth. Dixon, as a cop, is adversarial with the police; he is deceptive and moves freely between the underworld and respectable society. He is deeply involved with the dead man's wife, and his love for her complicates his situation. He essentially is the very image of the P.I. working as a sworn police detective.

Featuring homicide detectives as protagonists working to solve the murder of an attractive young blonde model, *The Naked City* was shot on location on the streets of New York in a pseudo-documentary style, with a voice-over narrator, and is laden with police procedure. The storyline portrays the police as the good guys, working day and night to capture violent criminals. The film follows a murder investigation, which ultimately leads to a police pursuit of the murderer. The police trap him in a corner, on the pedestrian walk on the Williamsburg Bridge, with no chance of escape, leaving the murderer with the only option of climbing up the tower of the bridge. In a shootout, the police fatally shoot the murderer, who dramatically falls from the bridge, illustrating the Code compliance ending that crime does not pay and that the police will win. *The Naked City* is another classic noir police tale that provides an up-close look at traditional law enforcement detectives in New York City during the 1940s.

The private investigators of 1940s film noir originated in the hard-boiled crime fiction published decades earlier in cheap pulp magazines that grew as an expansion of the dime novel. *Detective Story Magazine* was the first of its kind in the genre. Its publication began in 1915 and ran until 1949. It featured such notable writers as Agatha Christie, Arthur Conan Doyle, and Johnston McCulley.[8] *Detective Story* focused on short crime fiction stories that frequently featured tough-guy detectives and Robin-Hood-type criminals, as well as unique, costumed crime fighters.

Another successful hard-boiled fiction publication that ran for 67 years (1920–1987) was *Black Mask* the most substantial magazine for the genre.[9] The magazine featured stories written by hard-boiled writers, including Raymond Chandler, Dashiell Hammett, and several other famous writers. Magazine issues of *Black Mask* that feature stories by Chandler and Hammett today command high prices because of their rarity and popularity as among the best hard-boiled writers of their time.[10] Chandler's *The Big Sleep*, published in 1939 in *Black Mask*, is the story on which the 1946 film of the same name is based. Hammett's *The Maltese Falcon*, released on film for its third version in 1941 and produced by Warner Bros., was the first "faithfully hard-boiled film" of the decade, originally serialized in *Black Mask* at the end of the 1920s and released as a novel by the same name in 1930.[11]

Many of the P.I.s found in 1940s film noir are also reflections of those found in the literature of the 1920s and 1930s, where the P.I. was routinely depicted as a smooth and sophisticated character regularly dressed in tuxedos, who smoked cigarettes, drank heavily, and who often solved a crime or murder ahead of the police. Philo Vance, the private eye whose mysteries series ran from 1926 to 1939 when its writer S.S. Van Dine (the pseudonym used by Willard Huntington Wright) died, was widely popular. In Van Dine's first book that featured Vance, *The Benson Murder Case*, Van Dine describes details about him. Through this description, many similarities correlate with private investigators of the 1940s film noir—their intelligence is superior to the detective working for the police department, and their tough judgment is unmatched:

V. Shadows of Law Enforcement in Film Noir

Vance was what many would call a dilettante, but the designation does him an injustice. He was a man of unusual culture and brilliance. An aristocrat by birth and instinct, he held himself severely aloof from the common world of men. In his manner there was an indefinable contempt for inferiority of all kinds. The great majority of those with whom he came in contact regarded him as a snob. Yet there was in his condescension and disdain no trace of spuriousness. His snobbishness was intellectual as well as social. He detested stupidity even more, I believe, than he did vulgarity or bad taste. I have heard him on several occasions quote Fouché's famous line: *C'est plus qu'un crime; c'est une faute.* And he meant it literally.

Vance was frankly a cynic, but he was rarely bitter; his was a flippant, Juvenalian cynicism. Perhaps he may best be described as a bored and supercilious, but highly conscious and penetrating, spectator of life. He was keenly interested in all human reactions; but it was the interest of the scientist, not the humanitarian.

Vance's knowledge of psychology was indeed uncanny. He was gifted with an instinctively accurate judgment of people, and his study and reading had coordinated and rationalized this gift to an amazing extent. He was well grounded in the academic principles of psychology, and all his courses at college had either centered about this subject or been subordinated to it...

He had reconnoitered the whole field of cultural endeavor. He had courses in the history of religions, the Greek classics, biology, civics, and political economy, philosophy, anthropology, literature, theoretical, and experimental psychology, and ancient and modern languages. But it was, I think, his courses under Münsterberg and William James that interested him the most.

Vance's mind was basically philosophical—that is, philosophical in the more general sense. Being singularly free from the conventional sentimentalities and current superstitions, he could look beneath the surface of human acts into actuating impulses and motives. Moreover, he was resolute both in his avoidance of any attitude that savoured of credulousness and in his adherence to cold, logical exactness in his mental processes.[12]

From Van Dine's description of his private investigator Philo Vance, it is clear he is not the traditional police detective of his time. Vance was an outsider, one the police departments were unfamiliar with; he had worked for them but they could not retain him because he was beyond the monotony of routine police investigations—he was beyond the expectations of a uniformed cop working the beat and was a free-spirit who could not hold a career where punching a clock, so to speak, was part of the daily routine. He needed to march to his beat, utilizing his cultural brilliance and innate ability to see through deception, where other investigators would easily be misled. He is characteristically always many investigative steps ahead of the police. He seemingly knows the criminal's next move before the criminal even makes it. He desires to investigate the most complex and dangerous cases, answering only to himself. Police commanders and supervisors, and even district attorneys, cannot counsel him because they are unfamiliar with his alignment with his moral code and his ambivalent approach to the law. He goes against all the belief systems and paradigms they stand for. Philo Vance's superiority to the traditional police detective, and his brilliance by comparison, sustained his popularity for twelve novels, fifteen adaptions in film, and a radio program. The P.I.'s degrees of separation from the traditional police detective are embodied in film noir.

Another private detective found in literature with similar attributes to Philo Vance, and whose character subsequently appeared in film, is Dashiell Hammett's private detective Nick Charles, whose story materializes in *The Thin Man*, published in 1934. Hammett sets Charles in New York City during the late Prohibition period. Often writers who tell stories about investigations need to have, or have had, some experience in the field. Many are investigative journalists, or former investigators, such as Hammett, who was a former private detective at the notable Pinkerton National Detective Agency.[13] Charles is *The Thin Man*'s protagonist, a retired detective with the Trans-American Detective Agency who unwillingly takes on a murder investigation while vacationing in New York City. Although Charles is a hard-boiled detective, the book is unique with its light comic tone.[14] Hammett's *Thin Man* was successful in its adaptions for film in 1934, with several sequels, a 1940s radio program *The Adventures of the Thin Man*, and an NBC TV series which ran from 1957 to 1959.

The films discussed below illustrate the role of the P.I. alternatively as an adversary to law enforcement, an asset to law enforcement, and either as a police detective or as the quintessential P.I. working as a member of law enforcement.

The Maltese Falcon (1941)

A film noir written and directed by John Huston, *The Maltese Falcon* is a Warner Bros. production based on the novel of the same title by Dashiell Hammett. The Hays Office, because of the film's "lewd" content, had previously prevented its production. However, its 1941 remake more closely complied with the Production Code, yet with many instances of innuendo in the film, for instance in the scene where detectives question Spade and he displays homophobia, asking, "What's your boyfriend getting at, Tom?"[15] (The Production Code would have condemned any character during this period that was openly homosexual.)

V. Shadows of Law Enforcement in Film Noir

The Maltese Falcon was warmly received by viewers and critics, earning three nominations at the 14th Academy Awards: Best Picture; John Huston, for Best Adapted Screenplay; and Sydney Greenstreet, for Best Supporting Actor. Film critic Bosley Crowther claimed *The Maltese Falcon* is "the slickest exercise in cerebration that has hit the screen in many months, and it is also one of the most compelling nervous-laughter provokers yet."[16]

Early in the film, P.I. Sam Spade's (Humphrey Bogart) first interaction with a policeman (Robert Homans) occurs when the policeman is securing the crime scene of Spade's partner, Miles Archer.[17] The policeman confronts Spade and questions what he is doing at the crime scene. This short scene reveals a boundary between law enforcement and the P.I., who is not permitted into the crime scene. The police are the authority over the crime scene, and the P.I. has no movement into that sphere, regardless if he is investigating a case involving the deceased. However, Spade informs the policeman he was contacted by Detective Tom Polhaus (Ward Bond). Satisfied with Spade's response, the policeman allows him into the crime scene. Spade is next seen with Polhaus discussing the crime scene. Polhaus shows Spade the handgun that killed Archer. Polhaus appears unfamiliar with the firearm. This signals Spade has a superior intellect. Spade discusses the gun with expertise. Moreover, he analyses the crime scene, illustrating how that firearm was used in the murder. However, Polhaus also displays his proficiency through his investigative assessment, and the two men at the moment appear to be somewhat equals. Their competition is evidenced when Polhaus questions Spade about Archer: Spade informs him but holds back information: "Don't crowd me, Tom," Spade tells him. This scene twists the view of their sort of partnership, subtly showing competition to solve crimes—one on behalf of the state, the other for profit. The P.I.'s for-profit investigation is revealed in the scene with Brigid O'Shaughnessy (Mary Astor), where Spade demands $500 for his services, telling her to raise some more money by "hocking" her furs and jewelry.

In the following scene the loose affiliation between the police and the P.I., as with many of the relationships in the film, take a turn, with Detective Lieutenant Dundy (Barton MacLane) and Polhaus questioning Spade at his home. Dundy presses Spade about what kind of gun he carries. Spade gets upset: "Why are you suckin' around here? Tell me or get out!" Polhaus responds: "You can't treat us like that, Sam. It ain't right. We got our work to do."

This statement by Polhaus shows the legitimacy of the P.I. and his involvement in law enforcement as a pay-for-service detective. It also reveals a superiority of the P.I. over the police. The film continues to show this dominance when the arguing continues, and Polhaus says, "Be reasonable, Sam. Give us a break, will you? How can we turn up anything if you don't tell us what you got?" This statement allows the P.I. to be seen a superior investigator, one who plays an integral role in the solving of a crime, even if competition is at play. The end of the scene presents law enforcement in a favorable light, with Dundy telling Spade, "Don't know if I blame you as much, a man that killed your partner. But that won't stop me from nailing ya." Dundy represents the law and its superiority, with the power to arrest the P.I., whereas the P.I. is powerless in this respect. The P.I., therefore, can work alone but needs the police and the justice system after detecting a criminal. Procedurally, the police do not need the P.I., and if so, his role would be purely as a witness.

Spade meets gunman Joel Cairo (Peter Lorre) who endeavors to search Spade's office. With a cigarette pressed between his lips, Spade punches out the gunman and then searches Cairo for any intelligence he can gather from his pockets. Spade's cool-headedness presents the P.I. as a tough guy, smooth in the way Philo Vance was depicted in the late 1920s and 1930s. The tough-guy, intelligent P.I. is superior to the criminal, as he can fight and disarm criminals with ease.

When Cairo awakes from his brief unconsciousness, he offers to hire Spade to find the Maltese Falcon. Cairo's proposition evidences the P.I.'s ability to move freely in the criminal underworld, while also working with police. The P.I. can work for either, if that leads him to where he needs to be to gather more investigative intelligence. Therefore, the P.I.'s loyalty is only to his profession, reputation, and earnings. The police, although they historically use informants and undercover detectives to infiltrate crime factions, do not have this freedom of mobility and must always sit on the right side of the law. The P.I., however, can blur the lines as someone working for a client. Films such as *The Maltese Falcon* thus demonstrate the murkiness of the law at play in the 1940s. To maintain a balance, Spade tells Cairo, "You're not hiring me to do any murders or burglaries, but simply to get it back, if possible, in an honest, lawful way." Cairo responds, "If possible, but in any case with discretion." Cairo's signal to use discretion shows he is familiar with the P.I. meandering with the law as he sees fit.

The scene follows with Spade returning Cairo his pistol and Cairo again forcing Spade to put his hands up while he searches his office. Spade laughs, "Go ahead. I won't stop ya." The scene fades out, but Cairo

V. Shadows of Law Enforcement in Film Noir

is without question a criminal, and Spade intends to work with criminals or anyone who is willing to pay him for his services and assist him in solving a case. In contrast, the police do not have this freedom of movement. However, the cops depicted on films in the 1940s are also not without sin. Sometimes, they, too, work outside of the law to solve cases, as discussed further on.

The following scene opens at Spade's home door. Dundy and Polhaus return to visit Spade in the middle of the night. The men begin to argue, and Dundy asserts his authority. Cairo and O'Shaughnessy are in the parlor when they fight, and the policemen are alerted and enter the apartment. The story shows Spade's superior knowledge of the criminal justice system. Spade appears to play the role of a criminal defense attorney, to counter any arrests or positions on behalf of the police. Dundy gets upset with Spade and punches him in the throat. This scene shows that the police are willing to assault a person who challenges them. It also depicts police brutality and how the citizen P.I. is powerless to punch back. Had Spade punched Dundy back, he would have likely faced arrest. The power struggle in this scene, again, shows the superior dominance of law enforcement over the P.I.; however, yet again the police are unable to solve the crimes without the help of the P.I. This scene shows that the police in the 1940s, in ways similar to the P.I., work outside of the law, and break it when it suits them. However, the mindset of the police at the time as to whether or not this was a violation of the law, as opposed to a mere extension of a sense of justice, is essential to consider. Many heinous criminals, such as those who raped or killed children, sometimes "fell down the stairs" on their way to and from the police stations, and when their injuries appear in the press or visible before the court of law, they often conjured little sympathy from the public who were horrified by the actions of the criminal.[18]

The Maltese Falcon portrays the interplay between the P.I., the police, and the justice system. The scene with Spade arguing with the district attorney (D.A.), assistant district attorney, and a stenographer is very telling. The D.A. is questioning Spade about who killed Floyd Thursby. Spade is evasive with his testimony. Spade's dialogue in this scene shows how law enforcement and the P.I. are at odds and how the P.I. is licensed under law enforcement and must comply with law enforcement. It also illustrates how the P.I. views the law as both adversarial and ambivalent. Moreover, it displays how his investigative ability is working ahead of law enforcement in the hope of getting the conclusion of the investigation correct. According to Spade:

Law Enforcement in American Cinema, 1894–1952

> Everybody has something to conceal.... And as far as I can see, my best chance of clearing myself from the trouble you're trying to make for me is by bringing in the murderers all tied up. And the only chance I've got of catching them and tying them up and bringing them in is by staying as far away as possible from you and the police because you'd only gum up the works.

Spade takes a moment of light humor and sarcasm and turns to the stenographer: "You getting this all right, son. Or am I going too fast for you?" The stenographer replies: "No, sir. I am getting it all right." This exchange gestures that Spade is comfortable; he is not afraid in the presence of authority figures, even when he is apparently their subject of inquiry. Moreover, it shows the prowess and intellect of the private investigator, knowing he will leave the D.A.'s office without incident.

Spade nods to the stenographer, "Good work," and turns back to the D.A. leaning over his desk:

> Now if you want to go to the board and tell them I'm obstructing justice and ask them to revoke my license—hop to it! You tried it once before, and it didn't get you anything but a good laugh all around.... And I don't want any more of these informal talks. I have nothing to say to you or the police. And I'm tired of being called things by every crackpot on the city payrolls. So if you want to see me, pinch me or subpoena me or something and I'll come down with my lawyer. I'll see you at the inquest—maybe.

The reality that the district attorney had once unsuccessfully attempted to have his private investigator's license revoked for obstructing justice exemplifies how law enforcement views the private investigator as a menace, one that needs to be shut down. However, considering the board failed to revoke Spade's license means the committee believes there is a need for the separate services of the P.I., and the competing ventures between P.I.s and the police do not amount to obstruction on the part of the P.I. because he is not obligated to disclose the progress of his investigation while the police simultaneously pursue their own. This scene also reveals that the P.I. is intimately aware of the legal procedures involving interrogations as "informal talks," as well as how he is not required by law to partake in them, therefore signaling his lawyer's notification. Thus the P.I. essentially stonewalls further discussions, unless he is either charged or subpoenaed by the court, revealing how the justice community, or "every crackpot on the city payrolls," is against the P.I., seeking to slander his profession by indulging in gossip and character assassination.

Toward the end of the film a discussion between criminals Kasper Gutman (Sydney Greenstreet), Cairo, Wilmer Cook (Gutman's hired gun, played by Elisha Cook, Jr.), and O'Shaughnessy reveal a significant flaw in the P.I.'s character when he discusses giving the police a "fall guy" to take responsibility for the murders, while they split the proceeds. This illegality indicates that the P.I. is also part of the criminal underworld, willing to pervert the justice system if it works toward his advantage. As a surrogate of law enforcement, this again shows the murkiness of those involved as extensions of the law and justice during the period of film noir.

The P.I.'s integrity is remedied at the end when he phones the police and informs Det. Polhaus of the investigation and the persons responsible. He interrogates O'Shaughnessy and determines that she was the one who killed his partner, Miles Archer. The scene shows the P.I.'s excellence as a detective, how he can uncover the crimes. His romance with O'Shaughnessy is challenged when he won't play the "sap" for her. This scene also shows how the femme fatale complicates the P.I.'s character by pulling on his heartstrings. Spade ultimately decided that it was bad business to allow a man's partner to be killed, with the killer not being brought to justice. He relates how it may be bad for private detectives, but he confesses a love for O'Shaughnessy. The scene ends with the P.I. both as an agent of the law and in total love with another woman. Spade thus turns O'Shaugnessey over to the authorities and then heads to the stationhouse with the officers, resolving that law enforcement and the P.I. are both parts of the same system in pursuit of justice; however, they are also both enmeshed in the shadowy use of the law in the 1940s.

The Big Sleep (1946)

A film noir directed by Howard Hawks and adapted from Raymond Chandler's book of the same name, *The Big Sleep* stars Humphrey Bogart as P.I. Phillip Marlowe, and Lauren Bacall as Vivian Rutledge. Marlowe's love for Rutledge, who is his client and General Sternwood's (Charles Waldron) daughter, complicates his investigation. Rutledge is deeply involved with the criminal syndicate; however, she moves smoothly between her association with the criminals and Marlowe as the private detective. Marlowe is endeavoring to resolve gambling debts that the General's other daughter, Carmen (Martha Vickers), owes to a bookie, Arthur Gwynn Geiger (Theodore von Eltz, uncredited). Rutledge is suspicious of her father's hiring Marlowe, suspecting his actual reason for hiring Marlowe is to locate his protégé, Sean Regan, who had disappeared without notice a month earlier. The plot quickly turns into a whodunit murder mystery, with the murder of Geiger inside his home while Marlowe conducts outside surveillance.

Toward the end of the film when Marlowe is speaking with Agnes Lowzier (Sonia Darrin), she makes sure to call him a "copper," illustrating that Marlowe is a law enforcement representative, just not traditional in the sense of a sworn officer employed by the city. From the outset of the film, viewers learn Marlowe was a former member of law enforcement who turned private detective after being fired for, not surprisingly, insubordination. Using Marlowe as a representative of law enforcement also provides for flexibility in his interactions with criminals and their associates. Early on in the film when Geiger is murdered, Marlowe examines his body on the floor, quickly searches his apartment, but does not report the murder to the police.

Chief Inspector Bernie Ohls (Regis Toomey) makes a late-night visit to Marlowe's home. Marlowe and Ohls are friends, and Ohls invites Marlowe to the crime scene where there is a vehicle owned by his client, which was found in the lake with a dead body in it. This scene portrays the police as inept because using a private detective as a surrogate member of law enforcement shows that the P.I. has the expertise, whereas the police detective does not. Police ineptness is reaffirmed in Marlowe's statement to Ohls: "Give me another day, Bernie. I may have something for you." The detective appears satisfied with Marlow helping on the investigation. However, the crime scene also portrays the police processing as intelligent and technical, thus showing viewers that the police are professionals capable of solving crimes, but cases like these take an insider such as Marlowe to develop leads and additional information. The P.I. is thus viewed as an additional way to gather intelligence because he is the go-between the police and criminal underworld.

In the scene where Marlowe is questioning Joe Brody (Louis Jean Heydt), the doorbell rings; Brody answers it, and he is shot in the chest as he opens the door. Marlowe chases the shooter and confronts him on the sidewalk with a gun in hand: "What will it be, kid? Me or the cops?" Marlowe kidnaps the shooter and brings him back to Geiger's house, where he contacts the police (Ohls) and turns him in. This scene illustrates that the private investigator can commit crimes in pursuit of solving an investigation; he is clearly an anomaly from the police; however, they are still portrayed as working in tandem. When an armed criminal attempts to rob Rutledge of her purse, Marlowe intervenes, takes the robber's gun, and then punches the robber out. Marlowe and Rutledge

V. Shadows of Law Enforcement in Film Noir

casually leave the area, and, again, the police are not contacted to report the robbery. Had Marlowe been a police detective, and not a private for-profit investigator, he would have been obliged to report the crime, even if Rutledge was not a willing participant in the investigation. It also shows that Marlowe is not concerned with justice for any crimes he has not been paid for his services to investigate. In contrast, justice, and the arrest and detection of all criminals, concern the police officers, whereas pay for services is not a deciding factor in the performance of their duties.

When Ohls contacts Marlowe and asks him to report to the police station, the film portrays the police department as having political involvement with the district attorney's office that borders on corruption. Ohls tells Marlowe to stop working on the Sternwood case per the district attorney and conveys how General Sternwood's daughter approached the district attorney and persuaded him to have Marlowe lay off the case. This interaction is an example of how Marlowe is not an employee of the police department and does not have to take orders from the district attorney. Marlowe discusses his investigation with Ohls, who informs him again that the district attorney wants him to lay off the case, but he usually does an excellent job following his hunches. Traditional law enforcement in this scene is represented through Ohls still pursuing justice; however, he does so in secrecy so not to garner the district attorney's attention. The district attorney as a symbol of the legal system portrays corruption and a perverting of justice. Marlowe, as the private detective, as well as both law enforcement insider and outsider at the same time, is viewed as pursuing truth, even as politics complicate the law enforcement system. Marlowe's contempt for the justice system is seen in the following scene when Harry Cook (Elisha Cook, Jr.) approaches him with information about the case. He tells Cook the information can easily be given to the police—in other words, why him?

> COOK: I came here with a straight proposition. Take it or leave. One right guy to another. You start waving cops at me. You ought to be ashamed of yourself.
> MARLOWE: I am.

This dialogue portrays the police as corrupt. Essentially, a person who is offering information to a private investigator, and thus hindering the police's investigation, is representing himself as righteous, while the police are not. Marlowe's agreement shows viewers that he also holds similar views about the police.

The ending is resolved with Marlowe solving the investigation, as well as murdering an unarmed man. Marlowe shoots criminal Eddie Mars (John Ridgley) in the arm, forcing him to run out the front door of Geiger's home where his henchmen are waiting. Marlowe tells Mars that when he runs out that door, his henchmen will shoot him reflexively; therefore, clearly Marlowe knows he is setting up Mars's murder by proxy. This illegality shows the P.I. often moves outside of the law and follows his own moral compass that, at times, contradicts the morality of law. Marlowe phones the police (Ohls) to get him out because there are gunmen outside surrounding the house. Marlowe uses the police to rescue him by informing Ohls he has the information he desires; however, Marlowe does not tell Ohls there is also information he will hide. The viewer is left with the understanding that Marlowe and Rutledge are in love, and at the end of the day, love wins. And also that law enforcement on both sides in terms of professional and private investigators are hopeless in their pursuit of justice because each side can, and often is, conniving, working in the shadows of the law during the period of film noir.

Where the Sidewalk Ends (1950)

A 20th Century–Fox film directed by Otto Preminger, *Where the Sidewalk Ends* stars Dana Andrews, an undervalued actor in film history, as Detective Mark Dixon of the New York City Police Department.[19] Dixon is set in contrast to his father who was a career criminal. However, as a detective, Dixon's reputation is marred by conflict. Dixon is an intelligent and capable investigator but is routinely in trouble with his superiors for the brutality he inflicts upon the criminals he is investigating. Thus the film is a fictionalized portrait of law enforcement during the period of film noir that confronts many issues of policing, including police brutality, corruption, and the use of the third degree (torture) to garner confessions during suspect interrogations. The third degree, as aforementioned, is a euphemism for torture when confessions fail through communication. It is the "inflicting of pain, physical or mental, to extract confessions or statements."[20] This film also creates an opposition between the construct of the ideal male of the 1940–1950s who settles down with a wife and family and represents wholesome family values, and the character of Dixon, who is a bachelor and is promiscuous, and hopeless, in conforming to the social norms as the patriarch

V. Shadows of Law Enforcement in Film Noir

of a wholesome family. While he almost gets there at the end, an awaiting stretch in prison stalemates any chance of redemption.

The film begins with Dixon investigating the murder of wealthy Ted Morrison (Harry von Zell, uncredited) at a New York City hotel. The crime involves a criminal underworld boss Tommy Scalise (Guy Merrill) whose illegal dice game was a set up to make a fool of Morrison. Scalise's henchman Ken Paine (Craig Stevens) brought Morrison to the hotel to gamble with the aid of his wife, Morgan Taylor (Gene Tierney), who was deceived by Paine into bringing Morrison there. When Morrison attempts to leave with his $19,000 in profits, Paine gets angry, smacks his wife, and punches Morrison. That is where the fight seems to end; however, Morrison ends up dead, and Paine appears to be the person responsible. This scene of domestic violence that goes unpunished reinforces how Taylor's minimizing of her husband's actions is both jarring and a sad reflection of the times. The film misses its opportunity to condemn domestic violence.

From the start, the film portrays Dixon's investigative intelligence as being superior to that of the newly appointed Lieutenant Thomas (Karl Malden), who is commander of the detective bureau. While at the hotel analyzing the crime scene and speaking with the criminals, Dixon knows the investigation is headed down the wrong path, and he takes it upon himself to solve it, while his colleagues head in a different investigative direction. Lieutenant Thomas tells Dixon to locate Paine, so he goes alone to the Paine's apartment. Dixon's vicious nature, perhaps a trait he got from his father, gets the better of him. Paine punches Dixon, who slugs the man back, not knowing that Paine is a war hero turned small-time criminal with a metal plate in his head. The punch kills Paine and Dixon finds himself in a difficult situation. He could notify his supervisors and explain what happened. If he had his partner with him, there would have been a witness to certify that it was a justifiable act. However, they were already onto him as a cop quick to use brutality, so he decides to cover up the incident. What follows is Dixon's efforts to dispose of the body, conceal his actions (thus hindering the investigation), and find the man who killed Morrison, while also framing him for the death of Paine.

The film portrays Dixon as corrupt. Throughout the film, he is depicted as willing to break the law whenever it suits him. He is similar to a P.I. who can become involved in situations that would typically require proper documentation and investigating by the police. Unlike P.I. Marlowe in *The Big Sleep*, who unjustifiably shot an unarmed man and forced him out a door that led to his death, Detective Dixon must pay for his violations of the law. At the end of the film Dixon's superior, Inspector Nicholas Foley (Robert F. Simon, uncredited), arrests Dixon, personally signing the charges against him. Dixon's admission causes his detection. Even though he is under arrest, he wins the heart of the beautiful woman, Morgan Taylor, who desperately declares her love for him. This arrest is a significant contrast from the usual P.I. character of film noir, who seldom had to pay for violations of the law as did Dixon. Dixon's role as a sworn officer of the law forced this ending.

In the opening of the film, after newly appointed Lieutenant Thomas is introduced as the commander of the 16th Precinct detective bureau by Inspector Foley, he brings Dixon into Lieutenant Thomas's new office to speak with him privately. Foley reprimands Dixon for "12 more legitimate citizens' complaints against you [Dixon] this month for assault and battery." Dixon challenges him, "From who? Hoods, dusters, mugs, a lot of nickel rats." Inspector Foley tells Dixon how he just saw the promotion of an officer (Lieutenant Thomas), who started at the same time on the force as Dixon; however, Dixon will never move ahead unless he gets a hold of himself. "I know what to get a hold of," Dixon says. "A little more pull." From this tense interaction, the viewer learns that officers can use brutality with little punishment and are thus corrupt. Twelve legitimate citizens' complaints for assault was still not enough to warrant further discipline, other than the demotion Foley gave Dixon, all the while still telling him that he is a good man with a good brain, and if he gets any more complaints for assaulting citizens, he will have no choice but to transfer him back into uniform and place him back on the beat. In other words, police brutality is acceptable in the police department because it only warrants internal punishments and the transfer of duty of officers who are brutal with the public. This scene also shows the political corruption involved in the promotional processes of the police department. Dixon's need for "more pull" to get ahead signals his contempt for a promotional process that is compromised by political affiliations.

There is a further reference of police brutality in interrogations in a later scene where Dixon approaches Paine's wife, Morgan Taylor, and questions her. She tells him she is on her way home. Dixon asks if she would mind if he joined her. "That's a nice way to put it when you're out to give me the third degree," Morgan says. As discussed earlier, the third degree was widely practiced by the police during the late nineteenth century and early twentieth century, as reported by the Wickersham

V. Shadows of Law Enforcement in Film Noir

Commission in 1931. In addition to the Wickersham Commission's finding that the police used the third degree to coerce confessions, it equally noted their participation in corruption.[21] The commission found that in New York City police "played in and robbed floating crap games, hijacked trucks, and took bribes for every conceivable regulatory violation."[22] It also showed that during Prohibition, the police were paid a dollar for every half-barrel of beer in New York City, where over thirty-two thousand speakeasies operated.[23]

During the 1940s era of film noir, using the third degree to interrogate suspects was a significant motif in crime film. In the previous decade, the movie *Behind the Green Lights* (1935) was derived from the autobiography of New York City police captain Cornelius W. Willemse, published in 1931 under the same name. In the book, Willemse reveals his use of the third degree: "Against a hardened criminal I never hesitated. I've forced confessions—with fist, black-jack, and hose—from men who would have continued to rob and to kill if I had not made them talk. The hardened criminals know only one language and laughs at the detective who tries any other. Remember this is war after all! I am convinced that my tactics saves many lives."[24] Willemse's published declaration was indicative of a police force at the time that was willing to go outside of the law to solve cases, thus contributing to the belief that the boundaries of law were ineffective for police interrogations.

Where the Sidewalk Ends is keenly aware of brutal interrogation police tactics and tries to show how a modern police force was moving away from these. In the aforementioned scene where Dixon and Lieutenant Thomas are questioning Scalise in the hotel room, Dixon represents the old ways of policing when he tells Lieutenant Thomas that he will smack the truth out of Scalise. Lieutenant Thomas, aware of the illegal practice of beating suspects for confessions, rebukes Dixon. This scene shows the tension between old representations of law enforcement in Dixon being quick to use the third degree to gain confessions of criminals, and the new approach of law enforcement in Lieutenant Thomas who abides by the law and endeavors to do his job within its boundaries. However, later in the film, when Inspector Foley forces Dixon into a week's vacation for beating another criminal and insubordination, he dismisses Dixon, and then turns to Lieutenant Thomas instructing him to question a man at the hotel on the night Morrison was murdered. However, he tells Lieutenant Thomas to interrogate him "like Dixon would." The scene continues with Lieutenant Thomas pushing the man to the corner of the room, giving him the third degree.

Law Enforcement in American Cinema, 1894–1952

Clearly, in *Where the Sidewalk Ends*, the struggle over police use of force as an efficient way to gain information in interrogations is played out.

Toward the end of the film, Dixon is portrayed like a P.I. who moves freely into the underworld. He becomes a detective working alone to solve the murder. He risks his life, gets shot in the arm, and wins the beautiful lady; however, unlike other P.I.s, he is punished for covering up the incident and deceiving the police. Dixon thus represents the quintessential film noir P.I., one who is unwelcome in the professional police force. Definitely not the ideal male of the era, Dixon is neither wholesome, has any family values, or is a representation of the traditional family man of the 1940s and 1950s. Instead, he is a renegade, a man who exists outside of societal norms, is promiscuous, and outside of the law. However, at the end, through his love for Taylor there exits the possibility that Dixon may conform to the construct of the ideal male of the era; ultimately, this redemption is thwarted due to his arrest.

The Maltese Falcon, *The Big Sleep*, and *Where the Sidewalk Ends* present a variety of representations of law enforcement. In *The Maltese Falcon*, the P.I. Sam Spade competes with police detectives. He argues with police detectives, clearly working in a competing role, where the detectives believe he may be the criminal himself, even though he was once working on the side of the law. When comparing this posturing between the P.I. and the detectives in *The Big Sleep*, the interactions are far more professional, and at times both are working in concert. In both films, the P.I. was a former member of the law enforcement community, thus signaling that it takes an insider of sorts to earn the respect of law enforcement and to lessen the competition among the bilateral investigations. In *The Big Sleep*, Marlowe, while working for himself, was constantly in contact with the police, essentially solving the case for them. In contrast, the police are portrayed as a team, with several detectives working a case, whereas Marlowe's resources are himself and any information he can get from his police contacts. In *Where the Sidewalk Ends* the police detective resembles the unethical private investigator so deep into his work that he commits crimes himself. He is similar to a P.I. but does not get the same treatment. His partaking in criminal activity is interpreted as neither clever nor an acceptable means to accomplish an objective. He is technically a sworn officer and does not get to march to the beat of his own drum.

As the decades ahead continue both to shape and reflect the public's perception of law enforcement through film, one thing is certain: the representations of the police (and their surrogate of the private

V. Shadows of Law Enforcement in Film Noir

investigator) in film noir paved the way for numerous movies and television series featuring police officers working on both sides of the law. The figures of the P.I. and the police detective transitioned mainly into television series, and as the national mood improved with the U.S. victory in World War II, and its new distinction as the superpower of the world, so did the representations of law enforcement in films. As the public became more sympathetic and trustworthy of police authority, the following decade of the 1950s held more favorable depictions of law enforcement in cinema. Now the police were the good guys, endeavoring to restore order and to protect the wholesome American family. Criminals were only to be condemned, and the law was the way to bring them to justice.

Coda

Law Enforcement in Early Twentieth-Century Film: From a Subject of Suspicion to a Power for the Common Good

From the inception of motion pictures, the major arc for law enforcement depictions in film begins with the relative suspicion, fear, and distrust of the police. This reflects real-world, socio-cultural shifts from the Progressive era through Prohibition and the Depression, and the seeming collapse of the American Dream. During the Cold War, the post–World War II period when the United States was a superpower of the world, the national mood improved, and as it did so did the representations of the police on film.

In every period of film social issues of the time found their way into film narratives, and many of these narratives include illustrations of the police and the justice system. While the films discussed in this study are not a comprehensive view of every movie that featured a symbol of law enforcement from inception through the first half of the twentieth century, the films presented here do represent an evolving narrative of depictions of police in film.

From inception through the early 1910s (when films were short in length), depictions of law enforcement in cinema portrayed the police as brutes who were quick to use force, or their pistols, to overpower the seemingly innocent public into compliance. They were sometimes symbols adversarial to the people they served. They were, at times, depicted in bland procedural roles, as agents of an unfair justice system that favored the rich over the poor, the powerful over the weak, and who cared more for self-gain than the safety and security of the community. The counter-narratives found in films such as *Life of an American Policeman* (1905) paled in comparison to the dominant narratives that the law could not be trusted, and justice was seldom realized for the victim. This was an unfortunate reality for representations of law enforcement film during the Progressive era when social reform initiatives and anxieties occupied the American consciousness; nonetheless, it is still a negative view of the police. In fact, the police themselves were a target of social reform initiatives during this period, so it is not surprising that their shortcomings found their way into the cinema.

By the 1910s, when longer feature films appeared, the accounts of the police in film evolved to include their portrayals as the dense, but sometimes good, guys worthy of lampoon, even as they filled protagonist roles. Popular serials, such as the Keystone Kops, and subsequent films, such as Charlie Chaplin's *Easy Street* (1917) and Buster Keaton's *Cops* (1922), challenged the effectiveness of the police and openly criticized them through slapstick or other comedy. *Easy Street* criticizes the police as ineffective in addressing social conditions in the inner cities and illustrated the need for a police outsider/community insider mindset to solve the problems the citizenry needed fixing. It pokes fun at the police's ineptness and inability to quell the community blight. Although *Easy Street* was not as explicitly critically of the police as was *Cops'* outright disdain for them and the justice system, films of this type occupied the public sphere and mirrored the public's distrust of police authority as agents of the law. This correlates to the emerging expansion of the police as an occupying force, extending from cities into suburban America. During these early years of modern law enforcement, the public's uneasiness and hesitation to trust the police was seemingly natural as memories (whether positive or negative) built through these new interactions between the police and the community. Some of the public's suspicion was from the stereotypes derived from the heavily reported corruption of city police departments in newspapers across the nation around the turn of the century, and from individual encounters with rough cops, thus welcoming the films that supported their life experiences.

The 18th Amendment to the Constitution, which banned alcohol across the nation, cast the police on film into the shadows of the more sympathetic criminal, who maintained the spotlight as the protagonist in many films into the early 1930s—a time when the gangster films were among the most popular and most violent films of the day. This move toward a more sympathetic criminal and the expansion of organized crime in cities across America was the result of Prohibition, which allowed access to the American Dream by way of their criminal enterprise and conversely made criminals out of ordinary Americans

Coda

who indulged in the banned libations. The film industry took advantage of these popular public perceptions, and thus movie plots throughout the 1920s and into the 1930s show gangsters as the embodiment of the American Dream. This reality also speaks to the film industry enterprise as American capitalists.

During this period, film also moved from the silent to the sound era. In the new age of the "talkies," the thoughtless detective was routinely giving way to the romanticized criminal protagonist. Movies such as *Little Caesar* (1931), *The Public Enemy* (1931), and *Scarface* (1931) are all told from the view of a criminal protagonist and offer the viewer a romanticized look into the criminal underworld. Many of these criminal characters are portrayed as a victim of circumstance. Often, their willingness to engage in crime is no fault of their own. The economy, poverty, unfair moral laws, or the government keeping them down was to blame. The American Dream, for honest citizens, had seemingly collapsed during the Depression, and it seemed the Republic would soon follow. However, the urban gangster or the rural outlaw had access to the American Dream through criminality—a paradoxical reality that is represented over and over in films and throughout popular culture.

Characterizing the police in many of the early crime films as essentially another gang, willing to use similar extralegal methods to arrive at the conclusions of investigations, was routine. The police in 1930s cinema often live by their own moral code and take the fight on crime personally. They are locked in rivalries with gangs for turf or respect from the public. Their representations evolve once again during the mid–1930s when films, courtesy of the Production Code Administration and demands from law enforcement and civilian activists to stop glamorizing criminals and violence, changed the storylines of the movies. During the mid–1930s, films that heroicized law enforcement as the good guys, tasked with ridding the world of violence and maintaining the safety of the community, sprang up. In these films, the condemning of the despicable villain appeared. Actors who had previously played roles as villains were now the brave lawman. Movies, such as *"G" Men* (1935), *Public Hero Number 1* (1935), *Whipsaw* (1935), *36 Hours to Kill* (1936), and *Midnight Taxi* (1937), were sympathetic to law enforcement and strictly followed the moral understanding that criminals are to be punished and the law exists for the greater benefit of society. This new narrative was a significant shift from the preceding decades where the police in film were overshadowed by the romanticized criminal protagonist.

During 1940s film noir, representations of law enforcement and the

Law Enforcement in Early Twentieth-Century Film

law return to a previous ambivalence. The private investigators are routinely depicted as similar to gangsters of the prior decade who live by their own moral philosophy outside the authority of the law. Even considering that many noir films end with legal justice, the detectives who arrive at that point first have to go outside of the law to get there. The P.I. of film noir is dissimilar from the police investigator of the late 1930s. He is sometimes deceitful with the police and commits crimes himself, often bending and breaking the law as he deems necessary to achieve investigative objectives, or is looking to redeem the heart of the femme fatale, such as P.I. Sam Spade pursues in *The Maltese Falcon*. The P.I. of film noir can move back and forth between the respectable world and the criminal underworld, while seemingly acting as a surrogate for law enforcement. However, through his interactions with criminals, he is often seen as working for both sides of the law.

The 1950s was a time of strong American exceptionalism. It was the decade of respect for law enforcement and order. *The Adventures of Superman* television series starring George Reeves, which ran from 1952 to 1958, showcased the "Man of Steel" who rid the streets of crime and saves the planet, much as the United States had done for the world. Superman's respect for authority is shown throughout the series, with scenes of Superman respecting the police and the authority their work represents, sending a clear message that the public should also respect the police. *Superman* exhibits how there is room for everyone to work together to fight crime, as is evidenced in the Police Inspector Henderson character who worked for the Metropolis Police Department and befriended the staff at the *Daily Planet* where they often worked side-by-side to solve crimes. The police no longer needed to go at crime-fighting alone because they were on the public's side, and both had a stake in the fight against crime.

In the 1950s, the detectives of the previous decades were now appearing on television in series such as *Dragnet*, which began in 1951 and depicts detectives as honest, trustworthy, wholesome paternal figures, working within the limitations of the law to solve cases and to protect the community. They were no longer the brash cops using the third degree to beat confessions out of suspects. They solved cases by outsmarting the criminals and maintained strict respect and admiration for the law. There were lots of bad people out there in the world, and the police officer was the means to corral these criminals and to keep the neighborhood safe.

Cinema in the 1950s, especially in terms of law enforcement

Coda

representations, was distinct from all previous decades. Movies such as *High Noon* (1952) were widely successful and demonstrated that the local lawman can save the world. *High Noon* earned Gary Cooper an Academy Award and Golden Globe Award as best actor and of the seven nominations for Academy Awards, it won four. It was among the most critically acclaimed and popular movies that year.[1] *High Noon* was derived from John Marshall Cunningham's short story "The Tin Star," which was published in *Collier's Magazine* in 1947. The movie begins with the lawman, Marshall Will Kane (Gary Cooper), marrying community outsider Amy Fowler (Grace Kelly). The newlywed couple is leaving town, since Kane had given up his position as marshal, and are planning on building their new life together somewhere else. However, Kane soon learns that the imprisoned notorious criminal, Frank Miller (Ian MacDonald), who was pardoned and no longer faces the gallows is on his way back to town on the noon train. Miller had vowed that he would one day return to kill Kane. The townspeople are terrified when they learn Miller is returning. Kane decides his only option is to stand up to Miller, since running away like a coward would get him killed, and the townspeople needed him to protect them. However, Kane shortly learns that the townspeople have turned their back on him, believing that if Kane had left town, Miller would have no issue with them, and they would thus possibly be safe. All of Kane's attempts to swear in new deputies and build a force to confront Miller and his men are futile—Kane must go at it alone.

When Kane walks into the church, the church members are singing the patriotic "Battle Hymn of the Republic," in a similar way to that in *Life of an American Policeman* (1905), which arguably used the song as a musical accompaniment to the silent film, to celebrate the heroism of the police. The church scene also praises law enforcement as an effective force to maintain the safety and security of the community through residents declaring Kane was the lawman that tamed the town and made it a safe place to raise children—that he was the best marshal that they had ever had and that his efforts were both worthy and needed. This signals that the relationship between law enforcement and the community had grown to a point where partnerships were formed; law enforcement was met with less suspicion and was held in esteem. It can be posited that perhaps directors Wallace McCutcheon and Edwin S. Porter, and the New York City police officers who collaborated on *Life of an American Policeman* forty-seven years earlier, would be proud to see that their message had finally caught on. However, the townspeople are

Law Enforcement in Early Twentieth-Century Film

still terrified and find creative ways to rationalize their cowardice in not helping Kane. Nevertheless, there is evidence that the American mood toward law enforcement had greatly improved during the 1950s when actor John Wayne (a friend of Cooper happy for Cooper's success with the film), who was upset with the plot, said, "No American would turn his back on the sheriff and allow criminals to run the town."[2]

High Noon also makes certain to remedy displays of police corruption found in earlier decades on film. When Kane is endeavoring to raise a posse, a townsperson blames Kane for the imminent doom the town faces with the soon-to-be-arriving Miller. The man blames Kane for not arresting Miller's men who are waiting for him. Kane explains that he cannot arrest a man for sitting at the train depot; hence he follows a strict adherence to, and respect for, the law. In the saloon scene, where patrons are speaking with saloon owner Gillis (Larry J. Blake) about the looming showdown between Kane and Miller, Kane enters and overhears Gillis telling how Kane will be dead five minutes after Miller disembarks from the train. Kane approaches Gillis, punches him in the face, knocking him to the ground. Gillis, rubbing his jaw, says, "You carry a badge and a gun, marshal. You ain't no call to do that." Kane nods, "You're right." He then attempts to help Gillis up from the floor. This demonstration illustrates how the police have transitioned from the yesteryears' quick use of brutality, and while Kane uses it in this scene, his acknowledgment of it as wrong confers that it is not the right approach for modern law enforcement.

High Noon ends in a classic battle of good versus evil. Kane is outmatched and bravely stands up to Miller and his gang, eventually killing all of them, albeit with the help of his wife Amy—the Quaker who despises violence—who, from the window of Kane's office, kills one of the gang members as he is attempts to shoot Kane. Kane, disgusted with the townspeople, throws his badge in the dirt, and rides out of town with his wife. Interestingly, previous film criticism connects *High Noon* to McCarthy-era blacklisting. The film that was scripted by blacklisted writer Carl Foreman was not another typical Western.[3] The film, as M. Ray Lott discusses, was a metaphor for the threatened Hollywood blacklist artists standing up against the system.[4] As a sign of the strength of the pro–American narrative of the 1950s, the casting of star Gary Cooper and the use of an American Western was by design because it allowed for very little pushback from the public or the House Committee on Un-American Activities (HUAC) and ensured that if the HUAC attacked, the studio could spin it as an attack against America itself.[5]

Coda

High Noon's famous tune, "The Ballad of High Noon" (or "Do Not Forsake Me, O My Darlin'")—a popular theme song published in 1952—with music by Dimitri Tiomkin, lyrics by Ned Washington, and sung over the opening credits by Tex Ritter, is used as a leitmotif throughout the film, pointing to how the police evolved from their early depictions on film, to the 1950s.

In ways similar to America, the new superpower of the world, standing up against evil and overcoming against all the odds, these lyrics are also a symbol of law enforcement. The 1950s' lawman had evolved in film from its first appearance of a uniformed officer in *Chinese Laundry* (1894) being beat up or from disregarding a robbery victim lying unconscious on the sidewalk, opting instead to steal the victim's money the robber inadvertently left behind in *How They Rob Men in Chicago* (1900), into a legitimate force for good—strong-willed, brave, capable of saving the world. The former decades of the police as mere representations of the law were replaced as they now became the embodiment of the nation. Thus, the police must be good because the nation must also be presented as good.

This study seeks to address the dearth of scholarship on law enforcement in American film from inception through the first half of the twentieth century, and by doing so reveals the arc of the evolution of representations of police in cinema, demonstrating both the changes and progress of representations of early law enforcement in tandem with rapidly shifting social and cultural conditions. Far from exhaustive, this study reveals the need for much further research in this area. For example, of the thousands of films produced in the early silent film era, there is an abundance of movies where law enforcement appears, whether in purely procedural roles or as characters actively engaging in the development of the narrative. Therefore, an encyclopedic-type individual study of all of these surviving films can lead to an overall stronger understanding of the police and their role in society and film during this period, thus extending the work of this study in both breadth and depth.

Recommended areas for further study include more in-depth research on the portrayals of law enforcement in film during Prohibition and the Depression, which would further explain the public's ambivalence regarding the law and its agents as portrayed in cinema. A study of this kind could further contribute to popular culture studies on the romanticization of criminals, who were seeking to realize the American Dream by way of crime. These studies can also answer what the American police officers had at stake during this period, and how was their plight for a better life symbolized in film? Were the police, too, a victim of the government, and if so, to what extent did their experience compare to the populace whose jobs were not as stable as those in government? Further considerations of the citizen's appraisal of the police are needed, especially in suburban communities where police departments were new forces in the neighborhood.

Studies that scrutinize the range of pro-law enforcement films made during the 1930s can offer profound interpretations of a more accurate assessment of the public's viewing of the police in the community, since at present no such study exists and only inferences can be made through representations of police interactions with the reoccurring criminal protagonist. This study can contribute to further understandings of the significant shifts regarding favorable police depictions on screen during the mid–1930s and how this influenced Americans' relationship with the now firmly grounded round-the-clock police officers active in their communities. Also, a complete study of every pro-criminal protagonist film from the viewpoint of police characters can reveal a counter-narrative to that of the romanticized criminal during this period. Much has been written about the criminal of the 1930s film. More works need to follow on the foil of the criminal—the police officer. This area of study is plentiful with material and only waiting for a future researcher to grab hold of it.

Moreover, a study to examine how police characters (private investigators and police detectives) in film noir used the third degree (torture) for police interrogations versus those employing dependable rational methods of deduction could provide additional insight into the police culture at the time and how these tactics of interrogations evolved as represented in film during the 1940s. This study would be highly focused and can provide extra layers of interpretations of the police. Independent works researching both the private investigator and the police detective of the 1940s can offer additional layers of analysis and comprehension. At present, there are no comprehensive works that look individually at either of these representations of law enforcement in film, and therefore, much scholarly attention is warranted.

This study has revealed that representations of early law enforcement in film in the first half of the twentieth century, in general, have been neglected by scholars. While this work helps to ameliorate this lack of scholarship, much more study must be conducted to open up further avenues of inquiry to build upon its thesis. It is hopeful these studies will commence shortly.

Filmography

Angels with Dirty Faces. Directed by Michael Curtiz. Performed by James Cagney, Pat O'Brien, Humphrey Bogart. 1938. Burbank, CA: Warner Bros.
Appointment by Telephone. Directed by Edwin S. Porter. Performed by unknown. 1902. New York: Edison Manufacturing Company.
The Assassination of Jesse James by the Coward Robert Ford. Directed by Dominick Andrew. 2007. Burbank, CA: Warner Bros.
The Bangville Police. Directed by Henry Lehrman. Performed by Mabel Normand, Fred Mace, Nick Cogley. 1913. Edendale, Los Angeles: Keystone Film Company.
Behind the Green Lights. Directed by Christy Cabanne. Performed by Norman Foster, Judith Allen, Sidney Blackmer. 1935. Los Angeles: Mascot Pictures.
The Big Heat. Directed by Fritz Lang. Performed by Glenn Ford, Gloria Grahame, Jocelyn Brando. 1953. Culver City, CA: Columbia Pictures Corporation.
Big Jim McLain. Directed by Edward Ludwig. Performed by John Wayne, Nancy Olson, James Arness. 1952. Burbank, CA: Warner Bros.
The Big Sleep. Directed by Howard Hawks. Performed by Humphrey Bogart, Lauren Bacall, John Ridgely.1946. Burbank, CA: Warner Bros.
Billy the Kid. Directed by Laurence Trimble as "Larry Trimble." Performed by Tefft Johnson, Edith Storey. 1911. New York: Vitagraph Company of America.
The Birth of a Nation. Directed by D.W. Griffith. Performed by Lillian Gish, Mae Marsh, Henry B. Walthall. 1915. Los Angeles: D.W. Griffith Corp, Epoch Producing Corporation.
The Black Hand. Directed by Wallace McCutcheon. Performed by Anthony O'Sullivan, Robert G. Vignola. 1906. New York: American Mutoscope & Biograph.
The Blue Dahlia. Directed by George Marshall. Performed by Alan Ladd, Veronica Lake, William Bendix.1946. Los Angeles: Paramount Pictures.
Bullets or Ballots. Directed by William Keighley. Performed by Edward G. Robinson, Joan Blondell, Barton MacLane. 1936. Burbank, CA: Warner Bros.
The Celluloid Closet. Directed by Rob Epstein and Jeffrey Friedman. Performed by Lily Tomlin, Tony Curtis, Susie Bright. 1996. New York: Channel Four Films HBO Pictures/Sony Pictures Classics.
Cops. Directed by Edward F. Cline and Buster Keaton. Performed by Buster Keaton, Edward F. Cline, Virginia Fox. 1922. Los Angeles: Joseph M. Schenck Productions.

Filmography

A Corner in Wheat. Directed by D.W. Griffith. Performed by Frank Powell, Grace Henderson, James Kirkwood. 1909. New York: Biograph Company.

Criss Cross. Directed by Robert Siodmak. Performed by Burt Lancaster, Yvonne De Carlo, Dan Duryea. 1949. London, UK: Universal International Pictures (UI).

The Dark Corner. Directed by Henry Hathaway. Performed by Lucille Ball, Clifton Webb, William Bendix.1946. Los Angeles: Twentieth Century–Fox.

Dead End. Directed by William Wyler. Performed by Sylvia Sidney, Joel McCrea, Humphrey Bogart. 1937. Hollywood, CA: The Samuel Goldwyn Company.

Destry Rides Again. Directed by George Marshall. Performed by Marlene Dietrich, James Stewart, Mischa Auer. 1939. Universal City, CA: Universal Pictures.

D.O.A. Directed by Rudolph Maté. Performed by Edmond O'Brien, Pamela Britton, Luther Adler. 1949. Beverly Hills, CA: United Artists (Distributor). Producer: Harry Popkin Productions/ Cardinal Pictures.

Don Juan. Directed by Alan Crosland. Performed by Jane Winton, John Roche, Warner Oland. 1926. Burbank, CA: Warner Bros.

The Doorway to Hell. Directed by Archie Mayo. Performed by Lew Ayres, James Cagney, Charles Judels. 1930. Burbank, CA: Warner Bros.

Double Indemnity. Directed by Billy Wilder. Performed by Fred MacMurray, Barbara Stanwyck, Edward G. Robinson. 1944. Los Angeles: Paramount Pictures.

Dragnet. Creator: Jack Webb. Performed by Jack Webb, Ben Alexander, Olan Soule. 1951. Burbank, CA: Warner Bros./ Mark VII Ltd.

Dragnet. Directed by Jack Webb. Performed by Jack Webb, Ben Alexander, Richard Boone. 1954. Burbank, CA: Warner Bros./ Mark VII Ltd.

A Drunkard's Reformation. Directed by D.W. Griffith. Performed by Arthur V. Johnson, Linda Arvidson, Adele DeGarde. 1909. New York: American Mutoscope & Biograph.

Easy Street. Directed by Charlie Chaplin. Performed by Charles Chaplin, Edna Purviance, Eric Campbell. 1917. Edendale, CA: Mutual Film Company/Lone Star Corporation.

A Gesture Fight in Hester Street. Directed by Marvin W. Arthur. Performed by unknown. 1900. New York: American Mutoscope and Biograph Company.

"G" Men. Directed by William Keighley. Performed by James Cagney, Margaret Lindsay, Ann Dvorak. 1935. Burbank, CA: First National Pictures.

The Great Train Robbery. Directed by Edwin S. Porter (uncredited). Performed by Gilbert M. "Broncho Billy" Anderson, A.C. Abadie, George Barnes. 1903. New York: Edison Manufacturing Company.

He Walked by Night. Directed by Alfred L. Werker (as Alfred Werker) and Anthony Mann (uncredited). Performed by: Richard Basehart, Scott Brady, Roy Roberts. 1948. Bryan Foy Productions.

The Heathen Chinee and the Sunday School Teacher. Director unknown. Director of Photography A.E. Weed. Performed by unknown. 1903. New York: American Mutoscope & Biograph.

High Noon. Directed by Fred Zinnemann. Screenplay by Carl Foreman. Per-

Filmography

formed by Gary Cooper, Grace Kelly, Thomas Mitchell. 1952. Beverly Hills, CA: United Artists (Distributor), Produced by Stanley Kramer Productions.
How They Do Things on the Bowery. Directed by Edwin S. Porter. Performed by anonymous. 1902. Orange, NJ: Thomas A. Edison.
How They Rob Men in Chicago. Directed by Wallace McCutcheon. Performed by anonymous. 1900. New York: American Mutoscope & Biograph.
In Old California. Directed by D.W. Griffith. Performed by Frank Powell, Arthur V. Johnson, Marion Leonard. 1910. New York: Biograph Company.
The Inside of the White Slave Traffic. Directed by Frank Beal. Performed by Edwin Carewe, Jean Thomas, Virginia Mann. 1913. Moral Feature Film Company.
Jack and the Beanstalk. Directed by Edwin S. Porter. Performed by unknown. 1902. New York: Edison Manufacturing Company.
The James Boys of Missouri. Directed by Gilbert M. "Broncho Billy" Anderson. Performed by Harry McCabe. 1908. Chicago, IL: Essanay Film Mfg. Co.
The Jazz Singer. Directed by Alan Crosland. Performed by Al Jolson, May McAvoy, Warner Oland.1927. Burbank, CA: Warner Bros.
Jesse James. Directed by Henry King and Irving Cummings. Performed by Tyrone Power, Henry Fonda, Nancy Kelly. 1939. Los Angeles: Twentieth Century-Fox.
King of the Underworld. Directed by Archie Mayo. Performed by Lew Ayres, James Cagney, Charles Judels. 1939. Burbank, CA: Warner Bros.
The Kiss. Directed by William Heise. Performed by May Irwin, John C. Rice. 1896. New York: Edison Manufacturing Company.
The Kleptomaniac. Directed by Edwin S. Porter. Performed by Aline Boyd, Phineas Nairs, Jane Stewart. 1905. New York: Edison Manufacturing Company.
Lady in the Lake. Directed by Robert Montgomery. Performed by Robert Montgomery, Audrey Totter, Lloyd Nolan. 1946. Los Angeles: Metro-Goldwyn-Mayer (MGM).
The Last Gangster. Directed by Edward Ludwig. Performed by Edward G. Robinson, James Stewart, Rose Stradner. 1937. Los Angeles: Metro-Goldwyn-Mayer (MGM).
Laura. Directed by Otto Preminger. Performed by Gene Tierney, Dana Andrews, Clifton Webb. 1944. Los Angeles: Twentieth Century-Fox.
Life of an American Policeman. Directed by Wallace McCutcheon, Edwin S. Porter. Performed by Jennie Bartlett, Bert Conneally. 1905. New York: Edison Manufacturing Company.
Little Caesar. Directed by Mervyn LeRoy. Performed by Edward G. Robinson, Douglas Fairbanks, Jr., Glenda Farrell. 1931. Burbank, CA: First National Pictures.
The Maltese Falcon. Directed by John Huston. Performed by Humphrey Bogart, Mary Astor, Gladys George. 1941. Burbank, CA: Warner Bros.
Midnight Taxi. Directed by Eugene Forde. Performed by Brian Donlevy, Frances Drake, Alan Dinehart. 1937. Los Angeles: Twentieth Century-Fox.
Mildred Pierce. Directed by Michael Curtiz. Performed by Joan Crawford, Jack Carson, Zachary Scott. 1945. Burbank, CA: Warner Bros.

Filmography

The Moonshiners. Directed by Wallace McCutcheon. Performed by Wallace McCutcheon, Harold Vosburgh. 1904. New York: American Mutoscope & Biograph.

Murder My Sweet. Directed by Edward Dmytryk. Performed by Dick Powell, Claire Trevor, Anne Shirley. 1944. Los Angeles: RKO Radio Pictures.

The Musketeers of Pig Alley. Directed by D.W. Griffith. Performed by Elmer Booth, Lillian Gish, Clara T. Bracy. 1912. New York: Biograph Company.

My Darling Clementine. Directed by John Ford. Performed by Henry Fonda, Linda Darnell, Victor Mature. 1946. Los Angeles: Twentieth Century–Fox.

The Naked City. Directed by Jules Dassin. Performed by Barry Fitzgerald, Howard Duff, Dorothy Hart. 1948. London, UK: Hellinger Productions, Universal International Pictures (UI).

Out of the Past. Directed by Jacques Tourneur. Performed by Robert Mitchum, Jane Greer, Kirk Douglas. 1947. Los Angeles: RKO Radio Pictures.

Paradise Canyon. Directed by Carl Person. Performed by John Wayne, Marion Burns, Reed Howes. 1935. Los Angeles: Lone Star Productions, Monogram Pictures Corp. / Paul Malvern Productions

Perils of the New Land: Films of the Immigrant Experience (1910–1915). Directed by Reginald Barker, George Loane Tucker. Performed by George Beban, Clara Williams, J. Frank Burke, Jane Gail, Ethel Grandin, William H. Turner. 2009. DVD. Los Angeles: Flicker Alley.

Police Force of New York City. Directed by James H. White. 1910. New York: Edison Manufacturing Company.

The Postman Always Rings Twice. Directed by Tay Garnett. Performed by Lana Turner, John Garfield, Cecil Kellaway. 1946. Los Angeles: Metro-Goldwyn-Mayer (MGM).

The Public Enemy. Directed by William A. Wellman. Performed by James Cagney, Jean Harlow, Edward Woods. 1931. Burbank, CA: Warner Bros.

Public Hero Number 1. Directed by J. Walter Ruben. Performed by Lionel Barrymore, Jean Arthur, Chester Morris. 1935. Los Angeles: Metro-Goldwyn-Mayer (MGM).

Rainbow Valley. Directed by Robert N. Bradbury. Performed by John Wayne, Lucile Browne, George "Gabby" Hayes. 1935. Los Angeles: Lone Star Productions, Monogram Pictures Corp. / Paul Malvern Productions.

The Roaring Twenties. Directed by Raoul Walsh. Performed by James Cagney, Humphrey Bogart, Priscilla Lane. 1939. Burbank, CA: Warner Bros.

Robetta and Doretto [No. 2] also known as *Chinese Laundry*. Directed by William K.L. Dickson and William Heise. Performed by Phil Doreto, Robetta. 1894. Thomas A. Edison.

Runaway in the Park. Directed by James H. White. Performed by unknown. 1896. Orange, NJ: Edison Manufacturing Company.

Salt of the Earth. Directed by Herman Biberman. Performed by Juan Chacón, Rosaura Revueltas, Will Geer. 1954. Independent Productions, International Union of Mine, Mill and Smelter Workers.

Scarface. Directed by Howard Hawks and Richard Rosson (co-director). Per-

Filmography

formed by Paul Muni, Ann Dvorak, Karen Morley. 1932. Beverly Hills, CA: United Artists (Distributor) Produced by The Caddo Company.
Sherlock Holmes Baffled. Directed by Arthur Marvin. Performed by anonymous. 1900. New York: American Mutoscope & Biograph.
The Silver Wedding. Cameraman F.A. Dobson. Performed by unknown. 1906. New York: American Mutoscope & Biograph.
Smart Money. Directed by Alfred E. Green. Performed by Edward G. Robinson, James Cagney, Evalyn Knapp. 1931. Burbank, CA: Warner Bros.
Sounder. Directed by Martin Performed by Cicely Tyson, Paul Winfield, Kevin Hooks, Carmen Matthews. 1972. Ritt Radnitz / Mattel Productions, Inc./ Twentieth Century–Fox.
The Star Packer. Directed by Robert N. Bradbury. Performed by John Wayne, Verna Hillie, George "Gabby" Hayes. 1934. Los Angeles: Lone Star Productions, Monogram Pictures Corp. / Paul Malvern Productions.
Suspense. Directed by Phillips Smalley and Lois Weber. Performed by Lois Weber, Val Paul, Douglas Gerrard. 1913. New York: Rex Motion Picture Company.
The Thin Man. Directed by W.S. Van Dyke. Performed by William Powell, Myrna Loy, Maureen O'Sullivan. 1934. Los Angeles: Metro-Goldwyn-Mayer (MGM).
36 Hours to Kill. Directed by Eugene Forde. Performed by Brian Donlevy, Gloria Stuart, Douglas Fowley. 1936. Los Angeles: Twentieth Century–Fox.
This Gun for Hire. Directed by Frank Tuttle. Performed by Alan Ladd, Veronica Lake, Robert Preston. 1942. Los Angeles: Paramount Pictures.
Traffic in Souls. Directed by George Loane Tucker. Performed by Jane Gail, Ethel Grandin, William H. Turner. 1913. New York: Independent Moving Pictures Co. of America (IMP).
Underworld. Directed by Josef von Sternberg, Arthur Rosson (uncredited). Performed by George Bancroft, Clive Brook, Evelyn Brent. 1927. Los Angeles: Paramount Pictures.
Weary River. Directed by Frank Lloyd. Performed by Richard Barthelmess, Betty Compson, William Holden. 1929. Burbank, CA: First National Pictures.
What Happened to Mary. Directed by Charles Brabin. Performed by Mary Fuller, Marc McDermott, Charles Ogle. 1912. New York: McClure Publishing Co., Edison Manufacturing Company.
Where Are My Children. Directed by Phillips Smalley (uncredited) and Lois Weber (uncredited). Performed by Tyrone Power, Sr., Mrs. Tyrone Power, Marie Walcamp. 1916. Los Angeles: Lois Weber Productions, Universal Film Manufacturing Company.
Where the Sidewalk Ends. Directed by Otto Preminger. Performed by Dana Andrews, Gene Tierney, Gary Merrill. 1950. Los Angeles: Twentieth Century–Fox.
Whipsaw. Directed by Director: Sam Wood. Performed by Myrna Loy, Spencer Tracy, Harvey Stephens. 1935. Los Angeles: Metro-Goldwyn-Mayer (MGM).
The Woman in the Window. Directed by Fritz Lang. Performed by Edward G. Robinson, Joan Bennett, Raymond Massey. 1944. Christie Corporation, International Pictures (I).

Chapter Notes

Introduction

1. Lee Grieveson's work *Policing Cinema: Movies and Censorship in Early-Twentieth-Century America* (Berkeley: University of California Press, 2004) provides a complete assessment of police involvement in censorship in the early years and how these forces shaped American cinema and its role in society. It also reveals the social function of cinema at the time and argues how it should function in society.
2. Charles Musser, *Before the Nickelodeon: Edwin S. Porter and the Edison Manufacturing Company* (Berkley: University of California Press, 1991), 308.
3. Ray M. Lott, *Police on Screen: Hollywood Cops, Detectives, Marshall and Rangers* (Jefferson, NC: McFarland, 2006), 4.
4. *Ibid.*
5. *Ibid.*, 5.
6. Though often classified as a Western, many scholars like Drew Todd argue that "early-twentieth-century viewers may well have considered *The Great Train Robbery* a movie about crime." While "Westerns" are about a mythical past, in 1903 the West was still real, and therefore for its audiences the film was a contemporary crime film and not a Western. Todd is supported in this view by Richard Maltby's study on genre recognition: "Contemporary audiences recognized *The Great Train Robbery* as a melodramatic example of one or more of the 'chase films,' the 'railway genre,' and the 'crime film.'" Richard Maltby, *Hollywood Cinema* (Cambridge, MA: Blackwell), 117, in Raftner, *Shots in the Mirror*, 23.
7. It is no surprise *The Great Train Robbery* idealizes the gun battles of the Old West— the days of train robberies along rural stretches of places like Iowa for the purposes of profit through robbery and violence. Americans at this time were familiar with the Old West. They witnessed the growing industrialization of America society eventually and unintentionally ousting social bandits like Jesse James and his exploits in the South and Southwest as cities sprung up on lands once roamed by massive herds of buffalo, Native American Indians, and in some areas thick forestry. These were developed into urban metropolises with hoards of newly arriving immigrant ethnic groups, leaving the exploits of these social bandits to be memorialized heavily in myth and legend.
8. Examining nickelodeons, Peter Roffman and Jim Purdy find that these early films offered "sympathy for the common man and the prevailing criticism of the corrupt and wealthy." From the start of moving pictures, films focused in cruel ways on criminals, and using these constructs ensured viewers of crime films an exposé of explicit violence. Peter Roffman and Jim Purdy, *The Hollywood Social Problem Film: Madness, Despair, and Politics from the Depression to the Fifties* (Bloomington: Indiana University Press, 1981), 10; quoted in Drew Todd, "The History of Crime Films," in Nicole Rafter, *Shots in the Mirror: Crime Films and Society* (New York: Oxford University Press, 2006), 22.
9. Ken Alder, *The Lie Detectors: The History of an American Obsession* (New York: Free Press, 2007), 19–20.
10. Ruth Mayer, "In the Nick of Time? Detective Film Serials, Temporality, and

Notes—Introduction

Contingency Management, 1919–1926," *The Velvet Light Trap* 79, no. 1 (2017): 21–35.

11. The central character in *What Happened to Mary* was played by actress Mary Fuller, who had previously starred in Edison Studio's *Frankenstein* (1910) before her career ended by 1917. Her life and film have an eerie parallel. After leaving acting, Mary Fuller allegedly suffered her first nervous breakdown, which hindered her 1926 attempt to reclaim her film career. After the death of her mother in 1940, she suffered another nervous breakdown. In 1947, she was admitted to Washington's Saint Elizabeth Hospital (America's first federally-operated psychiatric hospital) where she remained for twenty-six years, dying alone without any family. Indeed "What happened to Mary?" was a question for decades, as Fuller had vanished from public view, her whereabouts a mystery.

12. Mayer, "Nick of Time," 22.

13. Rob King, *The Fun Factory: The Keystone Film Company and the Emergence of Mass Culture* (Oakland: University of California Press, 2008).

14. "Chertoff castigated over Katrina: U.S. senators have lambasted homeland security chief Michael Chertoff for his department's response to Hurricane Katrina last August," *BBC News*, February 15, 2006, http://news.bbc.co.uk/2/hi/americas/4717916.stm.

15. John Cassidy, "The Keystone Kops in the White House," *The New Yorker*, March 31, 2014, https://www.newyorker.com/news/john-cassidy/the-keystone-kops-in-the-white-house.

16. James O'Kane, *The Crooked Ladder: Gangster, Ethnicity, and the American Dream* (New Brunswick: Transaction, 1992), 77.

17. For discussion on PCA approval see Stephen Prince, *Classical Film Violence: Designing and Regulating Brutality in Hollywood Cinema, 1930–1969* (New Brunswick: Rutgers University Press, 2003), 39.

18. See the Code as reproduced in Steven Mintz, Randy W. Roberts and David Welky, *Hollywood's America: Understanding History Through Film*, 5th ed. (Malden, MA: Wiley Blackwell, 2016), 122–33.

19. See Philippa Gates, *Detecting Women: Gender and the Hollywood Detective Film* (Albany: State University of New York Press, 2006) and Philippa Gates, *Detecting Men: Masculinity and the Hollywood Detective Film* (Albany: State University of New York, 2011).

20. Frank Krutnik, *In a Lonely Street: Film Noir, Genre, Masculinity* (New York: Routledge, 1991), 33–44.

21. Lott, *Police on Screen*, 97.

22. Frank Krutnik, *In a Lonely Street: Film Noir, Genre, Masculinity* (London: Routledge, 1991), 15.

23. Ibid.

24. However, not all film noir involves detectives, and some even cross into the genres of melodrama and the Western.

25. Paul Schrader, "Notes on Film Noir," *Film Comment* 8, no. 1 (1972): 10.

26. Since it is often argued that film noir is a style, and not a genre, realizing the German influence in these films complicates many ideas about reading "Americanism" in film noir.

27. Raymonde Borde and Etienne Chaumeton, *The Source of Film Noir*, trans. Bill Horrigan, *Film Reader* 3 (1977): 58.

28. For further explanation about law enforcement representations in film, see Patrick Anderson, *The Triumph of the Thriller: How Cops, Crooks, and Cannibals Captured Popular Fiction* (New York: Random House, 2007).

29. Frank Krutnik, *In a Lonely Street: Film Noir, Genre, Masculinity* (London: Routledge, 1991), 36.

30. Ibid.

31. Ibid., 39.

32. Ibid.

33. James Naremore, "A Season in Hell or the Snows of Yesteryear?" Introduction to

Notes—Chapter I

A Panorama of American Film Noir (1941–1953), by Raymond Borde and Etienne Chaumeton, trans. Paul Hammond (San Francisco: City Lights, 2002), xiv–xv.

34. *Ibid.*
35. The Wickersham Commission is the common informal name for the National Commission on Law Observance and Enforcement established by President Herbert Hoover on May 29, 1929. Former Attorney General George W. Wickersham (hence the informal name) chaired it with eleven members tasked with reviewing the criminal justice system during Prohibition and making recommendations for public policy based on their findings. It found, among many things, that the police were often brutal with interrogations of suspects, inflicting physical or mental pain to garner confessions. August Vollmer, the popular criminologist considered to be the father of American policing among contemporary criminologists, assisted with the writing of the commission's final report. For further readings see Willard M. Oliver, *August Vollmer: The Father of American Policing* (Durham: Carolina Academic Press, 2017) and United States Wickersham Commission, *Enforcement of the prohibition laws of the United States: Message from the President of the United States transmitting a report of the National Commission on Law Observance and Enforcement relative to the facts as to the enforcement, the benefits, and abuses under the prohibition laws, both before and since the adoption of the Eighteenth Amendment to the Constitution* (January 1, 1931). Available as a reprint at the University of Michigan Library.

Chapter I

1. Robert M. Regoli, John D. Hewitt, and Anna E. Kosloski, *Exploring Criminal Justice: The Essentials*, 3rd ed. (Burlington, MA: Jones & Bartlett, 2018), 68.
2. Punishment was also *lex talionis*, meaning retaliation authorized by law in the same kind and degree to the injury or harm the victim received.
3. Restorative justice involves rehabilitation of the offenders through reconciliation with crime victims and the community. It is a stark contrast to an "eye-for-an-eye" mentality of justice.
4. See Cody Benjamin, "WATCH: Father of three sex abuse victims tries to attack Larry Nassar in court: Police restrained Randall Margraves after he went after the disgraced doctor at his latest sentencing," *CBS Sports News*, last modified February 3, 2018, https://www.cbssports.com/olympics/news/watch-father-of-three-sex-abuse-victims-tries-to-attack-larry-nassar-in-court/.
5. Dean John Champion, *Police Misconduct in America: A Reference Handbook*, annotated ed. (Santa Barbara, CA: ABC-CLIO, 2001), 63.
6. Lott, *Police on Screen*, 3.
7. *Ibid.*
8. *Ibid.*
9. *Ibid.*
10. *Ibid.*
11. *Ibid.*
12. *Ibid.*
13. *Ibid.*
14. *Ibid.*
15. *Ibid.*
16. Bruce L. Berg, *Policing in Modern Society* (Boston: Butterworth-Heinemann, 1999), 23.
17. *Ibid.*, 23.
18. *Ibid.*, 24.
19. Lott, *Police on Screen*, 4.
20. *Ibid.*
21. *Ibid.*

Notes—Chapter I

22. Stephen Spitzer, "The Rationalization of Crime Control in Capitalist Society," *Contemporary Crises* 3, no. 1 (1979), 200.
23. Gary Potter, "The History of Policing in the United States, Part 1," *Police Studies Online*, June 25, 2013, http://plsonline.eku.edu/insidelook/history-policing-united-states-part-1.
24. *Ibid.*
25. *Ibid.*
26. See Hon. J.T. Headley, *The Great Riots of New York 1712 to 1873 Including a Full and Complete Account of the Four Days' Draft Riot of 1863* (New York: E.B. Treat & Co./Charles Scribner & Co., 1873), 130–131.
27. At the time of this writing, I have been in law enforcement for over twenty years and have witnessed firsthand many of these links between the police and politicians.
28. David Robinson, *From Peepshow to Palace: The Birth of American Film* (New York: Columbia University Press, 1996), 3.
29. *Ibid.*
30. *Ibid.*
31. *Ibid.*
32. Jordan Marche, *Theaters of Time and Space: American Planetaria, 1930–1970* (New Brunswick: Rutgers University Press, 2005), 11.
33. *Ibid.*
34. There were many other antecedents, such as shadowgraphy, camera obscura, and shadow puppetry; however, for this study, it is not necessary to go into the complete film history, as it is equally not necessary to go into the entire history of law enforcement. Therefore, the purpose is to provide a suitable background.
35. Robinson, *From Peepshow to Palace*, 6.
36. David Cook, *A History of Narrative Film*, 4th ed. (New York: W.W. Norton, 2004), 2.
37. John Pringle Nichol, *A Cyclopædia of the Physical Sciences* (London: Richard Griffin and Company, 1857), 571.
38. Hugo Münsterberg, *The Photoplay: A Psychological Study* (New York: D. Appleton, 1916), 43–71.
39. David Cook, *A History of Narrative Film*, 2.
40. *Ibid.*
41. *Ibid.*, 3.
42. *Ibid.*
43. *Ibid.*
44. *Ibid.*, 4.
45. *Ibid.*
46. *Ibid.*
47. *Ibid.*, 5.
48. Lott, *Police On Screen*, 5.
49. *Ibid.*
50. *Ibid.*
51. Richard Platt, *Film* (New York: Alfred A. Knopf, 1992), 16.
52. Lott, *Police On Screen*, 8.
53. Other seminal moments in film history included Edwin S. Porter's *The Great Train Robbery* (1903), the first film to move the camera and feature a narrative storyline. See Fritizi Kramer, "The Great Train Robbery (1903) A Silent Film Review," Movies Celebrate Silent Film, November 3, 2013, http://moviessilently.com/2013/11/03/the-great-train-robbery-1903-a-silent-film-review/.
54. Lott, *Police on Screen*, 5.
55. *Ibid.*
56. *Ibid.*, 5–9.
57. Fort Lee Film Commission, *Fort Lee: Birthplace of the Motion Picture Industry* (Charleston, SC: Arcadia Publishing, 2006), 9.

Notes—Chapter I

58. David Cook, *A History of Narrative Film*, 6–8.
59. Fort Lee Film Commission, *Fort Lee: Birthplace of the Motion Picture Industry*, 9.
60. Ibid.
61. Gerald A. Shiller, *It Happened in Hollywood: Remarkable Events That Shaped History* (Guilford, CT: Globe Pequot Press, 2010), 133.
62. Abby Ohlheiser, "Most of America's Silent Films are Lost Forever: Seventy-five percent of Silent era films have been lost forever to history, according to a new comprehensive study from the Library of Congress," *The Atlantic*, December 4, 2003, https://www.theatlantic.com/entertainment/archive/2013/12/most-americas-silent-films-are-lost-forever/355775/.
63. Ibid.
64. Dave Thompson, *Black and White and Blue: Adult Cinema from the Victorian Age to the VCR* (Toronto: ECW Press, 2007), 21.
65. Amanda Ann Klein, *American Film Cycles: Reframing Genres, Screening Social Problems, and Defining Subcultures* (Austin: University of Texas Press, 2011), 1.
66. *Mounted Police Charge* is the second surving film with uniformed police officers as recorded in the Library of Congress's film archive. The first film with a uniformed officer in the archives is Edison's *Robetta and Doretto [No. 2]*, also known as *Chinese Laundry*, 1894.
67. David Cook, *A History of Narrative Film*, 11.
68. Barak Y. Orbach, "Prizefighting and the Birth of Movie Censorship," *Yale Journal of Law & the Humanities* 21, no. 2 (2009), http://digitalcommons.law.yale.edu/yjlh/ vol21/iss2/3.
69. Gregory D. Black, *Hollywood Censored: Morality Codes, Catholics, and the Movies* (New York: Cambridge University Press, 1994), 10. See also Laura Keller, *Freedom of the Screen: Legal Challenges to State Film Censorship* (Lexington: University Press of Kentucky, 2008); Richard S. Randall, *Censorship of the Movies: The Social and Political Control of a Mass Medium* (Madison: University of Wisconsin Press, 1968).
70. Jody W. Pennington, *The History of Sex in American Film* (Westport, CT: Praeger, 2007), 1–2.
71. Ibid., 2.
72. Ibid.
73. Ibid.
74. Kathy Peiss, *Cheap Amusements: Working Women and Leisure in Turn-of-Century New York* (Philadelphia: Temple University Press, 1986), 160.
75. Jennifer Fronc, *Monitoring the Movies: The Fight Over Film Censorship in Early Twentieth-Century Urban America* (Austin: University of Texas Press, 2017). Additional excellent guides to further explain film censorship in the early years, mostly pre–Production Code era, are Black, *Hollywood Censored*; Thomas Doherty, *Pre-Code Hollywood: Sex, Immorality, and Insurrection in American Cinema, 1930–1934* (New York: Columbia University Press, 1999); Jeremy Geltzer, *Film Censorship in America: A State-by-State History* (Jefferson, NC: McFarland, 2017); Laura Witten-Keller, *Freedom of the Screen: Legal Challenges to State Film Censorship, 1915–1981* (Lexington: University Press of Kentucky. 2008); Mick LaSalle, *Complicated Women: Sex and Power in Pre-Code Hollywood* (New York: St. Martin's Griffin. 2002); and Prince, *Classical Film Violence*.
76. See Tim Newburn, *Handbook of Policing: 2nd Edition* (Portland, OR: Willan, 2012), 319.
77. See, Garth S. Jowett, "'A capacity for evil': The 1915 Supreme Court Mutual Decision," *Historical Journal of Film, Radio and Television*, 9, no. 1 (1989): 59–78; and John Wertheimer, "Mutual Film Reviewed: The Movies, Censorship, and Free Speech in Progressive America," *American Journal of Legal History* 37, no. 2 (1993): 158–89.
78. Also see Fronc, *Monitoring the Movies*. Fronc's scholarship on censorship sharpens between the years 1907 into the 1920s.
79. Samantha Barbas, "How the Movies Became Speech," *Rutgers Law Review* 64 (Spring 2012): 684.

Notes—Chapter II

80. *Ibid.*, 690.
81. See Douglas W. Churchill, "Hollywood Heeds the Thunder," *The New York Times* (New York, NY), July 22, 1934, as cited in Barbas, "How the Movies Became Speech."
82. *Ibid.*, 690.
83. Tom Gunning, "From the Opium Den to the Theatre of Morality: Moral Discourse and the Film Process in Early American Cinema," in *The Silent Cinema Reader*, ed. Lee Grieveson and Peter Kramer (London: Routledge, 2004), 145–54. Gunning has written extensively on film, approximately 100 publications, focusing on early cinema from its origins to World War 1.
84. *Ibid.*
85. *Ibid.*
86. See Kathy Peiss, *Cheap Amusements*, 139–62. See also Gail Bederman, *Manliness & Civilization: A Cultural History of Gender and Race in the United States 1890–1917* (Chicago: University of Chicago Press, 1995). Bederman's work is a brilliant discourse that shows the struggle over morality during the period.
87. Peiss, *Cheap Amusements*, 148.
88. See Lillian Faderman and Stuart Timmons, *Gay L.A.: A History of Sexual Outlaws, Power Politics, and Lipstick Lesbians* (Oakland: University of California Press, 2009), 57.
89. *Ibid.*
90. As reproduced in Steven Mintz, Randy W. Roberts, and David Welky, *Hollywood's America: Understanding History Through Film*, 5th ed. (Malden, MA: Wiley Blackwell. 2016), 122–33.
91. Richard Jewell, *The Golden Age of Cinema: Hollywood 1929–1945* (Malden, MA: Blackwell, 2007), 113.
92. *Ibid.*
93. Lee Jacobs, *The Wages of Sin: Censorship and the Fallen Woman Film, 1928–1942* (Oakland: University of California Press, 1997), 131.
94. Jewell, *The Golden Age of Cinema*, 113.
95. *Ibid.*, 117–18.
96. William H. Young and Nancy K. Young, *American Popular Culture through History: The 1930s* (Westport, CT: Greenwood Press, 2002), 190. It is important to note that this work is part of a series of which Ray B. Browne (arguably the initiator of the study of popular culture) serves as series editor.
97. Young and Young, *American Popular Culture through History*, 190.

Chapter II

1. *Report and Proceedings of the Senate Committee Appointed to Investigate Police Corruption of the Police Department of the City of New York. Vol. 1.* Transmitted to the State Legislature January 18, 1895 (Albany: James B. Lyon, State Printer, 1895), 7. This section also tells how strong public sentiment against police corruption sparked the need for the senate investigation.
2. *Ibid.*, Lexow Report, 6.
3. Daniel Czitrom, *New York Exposed: The Gilded Age Police Scandal That Launched the Progressive Era* (New York: Oxford University Press, 2016), 291.
4. Ken Alder, *The Lie Detectors: The History of an American Obsession* (New York: Free Press, 2007), 19–20. Here Alders discusses the remarks of August Vollmer who is considered the father of modern professional policing.
5. By criminologist definition, the later appearing Silent era of film appear synchronously with the "Reform Transition Era."
6. This cover appeared approximately a month prior to the New York City mayoral election on November 6, 1894, showing how influential these cartoons where when published to perform political objectives.

Notes—Chapter II

7. Bill Lamb, "Bill Devery," Society for American Baseball Research, accessed February 17, 2018, http://sabr.org/bioproj/person/500ba2d3.

8. On January 9, 1903, Devery and Frank J. Farrell, who was heavily involved in New York City gambling and owned pool halls and casinos, purchased the Baltimore Orioles for $18,000, moved them to New York City, and changed the team name. Twelve years later they sold their Yankees team for $460,000.

9. Bernard Whalen and David Doorey, "The Birth of the NYPD," *The Chief of Police: The Official Publication of the National Association of Chiefs of Police* (March/April 1998), http://www.bjwhalen.com/article.htm.

10. However, it briefly appeared Devery would be held accountable for his crimes. He had an interruption of police service on February 5, 1897, when he was arrested and charged with bribery and extortion. Devery was convicted and dismissed from the police department. He appealed his conviction in the New York Court of Appeals, successfully overturning it, and thereby was reinstated to the force and promoted to inspector on January 7, 1898, and deputy chief on February 14, 1898. He was subsequently appointed chief of police on June 30, 1898. The breakneck speed at which Devery was promoted to the top position is a testament to the strong political clout Devery was infamously known for.

11. Herbert Asbury, *The Gangs of New York: An Informal History of the Underworld* (New York: Vintage, 2008, originally published New York: Alfred A. Knopf, 1927), 217–18. Also stated nearly verbatim in Williams' obituary in The New York Times, March 26, 1917.

12. Lisa Elsroad, "Tenderloin," in Kenneth T. Jackson, ed., *The Encyclopedia of New York City* (New Haven: Yale University Press, 1995), 1161.

13. Asbury, *The Gangs of New York*, 219.

14. Ibid.

15. Ibid.

16. "Williams, 'Ex-Czar' of Tenderloin, Dies; Picturesque Former Inspector of Police Gave the District Its Sobriquet. Figured In Lexow Inquiry; Retired on Pension After That; Noted for His Love of a Fight; 77 Years Old. He Never Shunned a Fight. Appearance Before Lexow," *The New York Times*, March 26, 1917.

17. Ken Alder, *The Lie Detectors*, 19–20. There are conflicting accounts where the term third-degree originated. Darius Rejali offers the term was originally coined in 1910 by Major Richard Sylvester of Washington, D.C., the head of the International Association of Chiefs of Police. Sylvester explains the first degree is the arrest, the second is the transportation to jail, followed by the interrogation as the third degree. Shortly thereafter Americans began using the term synonymous with torture during interrogations to gain confessions of information. See Darius Rejali, *Torture and Democracy* (Princeton: Princeton University Press, 2007), 73.

18. LeRoy Lad Panek, *The Origins of the American Detective Story: An Anthology* (Jefferson, NC: McFarland, 2006), 9.

19. Musser, *Before the Nickelodeon*, 50. Tony Pastor, considered the "Dean of Vaudeville," featured an almost jingoistic brand of United States patriotism. Pastor was committed to attracting a "mixed-gender" audience, thereby making him a revolutionary in the male-oriented variety halls of the mid-century. For more on Pastor, see Robert W. Snyder, *The Voice of the City: Vaudeville and Popular Culture in New York* (New York: Oxford University Press, 1989).

20. Ibid.

21. Tom Gunning. *D.W. Griffith & The Origins of American Narrative: The Early Years at Biograph* (Chicago: University of Illinois Press, 1994), 41.

22. Ibid., 42.

23. Ibid.

24. Ibid., 8.

25. Ibid.

26. Musser, *Before the Nickelodeon*, 50.

Notes—Chapter II

27. Slapstick comedy that mocks the police became widely popular during the 1910s, as discussed in Chapter Two's feature of the *Keystone Kops*.

28. For *Sherlock Holmes Baffled* as first detective film see Jon Tuska *The Detective in Hollywood: The Movie Careers of the Great Fictional Private Eyes and Their Creators* (New York: Doubleday, 1978). Tuska's work showcases the growth of the detective film, tracing it back to the earliest *Sherlock Holmes Baffled* (1900). And also see Jim Harmon, *Radio Mystery and Adventure and Its Appearances in Film, Television and Other Media* (Jefferson, NC: McFarland, 2003),176. Additional early representations of law enforcement on film during the same year as *Sherlock Holmes Baffled* (1900) include *A Raid on 'Dago' Counterfeiters* (1900), *A Raid on a Woman's Poolroom* (1900), *Escape from Sing Sing* (1900), *A Raid on a Chinese Opium Joint* (1900), and *A Career of Crime* (1900).

29. See Elizabeth Ezra, *Georges Méliès: The Birth of the Auteur* (Manchester: Manchester University Press, 2000) for a thorough explanation of Méliès techniques, particularly his stop trick, and how these impacted film editing.

30. Michael Pointer, "Earliest Holmes Film," *Sherlock Holmes Journal* 8, no. 4 (Summer 1978), 138–140.

31. Anthony Slide, *The New Historical Dictionary of the American Film Industry*, 2nd ed. (Lanham, MD: Scarecrow Press, 2001), 22.

32. Jim O'Kane found in his research "The Crooked Ladder," which focused on 18th- and early 19th-century organized crime, that ethnic minority communities used organized crime as one vehicle of upward mobility to climb up from the bottom. O'Kane describes this reality as American as apple pie (see O'Kane, *The Crooked Ladder*, 158).

33. Walter C. Rucker Jr., and James N. Upton, eds., *Encyclopedia of American Race Riots: Greenwood Milestones in African American History, Volume 2 N–Z and Primary Documents* (Westport, CT: Greenwood Press, 2007), 475.

34. *Ibid.*

35. *Ibid.*

36. For more on the New York City Race Riot of 1900, see Gilbert Osofsky, "Race Riot, 1900: A Study of Ethnic Violence," *The Journal of Negro Education*, 32, no. 1 (Winter 1963), http://www.jstor.org/stable/2294487; Marilyn Johnson, *Street Justice: A History of Police Violence in New York City* (Boston: Beacon Press, 2003).

37. *Ibid.*

38. For more on McDonald, see Richard C. Lindberg, *The Gambler King of Clark Street: Michael C. McDonald and the Rise of Chicago's Democratic Machine* (Carbondale: Southern Illinois University Press, 2009) and Thomas J. Gradel and Dick Simpson, *Corrupt Illinois: Patronage, Cronyism, and Criminality* (Champaign: University of Illinois Press, 2015), 22–23.

39. See Musser, *Before the Nickeloden*, 176–177.

40. Charles Musser, *The Emergence of Cinema: The American Screen to 1907* (Oakland: University of California Press, 1994), 345.

41. Daniel Egan, *America's Film Legacy: The Authoritative Guide to the Landmark Movies in The National Film Registry* (New York: Continuum International, 2010), 523.

42. Charles H. Hoyt and Percy Gaunt, *The Bowery* (New York: Harms Incorporated, 1892).

43. Egan, *America's Film Legacy*, 523. For more on Stephen Foster's life see Ken Emerson, *Doo-Dah! Stephen Foster and the Rise of American Popular Culture* (Boston: Da Capo Press, 1998).

44. *Ibid.*

45. *Ibid.*

46. Lee Grieveson, Esther Sonnet and Peter Stanfield, *Mob Culture: Hidden Histories of the American Gangster Film* (New Brunswick: Rutgers University Press, 2005), 35.

47. For a detailed description of Mickey Finn and the process of drugging and robbing patrons of his saloon, see Herbert Asbury, *Gem of the Prairie: An Informal History of the Chicago Underworld* (New York: Alfred A. Knopf, 1940).

Notes—Chapter III

48. Lois Weber was a great director in her own right. Her notable works include *Hypocrites* (1915) and *Where Are My Children* (1916). Phillips Smalley, also an excellent earlier film director, directed over 100 films between 1911 and 1922 and was the husband of Lois Weber. Smalley and Weber were married in 1904 and divorced in 1922.

49. Other favorable views of law enforcement on film include *Runaway in the Park* (1896) which show a horse and carriage running away with a female in distress, when two mounted police officers pursue and save the woman, and the *Police Force of New York City* (1910) which demonstrates the heroism of officers and the dangers of their job. The Police Force of New York City is found on *Perils of the New Land* (1910), but the film says 1904 so it is likely it appeared earlier and was re-copywritten in 1910.

50. Musser, *Before the Nickelodeon*, 308.
51. Ibid.
52. Kerry Segrave, *Police Violence in America, 1869–1920: 256 Incidents Involving Death or Injury* (Jefferson, NC: McFarland, 2016), 110–111.
53. Ibid., 111.
54. Ibid., 112.
55. Ibid.
56. Ibid.
57. Ibid.
58. Alan A. Block, "Organized Crime: History and Historiography," in *Handbook of Organized Crime in the United States*, ed. Robert J. Kelly, Ko-lin Chin, and Rufus Schatzberg (Westport, CT: Greenwood Press, 1992).
59. Frank Browning and John Gerassi, *The American Way of Crime* (New York: Putnam, 1980), 71–72.
60. August Bequai, *Organized Crime: The Fifth Estate* (Toronto: Lexington Books, 1979), 29–30.
61. Charlie Keil, *Early American Cinema in Transition: Story, Style, and Filmmaking, 1907–1913* (Madison: University of Wisconsin Press, 2002), 118.
62. *The Kleptomaniac* was filmed in New York City during the winter. It offers historical scenes of snow-covered streets and Macy's department store, where the wealthy woman shoplifted.

Chapter III

1. David Robinson, *Chaplin: His Life and Art* (New York: McGraw-Hill, 1985), 192.
2. Todd, "The History of Crime Films," 23.
3. *The Birth of a Nation*, 1915. Adapted and directed by D.W. Griffith from the book *The Clansman* by T.F. Dixon, Jr. (New York: Doubleday, Page, 1905). D.W. Griffith also produced the movie and released it through Epoch Production Company. The film is now over 100 years old and is still one of the most highly referenced silent films to demonstrate a perceived white racial superiority and to showcase historical racism in the early twentieth century. This hysteria against blacks and their believed sexual aggression toward white woman was examined by scholar Gail Bederman in her assessment of the 1910 boxing match between African American Jack Johnson and white Jim Jefferies. See chapter one in Gail Bederman, *Manliness and Civilization: A Cultural History of Gender and Race in the United States, 1880–1917* (Chicago: University of Chicago Press, 1996).
4. Robert M. Folgeson, *Big City Police: An Urban Institute Study* (Cambridge: Harvard University Press, 1977), 72.
5. Stanley Cohen, *The Execution of Officer Becker: The Murder of a Gambler, the Trial of a Cop, and the Birth of Organized Crime* (Boston: Da Capo Press/Hachette, 2009).
6. Lewis E. Lawes, *Meet the Murderer!* (New York: Harper Bros., 1940), 25.
7. Marilyn Ferdinand, "Traffic in Souls," film essay (n.d.), https://www.loc.gov/programs/static/national-film-preservation-board/documents/traffic_souls.pdf.
8. The film was produced by Universal Studios, which at that time did not produce

Notes—Chapter IV

feature-length films. However, the success of *Traffic in Souls* provided a solid foundation for Universal, though they were initially cautious of producing it because of the nature and content it presented.

9. Reginald Wright Kaufmann, *The House of Bondage*, introduction (New York: Mofart, Yard and Company, 1910). Randall Clark also observed that *Traffic in Souls* was produced in the immediate aftermath of the Rockefeller Commission report on white slavery, see Clark, *At a Theatre or Drive-In Near You: The History, Culture, and Politics of the American Exploitation Film* (New York: Routledge, 1995), 35.

10. See Lee Grieveson, "Policing the Cinema: Traffic in Souls at Ellis Island, 1913," *Oxford Journals* 38, no. 2 (July 1, 1997): 149–71.

11. Ferdinand, "Traffic In Souls."

12. Another film that addresses class bias where the working class is viewed as victims is D.W. Griffith's gangster film, *Musketeers of Pig Alley*, produced the previous year. The *Musketeers of Pig Alley* depicts historical scenes of overpopulation and urban blight among the poor, mostly in the ghettos of New York City.

13. Robinson, *Chaplin: His Life and Art*, 192.

14. *Ibid.*

15. Even the NYPD—America's first police department—kept their requirements until the 1970s when Police Commissioner Donald F. Cawley removed the minimum height requirement. See "Height Requirement For Police Officers May Be Eliminated," *The New York Times*, July 23, 1973, http://www.nytimes.com/1973/07/23/archives/height-requirement-for-police-officers-may-be-eliminated.html.

16. Robinson, *Chaplin: His Life and Art*, 192.

17. Lott, *Police on Screen*, 11.

18. *Ibid.*, 12.

19. Scott McGee, "Buster Keaton: Cops," Turner Classic Movies, accessed February 17, 2018, http://www.tcm.com/tcmdb/title/438357/Cops/articles.html.

20. David Cook, *A History of Narrative Film*, 185.

21. Greg Merritt, *Room 1219: The Life of Fatty Arbuckle, the Mysterious Death of Virginia Rappe, and the Scandal That Changed Hollywood* (Chicago: Chicago Review Press, 2013), vii–xi.

22. Neda Ulaby, "Roscoe Arbuckle and the Scandal of Fatness," in Jana Evans Braziel and Kathleen LeBesco, *Bodies out of Bounds: Fatness and Transgression* (Berkeley: University of California Press, 2001), 153.

23. Nicholas Barber, "Deadpan but alive to the future: Buster Keaton the revolutionary: Buster Keaton wasn't just a born star—he was a revolutionary film-maker," *Independent Magazine*, January 5, 2014, https://www.independent.co.uk/arts-entertainment/films/features/deadpan-but-alive-to-the-future-buster-keaton-the-revolutionary-9037459.html.

24. See David Lobosco, "A Trip Down Memory Lane: A nostalgic journey to the past to relive the golden days of entertainment! The Last Days of Fatty Arbuckle," The Classic Movie Blog Association, October 25, 2103, http://greatentertainersarchives.blogspot.com/2013/10/the-last-days-of-fatty-arbuckle.html.

25. McGee, "Buster Keaton: Cops." Accordingly, the film's distributor was not fond of the anarchist bomb plot since two years prior, in 1920, an anarchist had bombed Wall Street, and thirty people were killed. However, the bomb plot did not cause any pushback because Keaton kept the fast pace of the film and many viewers didn't give it much thought.

26. Jude Sheerin, "'Fatty' Arbuckle and Hollywood's first scandal," *BBC News* (Washington, D.C.), September 4, 2011, http://www.bbc.com/news/magazine-14640719.

Chapter IV

1. Richard Jewell, *The Golden Age of Cinema: Hollywood 1929–1945* (Malden, MA: Blackwell, 2007), 91–92.

Notes—Chapter IV

2. E.J. Stephens and Marc Wanamaker, *Early Warner Bros. Studios* (Mount Pleasant, SC: Arcadia Publishing, 2010), 25.
3. Ibid.
4. Jewell, *The Golden Age of Cinema*, 93.
5. Ibid.
6. Douglas Gomery, *The Coming of Sound: A History* (New York: Routledge, 2005), 45.
7. An excellent work to understand the social bandit and the Robin Hood connection is found in the 1981 essay "Outlaw Guns of the Middle Border: American Social Bandit" by Richard White. The takeaway is that social bandits "preyed upon institutions that many farmers believed were preying on them." For more on social banditry, see Eric Hobsbawn's *Primitive Rebels* (1959) and *Bandits* (1969). Hobsbawn, a Marxist historian, is believed to have invented the term social bandit in his book *Primitive Rebels*. His other book, *Bandits*, inspired the field of historical social banditry study. Hobsbawn's work shows how bandits transcend the labels of criminals; they are outlaws and robbers to the status of avengers and champions of social justice.
8. Although *Billy the Kid* (1911) was the first appearance of the figure, it was not based on the real life of Billy the Kid. For a thorough discussion on this see, Johnny D. Boggs, *Billy the Kid on Film: 1911–2012* (Jefferson, NC: McFarland, 2011), 16.
9. Clearly, hordes of Americans were obsessed with the life and death of Dillinger. A solid source to understand how Dillinger's story grew larger and larger in the newspapers and newsreels, and even today, is found in Elliot J. Gorn's *Dillinger's Wild Ride*, 2011. Gorn details how this outlaw celebrity was the most famous and flamboyant of his time—more so than Baby Face Nelson, Pretty Boy Floyd, and Bonnie and Clyde. Gorn argues Dillinger represented an American fascination with primitive freedom against social convention. Gorn showcases this through a powerful and thought-provoking argument how Dillinger's story tells us about the complexity of American transformations from rural to urban life. He also details how Dillinger's story is much about the transformation of America during the Great Depression. In Gorn's view, Dillinger wasn't viewed as a Robin Hood; rather he was the man who symbolically attacked the rich. "His victims were banks, bastions of capitalism that were deeply unpopular in the 1930s. He came in blasting at a moment when many American felt betrayed." Gorn goes on to say, "To read about his [Dillinger's] gang's exploits in the papers or to see his image in newsreels was to feel both the fear and the excitement of taking matters into their own hands."
10. For this iconic image see "The Great Escape: Infamous gangster John Dillinger used a wooden pistol to break out of jail in 1934," *The New York Daily News*, March 2, 2016 (reprint of March 4, 1934), http://www.nydailynews.com/news/crime/dillinger-breaks-jail-wooden-pistol-1934-article-1.2548065.
11. When studying Dillinger, the premier publication for understanding him and others like him with a pragmatic lens is journalist Brian Burrough's work, *Public Enemies: America's Greatest Crime Wave and the Birth of the FBI, 1931–34*, 2005. In this *New York Times* bestselling masterpiece, and motion picture adapted book, Burrough's brings Dillinger to life by utilizing a timeline of fact, and less of a concentration of mythical accounts.
12. For a more thorough analysis, sociologist/criminologist James M. O'Kane uses the term "the crooked ladder," to explain how "crime served some useful function in American society as it enabled its practitioners to realize their peculiar version of the American Dream." See O'Kane, *The Crooked Ladder*, 25–50. Also see Richard Cloward, "Illegitimate Means, Anomie, and Deviant Behavior," *American Sociological Review* 24 (April 1959), 164–76, and Robert Merton, "Anomie, Anomia, and Social Interaction," in *Anomie and Deviant Behavior*, ed. Marshall B. Clinard (New York: Free Press, 1964), 218.
13. Ian Taylor, Paul Walton, and Jock Young, *The New Criminology: For a Social Theory of Deviance* (New York: Harper & Row, 1973), 102.
14. Fred D. Pasley, *Al Capone: The Biography of a Self-Made Man* (Garden City, NY: Garden City Publishing Company, 1930), 336.
15. As one of the most notorious American urban gangsters of the twentieth century,

Notes—Chapter IV

his legacy lived on long after his death in numerous books, films, articles, and songs—including "Al Capone" by the late Michael Jackson. In 1964 a Jamaican singer-songwriter named Prince Buster released a song also titled "Al Capone" which eventually became a hit and topped the record charts in the United Kingdom. The blue pinstriped suit and tilted fedora that has become the stereotypical attire of the Prohibition gangster is based on photos of Capone. Capone's life of celebrity and embellishments would take a fast personal turn in May of 1932 when at thirty-three he began his stretch in prison and the arduous life of dealing with complications from syphilis and gonorrhea. Upon his release in 1939, Capone received treatment for paresis caused by late-stage syphilis. He resigned his last days to his life in his mansion in Palm Island, Florida. By 1946 his physician concluded he had the mentality of a 12-year-old child. Shortly thereafter, on January 21, 1947, Capone suffered a stroke and subsequently contracted pneumonia. On January 25, 1947, Al Capone, 48, went into cardiac arrest and died.

16. Palisades Park Police Department Ledger 1930.

17. Although produced decades later, the movie *Sounder* (1972), adapted from the 1960 novel by William H. Armstrong, harnesses this reality, showing how the Morgans, a black family of sharecroppers in Louisiana in 1933, endured a severe family crisis when the husband and father, Nathan Lee Morgan, is sent to a prison camp for petty crime.

18. O'Kane, *The Crooked Ladder*, 25–50.

19. O'Kane views organized crime from an ethnic perspective, concentrating on behavior and criminal organizations, positing that each ethnic group "passes through six stages in its rise and fall from power." O'Kane's six stages in criminal mobility are (1) Individual Criminality; (2) Intra-Ethnic Gang Rivalry; (3) Inter-Ethnic Gang Rivalry; (4) Organized Criminal Accommodations; (5) Ethnic Gang Supremacy; and (6) Decline and Fall of the Ethnic Gang. O'Kane acknowledges these stages "present a reasonable interpretation of Irish, Jewish, and Italian crime; whether they will assist in explaining African American, Hispanic, Asian, and other ethnic minority organized crime in America remains to be seen..." See O'Kane, *The Crooked Ladder*, 79–82.

20. Daniel Bell's "Crime as an American Way of Life" is another excellent guide to understanding how crime is used as "a queer ladder of social mobility" from the poor immigrant beginning into successful businessman through criminality. Bell, "Crime as an American Way of Life," *Antioch Review* 13 (Summer 1953): 131–54.

21. Sutherland's Theory of Differential Association is that behavior is learned from interactions with others, especially family members. Criminal behavior occurs when excessively favorable definitions of crime are absorbed and outweigh those definitions against crime. For example, if a child grows up with a family whose older sibling is heavily involved with crime, they are likely to learn favorable definitions of crime, thus being differentially associated into criminal activity. Equally, if the community, such as neighbors, family members, or gangs, believes crime is nothing to be embarrassed by, the likelihood for juvenile delinquency is high because of these influences on a juvenile's development. Edwin H. Sutherland, *On Analyzing Crime*, ed. Karl Schuessler (Chicago: University of Chicago Press, 1973).

22. *Ibid.*, 6–7.

23. The Mongols were similar to the Huns, and for most of their early existence (until the time of Genghis Khan) preyed on weaker neighbors, living off tributes. In Europe during the crusades, organized criminals committed acts of brigandage and crime. The Knights of Saint John in the eighth century and the Teutonic Knights of the twelfth century, which were both initially derived to fight for religious and political objectives, eventually turned to pillaging the citizenry. History also provides proof that during the Middle Ages organized criminals came and went, such as groups of former soldiers who in some cases joined with landless knights and turned to banditry.

24. Otto J. Maenchen-Helfen, *The World of the Huns* (Berkeley: University of California Press, 1973).

25. A. Bequai, *Organized Crime: The Fifth Estate* (Toronto: Lexington Books, 1979), 10.

Notes—Chapter V

26. Ibid.
27. Ibid.
28. Howard Abadainsky, *Organized Crime*, 3rd ed. (Chicago: Nelson-Hall, 1990), 95.
29. Ibid.
30. As reproduced in Mintz, Roberts, and Welky, *Hollywood's America*, 122–33.
31. Richard Jewell, *The Golden Age of Cinema: Hollywood 1929–1945*, 117–18.
32. According to anomie theory, "some societies place much emphasis on the pursuit of certain goals, such as monetary success, but little emphasis on the norms regulating goal achievement. As a result, individuals attempt to achieve their goals in the most expedient manner possible, which for some is through crime. This anomie is said to be partly rooted in structural strain, with the inability to achieve cultural goals through legitimate channels reducing the commitment to norms regulating goal achievement." Robert Agnew and Joanne M. Kaufman, *Anomie, Strain and Subcultural Theories of Crime* (New York: Routledge, 2010), 1. For further explanations how anomie explains the usage of crime as a route for upward mobility, see O'Kane, *The Crooked Ladder*.
33. Robert Merton, "Social Structure and Anomie," *American Sociological Review* 3 (1938): 681.
34. Robert Merton, "Anomie, Anomia, and Social Interaction," in *Anomie and Deviant Behavior*, ed. Marshall B. Clinard (New York: Free Press, 1964), 218.
35. The theory of differential opportunity by Richard Cloward and Lloyd Ohlin is equally at play here as evidenced by Rico's behavior in the diner. Cloward and Ohlin further advance the work of Merton. They reveal that when legitimate ladders of success are blocked by intense deprivation and extremely limited legitimate pathways to success, collective adaptions of delinquent subcultures develop in three distinct types: the criminal subculture, the conflict subculture, and the retreatist subculture.
36. Other attempts to explain organized crime derive from Travis Hirschi's social control theory, originally known as The Social Bond Theory in 1969. This theory attempts to explain how people engage in criminal activity when their bond to society has weakened. In other words, when social constraints on antisocial behavior are absent or impaired, delinquent behavior evolves. See Travis Hirschi, *Causes of Delinquency* (Berkeley: University of California Press, 1969).
37. See Jewell, *The Golden Age of Cinema*,118.
38. William McAdams, *Ben Hecht: The Man Behind the Legend* (New York: Scribner, 1990), 128.
39. Henry M. Holden. *FBI 100 Years: An Unofficial History* (Minneapolis: Zenith Press, 2008), 232.
40. On January 21, 1947, Capone suffered a stroke and subsequently contracted pneumonia. On January 25, 1947, at age 48, he went into cardiac arrest and died. See "Famous Cases and Criminals—Al Capone." *Federal Bureau of Investigation*. www.fbi.gov. https://web.archive.org/web/20101019213135/http://www.fbi.gov/about-us/history/famous-cases/al-capone.

Chapter V

1. Cornelius William Willemse, *Behind the Green Lights* (New York: Alfred A. Knopf, 1931), 354.
2. Lott, *Police on Screen*, 97.
3. Ibid.
4. Ibid.
5. Karen Burroughs Hannsberry, *Femme Noir: Bad Girls of Film* (Jefferson, NC: McFarland, 2009), 2.
6. Ibid.
7. The "sex goddess" was similar in appearance to femme fatale in film, but markedly dif-

Notes—Chapter V

ferent. Jessica Hope Jordan's *Sex Goddess in American Film, 1930–1965: Jean Harlow, Mae West, Lana Turner, and Jayne Mansfield* is an excellent guide. Arguably all femme fatale were sex goddesses because of their appearance and attributes that are similar regarding seduction and sex appeal. However, the major difference is found in the seemingly endless power of the sex goddess to "influence and fascinate, to achieve in a sense her own self-reproduction through many decades of "re-makeovers" reveals her position in America culture as not only a lasting image but also a potentially powerful and subversive force" (2). Jordan continues to argue by highlighting the differences with the cinematic constructs of the femme fatale, showing how arguments played out that the femme fatale "represents a true projection of male castration anxiety and, therefore, must die at the end of the film for the anxiety she embodies, the sex goddess always triumphs in the end in getting what she wants, whether it be a husband (Blonde Crazy), diamonds (Gentlemen), or just persuading all the men around her to see things from her particular feminine perspective n(The Misfits)" (13).

8. See Randolph J. Cox, *The Dime Novel Companion: A Source Book* (Westport, CT: Greenwood, 2000), 79–80.

9. See Edward R. Hageman, *A Comprehensive Index to Black Mask, 1920–1951* (Bowling Green, OH: Bowling Green State University Popular Press, 1982).

10. Richard Bleiler, "Black Mask," in *The Oxford Companion to Crime and Mystery Writing*, ed. Rosemary Herbert (Oxford: Oxford University Press. 1999), 38–39.

11. Frank Krutnik, *In a Lonely Street*, 36, and Dashiell Hammett, *The Maltese Falcon* (New York: Alfred A. Knopf, 1930).

12. S.S. Van Dine, *The Benson Case Murder* (Redditch, Worcestershire: Read Books, 2013). Description found in the opening chapter "Philo Vance At Home" (n.p.).

13. See Richard Layman, *Discovering the Maltese Falcon and Sam Spade* (San Francisco: Vince Emery Productions, 2005), 11–68. In the first part of Layman's work "Detective Days," there is a discussion of Hammett's biographical information and a history of work as a private detective, including an interview with one of his former colleagues at Pinkerton.

14. Dashiell Hammett, *The Thin Man* (New York: Alfred A. Knopf, 1934).

15. *The Celluloid Closet*, directed and produced by Rob Epstein and Jeffrey Friedman, discussed the censorship of homosexuality in *The Maltese Falcon* (Channel Four Films HBO Pictures/Sony Pictures Classics, 1996). *The Celluloid Closet* is a documentary about how films dealt with homosexuality. Also see Jessica Hope Jordan, *The Sex Goddess in American Film, 1930–1965: Jean Harlow, Mae West, Lana Turner, and Jayne Mansfield* (Amherst, NY: Cambria Press, 2009). Jordan argues in her study this use of innuendo, in fact, came out of the Code itself, as filmmakers worked around the Code.

16. Bosley Crowther, "The Maltese Falcon, a Fast Mystery-Thriller with Quality and Charm, at the Strand," *The New York Times*, October 4, 1941, http://www.nytimes.com/movie/review?res=990DE4D7113FE13BBC4C53DFB667838A659EDE.

17. Since 1923, Robert Homas spent more than two decades in film often playing judges and lawmen.

18. As a young police officer, I met many retired police officers who had worked during this period. I would often speak with these officers during police organization dinners, and they shared their yesteryear experiences. From these conversations, I determined there was a commonality: the saying, "Police brutality, guilty. But I never took a dime." Thus the police officer mindset at the time saw theft as a crime and police brutality as an acceptable extralegal method for meting out justice.

19. James McKay, *Dana Andrews: The Face of Noir* (Jefferson, NC: McFarland, 2010), 2. McKay's assessment of Dana Andrews is that he was a private person who seldom gave interviews and whose life is mostly referenced by his excessive drinking. Thus, McKay finds he is the most undervalued actor in film history. Without question, Andrews was a king of the B Movies, and, as McKay calls him, "the face of noir." Carl E. Rollyson also notes his dominance in the film noir: "no comprehensive discussion of film noir can neglect

Notes—Coda

his performances." See Carl E. Rollyson, *Hollywood Enigma: Dana Andrews* (Jackson, Mississippi: University Press of Mississippi, 2012), 3.

20. As defined by the Wickersham Commission, 1931.

21. Jerome Herbert Skolnick and James J. Fyfe, *Above the Law: Police and the Excessive Use of Force* (New York: The Free Press, 1994), 45.

22. Ibid.

23. Ibid. This information was according to former New York City police commissioner Grover A. Whelan.

24. Willemse, *Behind the Green Lights*, 354.

Coda

1. Lott, *Police on Screen*, 36.
2. Ibid., 63.
3. Ibid., 36–37.
4. This idea is most visible in the storyline where Marshall Will Kane (Gary Cooper) is abandoned by the townspeople and left to fight the outlaws himself. According to M. Ray Lott in his discussion of the film, the narrative here parallels the lives of Hollywood industry professionals who were left to challenge the HUAC themselves after their studios abandoned them. Also, at the end of the film, Marshall Kane saves the townspeople, then tosses his badge to the dirt, which mirrors the blacklisted actors own concern about law and government oversight in America. See Lott, *Police on Screen*, 36–38.
5. *High Noon* was produced when fears of communism and calls for anti-communist censorship were common. President Harry S. Truman created rules that made any sympathetic association with a communist or socialist group cause for immediate dismissal, denied employment, or legal action. The Loyalty Review Board, which administered this initiative, trampled on a suspect's Constitutional Rights, precisely by denying them the right to confront the prosecution's witnesses. The Board also considered even unsubstantiated accusations against the accused as the truth. The United States Congress countered the Board, opting to revive HUAC. However, HUAC was no better than the Board. They used beliefs, thoughts, and outright fallacies to "out" suspected American spies and communists. Because of HUAC's strategies of believing innuendo, presuming the accused guilty, and casting aspersion on the accused, they more closely resembled the judges at the Salem Witch Trials than United States Congressmen. These actions resulted in several challenges from Hollywood actors, screenwriters, producers. These brave men and women were blacklisted from working in Hollywood. See Lott, *Police on Screen*, 35.

Bibliography

Abadainsky, Howard. *Organized Crime*. 3rd edition. Chicago: Nelson-Hall, 1990.
Albanese, Jay S. *Organized Crime: From the Mob to Transnational Organized Crime*. New York: Routledge, 2014.
Albini, Joseph. L. *The American Mafia: Genesis of a Legend*. New York: Appleton-Century-Crofts, 1971.
Albini, Joseph L., and Jeffrey S. McIllwain. *Deconstructing Organized Crime: An Historical and Theoretical Study*. Jefferson, NC: McFarland, 2012.
Alder, Ken. *The Lie Detectors: The History of an American Obsession*. New York: Free Press, 2007.
Allen, Frederick Lewis. *Since Yesterday: The 1930s in America, September 3, 1929–September 3, 1939*. New York: Harper & Row, 1939.
Altman, Rick. *Film/Genre*. London: BFI, 1999.
Alvarez, Luis. *The Power of the Zoot: Youth Culture and Resistance during World War II*. Berkeley: University of California Press, 2009.
American Television. *Canadian Review of American Studies* 41, no. 1 (2011): 75–95.
Anderson, Christopher. *Hollywood TV: The Studio System in the Fifties*. Austin: University of Texas Press, 1994.
Anderson, Patrick. *The Triumph of the Thriller: How Cops, Crooks, and Cannibals Captured Popular Fiction*. New York: Random House, 2007.
Arntfield, Michael. "TVPD: The Generational Diegetics of the Police Procedural on American Television." *Canadian Review of American Studies* 41, no. 1 (2011): 75–95.
Aron, Cindy. *Working at Play: A History of Vacations in the United States*. New York: Oxford University Press, 1999.
Asbury, H. *Gem of the Prairie: An Informal History of the Chicago Underworld*. New York: Alfred A. Knopf, 1940.
Ashby, L. *With Amusement for All: A History of American Popular Culture Since 1830*. Lexington: University of Kentucky Press, 2012.
Barbas, Samantha. "How the Movies Became Speech." *Rutgers Law Review* 64 (Spring 2012): 645–745.
_____. *Movie Crazy: Fans, Stars, and the Cult of Celebrity*. New York: Palgrave MacMillan, 2002.
Barber, Nicholas. "Nicholas Barber, "Deadpan but alive to the future: Buster Keaton the revolutionary: Buster Keaton wasn't just a born star—he was a revolutionary film-maker." *Independent Magazine*, January 5, 2014. https://www.independent.co.uk/arts-entertainment/films/features/deadpan-but-alive-to-the-future-buster-keaton-the-revolutionary-9037459.html.
Bederman, Gail. *Manliness and Civilization: A Cultural History of Gender and Race in the United States, 1880–1917*. Chicago: University of Chicago Press, 1996.

Bibliography

Bell, Daniel. *Crime as an American Way of Life. Antioch Review* 13 (Summer 1953): 131–54.

———. *The End of Ideology.* Glencoe, IL: Free Press. 1964.

Bequai, August. *Organized Crime: The Fifth Estate.* Toronto: Lexington Books, 1979.

Berg, Bruce L. *Policing in Modern Society.* Boston: Butterworth-Heinemann, 1999.

Black, Gregory D. *Hollywood Censored: Morality Codes, Catholics, and the Movies.* New York: Cambridge University Press, 1996.

Bleiler, Richard. "Black Mask." *The Oxford Companion to Crime and Mystery Writing.* Ed. Rosemary Herbert. Oxford: Oxford University Press, 1999.

Block, Alan A. "Organized Crime: History and Historiography." *Handbook of Organized Crime in the United States.* Eds. Robert J. Kelly, Ko-lin Chin, and Rufus Schatzberg. Westport, CT: Greenwood Press, 1992.

Boggs, Johnny D. *Billy the Kid on Film: 1911–2012.* Jefferson, NC: McFarland, 2013.

Booth, Paul. *Playing Fans: Negotiating Fandom and Media in the Digital Age.* Iowa City: University of Iowa Press, 2015.

Borde, Raymonde, and Etienne Chaumeton. "The Source of Film Noir." Translated by Bill Horrigan. *Film Reader* 3 (1977): 58.

Bordwell, David. *The Way Hollywood Tells it: Story and Style in Modern Movies.* Berkeley: University of California Press, 2006.

Braziel, Janna Evans, and Kathleen LeBesco. *Bodies out of Bounds: Fatness and Transgression.* Berkeley: University of California Press, 2001.

Britto, Saera, Tycy Hughes, Kurt Saltzman, and Colin Stroh. "Does 'Special' Mean Young, White and Female? Deconstructing the Meaning of 'Special' in Law & Order: Special Victims Unit." *Journal of Criminal Justice and Popular Culture* 14, no. 1 (2007): 39–57.

Brown, Scott. "Scott Brown on Sherlock Holmes, Obsessed Nerds, and Fan Fiction." *Wired,* April 20, 2009. https://www.wired.com/2009/04/pl-brown-6/.

Browning, Frank, and John Gerassi. *The American Way of Crime.* New York: Putnam, 1980.

Burroughs, Bryan. *Public Enemies: America's Greatest Crime Wave and the Birth of the FBI, 1931–34.* New York: Penguin, 2005.

Bushman, Brad J., Patrick E. Jamieson, Illana Weitz, and Daniel Romer. "Gun Violence Trends in Movies." *Pediatrics* 132, no. 6 (2013): 1014–1018.

Cassidy, John. "The Keystone Kops in the White House." *The New Yorker,* March 31, 2014 https://www.newyorker.com/news/john-cassidy/the-keystone-kops-in-the-white-house.

Cavender, Gary, and Nancy C. Jurik. *Justice Provocateur: Jane Tennison and Policing in Prime Suspect.* Urbana: University of Illinois Press, 2012.

Cavender, Gary, and Sarah K. Deutsch. "CSI and Moral Authority: The Police and Science." *Crime, Media, Culture* 3, no. 1 (2007): 67–81.

Chaddha, Anmol, and William J. Wilson. "'Way down in the hole': Systemic Urban Inequality and *The Wire.*" *Critical Inquiry* 38, no. 1 (2011): 164–188.

Champion, Dean J. *Police Misconduct in America: A Reference Handbook.* Annotated edition. Santa Barbara, CA: ABC-CLIO, 2001.

"Charm, at the Strand." *The New York Times,* October 4, 1941. http://www.nytimes.com/movie/review?res=990DE4D7113FE13BBC4C53DFB667838A659EDE.

Charren, Peggy, and Martin W. Sandler. *Changing Channels: Living (Sensibly) with Television.* Reading, MA: Addison-Wesley, 1982.

Clark, Daniel A. *Creating the College Man: American Mass Magazines and Middle-Class Manhood, 1890–1915.* Madison: University of Wisconsin Press, 2010.

Bibliography

Clark, Randall. *At a Theatre or Drive-In Near You: The History, Culture, and Politics of the American Exploitation Film.* New York: Routledge, 1995.
Cloward, Richard. "Illegitimate Means, Anomie, and Deviant Behavior." *American Sociological Review* 24 (April 1959): 164–76.
Cloward, Richard A., and Lloyd E. Ohlin. *Delinquency and Opportunity: A Theory of Delinquent Gangs.* New York: Free Press, 1960.
Cody, Benjamin. "WATCH: Father of three sex abuse victims tries to attack Larry Nassar in court: Police restrained Randall Margraves after he went after the disgraced doctor at his latest sentencing." CBS Sports News, last modified February 03, 2018. https://www.cbssports.com/olympics/news/watch-father-of-three-sex-abuse-victims-tries-to-attack-larry-nassar-in-court/.
Cohen, Stanley. *The Execution of Officer Becker: The Murder of a Gambler, The Trial of a Cop, and the Birth of Organized Crime.* Boston: Da Capo Press/Hachette, 2009.
Colbran, Marianne. *Media Representations of Police and Crime: Shaping the Police Television Drama.* New York: Palgrave Macmillan, 2014.
Cole, Simon A., and Rachael Dioso-Villa. "CSI and Its Effects: Media, Juries, and the Burden of Proof." *New England Law Review* 41, no. 3 (2007): 435–469.
Congdon, Don. *The '30s: A Time to Remember.* New York: Simon & Schuster, 1962.
Cook, David A. *A History of Narrative Film.* 4th Edition. New York: W. W. Norton, 2003.
_____. *Lost Illusions: American Cinema in the Shadow of Watergate and Vietnam, 1970–1979.* New York: Scribner's, 2000.
Corrigan, Timothy. *A Cinema Without Walls: Media Culture After Vietnam.* Piscataway, NJ: Rutgers University Press, 1991.
Cox, Randolph J. *The Dime Novel Companion: A Source Book.* Westport, CT: Greenwood, 2000.
Cressey, Donald R. *Criminal Organization: Its Elementary Forms.* New York: Harper & Row, 1972.
_____. "Methodological Problems in the Study of Organized Crime as a Social Problem." *Annals* 374 (Nov. 1967): 101–12.
_____. *Theft of the Nation: The Structure and Operations of Organized Crime in America.* New York: Harper & Row, 1969.
Critchley, David. *The Origin of Organized Crime in America: The New York City Mafia, 1891–1931.* New York: Routledge, 2008.
Cromie, Robert, and Joseph Pinkston. *Dillinger: A Short and Violent Life.* New York: McGraw-Hill, 1962.
Crowther, Bosley. "The Maltese Falcon, a Fast Mystery-Thriller with Quality and Charm, at the Strand." *The New York Times*, October 4, 1941. http://www.nytimes.com/movie/review?res=990DE4D7113FE13BBC4C53DFB667838A659EDE.
Croy, Homer. *Jesse James Was My Neighbor.* Lincoln: University of Nebraska Press, 1997 (1949).
Cuklanz, Lisa M., and Sujata Moorti. "Television's 'New' Feminism: Prime-Time Representations of Women and Victimization." *Critical Studies in Media Communication* 23, no. 4 (2006): 302–321.
Currell, Susan. *The March of Spare Time: The Problem and Promise of Leisure in the Great Depression.* Philadelphia: University of Pennsylvania Press, 2005.
Daniel Czitrom, *New York Exposed: The Gilded Age Police Scandal That Launched the Progressive Era.* New York: Oxford University Press, 2016.
Debauche, Leslie Midkiff. *Reel Patriotism: The Movies and World War I.* Madison: University of Wisconsin Press, 1997.
Dixon, Thomas F., Jr. *The Clansman.* New York: Doubleday, Page, 1905.

Bibliography

Doherty, Thomas. *Pre-Code Hollywood: Sex, Immorality, and Insurrection in American Cinema; 1930–1934.* New York: Columbia University Press, 1999.

Duffett, Mark. *Understanding Fandom: An Introduction to the Study of Media Fan Culture.* New York: Bloomsbury Academic, 2013.

Dugan, Mark. *Bandit Years: A Gathering of Wolves.* Santa Fe: Sunstone Press, 1987.

Dunlop, M.H. *Gilded City: Scandal and Sensation in Turn-of-the-Century New York.* New York: William Morrow, 2000.

"Easy Street (1917)." DiscoveringChaplin.com, February 7, 2013. http://www.discoveringchaplin.com/2013/02/easy-street-1917.html.

Egan, Daniel. *America's Film Legacy: The Authoritative Guide to the Landmark Movies in The National Film Registry.* New York: Continuum International, 2010.

Elsroad, Lisa. "Tenderloin." *The Encyclopedia of New York City.* Ed. Kenneth T. Jackson. New Haven: Yale University Press, 1995.

Emerson, Ken. *Doo-Dah! Stephen Foster and the rise of American Popular Culture.* Boston: De Capo Press, 1998.

Enstad, Nan. *Ladies of Labor, Girls of Adventure, Working Women, Popular Culture, and Labor Politics at the Turn of the Twentieth Century.* New York: Columbia University Press, 1999.

Erie, Steven P. *Rainbow's End: Irish Americans and the Dilemmas of Urban Machine Politics, 1840–1985.* Berkeley: University of California Press, 1988.

Ezra, Elizabeth. *Georges Méliès: The Birth of the Auteur.* Manchester: Manchester University Press, 2000.

Faderman, Lillian, and Stuart Timmons. *Gay L.A.: A History of Sexual Outlaws, Power Politics, and Lipstick Lesbians.* Oakland: University of California Press, 2009.

Ferdinand, Marilyn. "Traffic In Souls." Date Unknown. https://www.loc.gov/programs/static/national-film-preservation-board/documents/traffic_souls.pdf.

Folgeson, Robert M. *Big City Police: An Urban Institute Study.* Cambridge: Harvard University Press, 1977.

Foltyn, Jaclyn L. "Dead Famous and Dead Sexy: Popular Culture, Forensics, and the Rise of the Corpse." *Mortality* 13, no. 2 (2008): 153–173.

Forshaw, Barry. *British Crime Film: Subverting the Social Order.* New York: Palgrave Macmillan, 2012.

Fort Lee Film Commission. *Fort Lee: Birthplace of the Motion Picture Industry.* Charleston, SC: Arcadia Publishing. 2006.

Fox, Stephen R. *Blood and Power: Organized Crime in Twentieth-Century America.* New York: William Morrow, 1989.

Fried, Albert. *The Rise and Fall of the Jewish Gangster in America.* New York: Holt, Rinehart and Winston, 1980.

Friedman, Lawrence M. *Crime and Punishment in American History.* New York: Basic Books, 1993.

Fronc, Jennifer. *Monitoring the Movies: The Fight Over Film Censorship in Early Twentieth-Century Urban America.* Austin: University of Texas Press, 2017.

Gates, Philippa. *Detecting Men: Masculinity and the Hollywood Detective Film.* Albany: State University of New York, 2011.

_____. *Detecting Women: Gender and the Hollywood Detective Film.* Albany: State University of New York Press, 2006.

_____. "The Meritorious Melodrama: Film Noir with a Female Detective." *Journal of Film and Video* 61, no. 3 (2009): 24–39.

Geltzer, Jeremy. *Film Censorship in America: A State-by-State History.* Jefferson, NC: McFarland, 2017.

Bibliography

Girardin, G. Russell, and William Helmer. *Dillinger: The Untold Story.* Bloomington: Indiana University Press, 1994.

Gomery, Douglas. *Shared Pleasures: A History of Movie Presentation in the United States.* Madison: University of Wisconsin, 1992.

Gorn, Elliot J. *Dillinger's Wild Ride.* New York: Oxford University Press, 2011.

Gradel, Thomas, J., and Dick Simpson. *Corrupt Illinois: Patronage, Cronyism, and Criminality.* Champaign: University of Illinois Press, 2015.

"The Great Escape: Infamous gangster John Dillinger used a wooden pistol to break out of jail in 1934." *New York Daily News*, March 4, 1934. http://www.nydailynews.com/news/crime/dillinger-breaks-jail-wooden-pistol-1934-article-1.2548065.

Grieveson, Lee. *Policing Cinema: Movies and Censorship in Early-Twentieth-Century America.* Oakland, CA: University of California Press, 2004.

_____. "Policing the Cinema: Traffic in Souls at Ellis Island, 1913." *Oxford Journals* 38, no. 2 (July 1, 1997): 149–171.

Grieveson, Lee, Esther Sonnet, and Peter Stanfield. *Mob Culture: Hidden Histories of the American Gangster film.* New Brunswick: Rutgers University Press, 2005.

Griswold, Wendy. "A Methodological Framework for the Sociology of Culture." *Sociological Methodology* 17 (1987): 1–35.

Gunning, Tom. *D.W. Griffith & The Origins of American Narrative: The Early Years at Biograph.* Chicago: University of Illinois Press, 1994.

_____. "From the Opium Den to the Theatre of Morality: Moral Discourse and the Film Process in Early American Cinema." *The Silent Cinema Reader.* Eds. Lee Grieveson and Peter Kramer, 145–154. London: Routledge, 2004.

Hageman, Edward R. *A Comprehensive Index to Black Mask, 1920–1951.* Bowling Green, OH: Bowling Green State University Popular Press, 1982.

Haley, Andrew P. *Turning the Tables: Restaurants and the Rise of the American Middle Class, 1880–1920.* Chapel Hill: University of North Carolina Press, 2011.

Hall, Stuart. "Cultural Studies: Two Paradigms." *Media, Culture and Society* 2, no. 1 (1980): 57–72.

Hammett, Dashiell. *The Maltese Falcon.* New York: Alfred A. Knopf, 1930.

_____. *The Thin Man.* New York: Alfred A. Knopf, 1934.

Hannsberry, Karen Burroughs. *Femme Noir: Bad Girls of Film.* Jefferson, NC: McFarland, 2009.

Hansen, Miriam. *Babel and Babylon: Spectatorship in American Silent Film.* Cambridge: Harvard University Press, 1994.

Hansen, Ron. *Assassination of Jesse James by The Coward Robert.* New York: Open Road Integrated Media, 1983.

Harmon, Jim. *Radio Mystery and Adventure and Its Appearances in Film, Television and Other Media.* Jefferson, NC: McFarland, 2003.

Harvey, Elizabeth, and Linda Derksen. "Science Fiction or Social Fact? An Exploratory Content Analysis of Popular Press Reports on the CSI Effect." *The CSI Effect: Television, Crime, and Governance.* Eds. Michael Byers and Val Marie Johnson, 3–28. Lanham, MD: Lexington Books, 2009.

Hayworth, Will. "A Story of Myth, Fame, Jesse James." *Seattle Times*, September 17, 2007.

Headley, Hon. J.T. *The Great Riots of New York 1712 to 1873 Including a Full and Complete Account of the Four Days' Draft Riot of 1863.* New York: E.B. Treat & Co./Charles Scribner & Co., 1873.

"Height Requirement For Police Officers May Be Eliminated." *The New York Times*, July 23, 1973. http://www.nytimes.com/1973/07/23/archives/height-requirement-for-police-officers-may-be-eliminated.html.

Bibliography

Helmer, William J. *Al Capone and His American Boys: Memoirs of a Mobster's Wife*. Bloomington: Indiana University Press, 2012.
Hirschi, Travis. *Causes of Delinquency*. Berkeley: University of California Press, 1969.
Hobsbawn, Eric. *Bandits*. New York: Delacorte Press, 1969.
_____. *Primitive Rebels: Studies in Archaic Forms of Social Movement in the 19th and 20th Century*. Manchester: Manchester University Press, 1959.
Hoffman, Dennis E. *Scarface Al and the Crime Crusades: Chicago's Private War Against Capone*. Carbondale: Southern Illinois University Press, 1993.
Holden, Henry M. *FBI 100 Years: An Unofficial History*. Minneapolis: Zenith Press, 2008.
Horan, James D. *Desperate Men: The James Gang and the Wild Bunch*. Lincoln: University of Nebraska Press, 1997 (1949).
Horowitz, Daniel. *The Morality of Spending: Attitudes toward the Consumer Society in America, 1875–1940*. Baltimore: Johns Hopkins University Press, 1985.
Hughes, Michael. "The Fruits of Cultivation Analysis: A Reexamination of Some Effects of Television Watching." *Public Opinion Quarterly* 44, no. 3 (1980): 287.
Ianni, Francis A.J. *The Black Mafia: Ethnic Succession in Organized Crime*. New York: Simon & Schuster, 1974.
Inciardi, James A., and Juliet L. Dee. "From the Keystone Cops to 'Miami Vice': Images of Policing in American Popular Culture." *Journal of Popular Culture* 21, no. 2 (September 1987): pp. 84–102.
Iorizzo, Luciano. *Al Capone: A Biography (Greenwood Biographies)*. Westport, CT: Greenwood, 2003.
Jacobs, Lea. *The Wages of Sin: Censorship and the Fallen Woman Film, 1928–1942*. Oakland: University of California Press, 1997.
Jeffords, Susan. *Hard Bodies: Hollywood Masculinity in the Reagan Era*. New Brunswick: Rutgers University Press, 1994.
Jermyn, Deborah. "Labs and Slabs: Television Crime Drama and the Quest for Forensic Realism." *Studies in History and Philosophy of Science Part C: Studies in History and Philosophy of Biological and Biomedical Sciences* 44, no. 1 (2013): 103–109.
Jewell, Richard B. *The Golden Age of Cinema: Hollywood, 1929–1945*. Hoboken: Wiley-Blackwell, 2007.
Johnson, Marilyn. *Street Justice: A History of Police Violence in New York City*. Boston: Beacon Press, 2003.
Jordan, Jessica Hope. *The Sex Goddess in American Film, 1930–1965: Jean Harlow, Mae West, Lana Turner, and Jayne Mansfield*. Amherst, NY: Cambria Press, 2009.
Jowett, Garth S. "'A Capacity for Evil': The 1915 Supreme Court Mutual Decision." *Historical Journal of Film, Radio and Television* 9, no. 1 (1989): 59–78.
Kahle, Shannon. "Sentimental Science, Somaticization, and Forensic Drama." *Critical Studies in Media Communication* 30, no. 3 (2013): 241–255.
Kaufmann, Reginald Wright. *The House of Bondage*. Introduction. New York: Mofart, Yard and Company, 1910.
Keil, Charlie. *Early American Cinema in Transition: Story, Style, and Filmmaking, 1907–1913*. Madison: University of Wisconsin Press. 2002.
Keller, Laura. *Freedom of the Screen: Legal Challenges to State Film Censorship*. Louisville: University Press of Kentucky, 2008.
Kendrick, James. *Hollywood Bloodshed: Violence in 1980s American Cinema*. Carbondale: Southern Illinois University Press, 2009.
King, Neal. "Calling Dirty Harry a Liar: A Critique of Displacement Theories of Popular Criminology." *New Review of Film and Television Studies* 11, no. 2 (2013): 171–190.

Bibliography

_____. "Generic Womanhood: Gendered Depictions in Cop Action Cinema." *Gender & Society* 22, no. 2 (2008): 238–260.

_____. *Heroes in Hard Times: Cop Action Movies in the U.S.* Philadelphia: Temple University Press, 1999.

King, Rob. *The Fun Factory: The Keystone Film Company and the Emergence of Mass Culture.* Oakland: University of California Press, 2008.

Kitch, Carolyn. *The Girl on the Magazine Cover: The Origins of Visual Stereotypes in American Mass Media.* Chapel Hill: University of North Carolina Press, 2001.

Klein, Amanda Ann. *American Film Cycles: Reframing Genres, Screening Social Problems, and Defining Subculture.* Austin: University of Texas Press, 2011.

Kobler, John. *Ardent Spirits: The Rise and Fall of Prohibition.* New York: Da Capo Press, 1973.

_____. *Capone: The Life and World of Al Capone.* New York: DA Capo Press, 1971.

Krutnik, Frank. *In a Lonely Street: Film Noir, Genre, Masculinity.* New York: Routledge, 1991.

Lamb, Bill. "Bill Devery." Society for American Baseball Research, accessed February 17, 2018. http://sabr.org/bioproj/person/500ba2d3.

LaSalle, Mick. *Complicated Women: Sex and Power in Pre-Code Hollywood.* New York: St. Martin's Griffin, 2002.

Lawes, Lewis E. *Meet the Murderer!* New York: Harper Bros., 1940.

Lawrence, Novotny. *Blaxploitation Films of the 1970s: Blackness and Genre.* New York: Routledge, 2007.

Layman, Richard. *Discovering the Maltese Falcon and Sam Spade.* San Francisco: Vince Emery Productions, 2005.

Leach, William R. *Land of Desire: Merchants, Power, and the Rise of a New American Culture.* New York: Vintage, 1994.

Lears, Jackson T. *No Place of Grace: Antimodernism and the Transformation of American Culture, 1880–1920.* New York: Pantheon, 1981.

Leitch, Thomas M. *Crime Films.* New York: Cambridge University Press, 2002.

Light, Ivan. "The Ethnic Vice Industry, 1880–1944." *American Journal of Sociology* 42 (June 1977): 464–79.

Lindberg, Richard C. *The Gambler King of Clark Street: Michael C. McDonald and the Rise of Chicago's Democratic Machine.* Carbondale: Southern Illinois University Press, 2009.

Lindenmeyer, Kristie. *The Greatest Generation Grows Up: American Childhood in the 1930s.* Chicago: Ivan R. Dee, 2005.

Linnell, Greg. "'Applauding the good and condemning the bad': The Christian Herald and Varieties of Protestant Response to Hollywood in the 1950s." *The Journal of Religion and Popular Culture* 12, no. 1 (2006): 4.

Lipsitz, George. *Rainbow at Midnight: Labor and Culture in the 1940s.* Champaign: University of Illinois Press, 1994.

Lobosco, David. "A Trip Down Memory Lane: A nostalgic journey to the past to relive the golden days of entertainment! The Last Days of Fatty Arbuckle." The Classic Movie Blog Association, October 25, 2103. http://greatentertainersarchives.blogspot.com/2013/10/the-last-days-of-fatty-arbuckle.html.

Lookingbill, Brad D. *Dust Bowl, USA: Depression America and the Ecological Imagination, 1929–1941.* Athens: Ohio University Press, 2001.

Lott, Eric. *Love and Theft: Blackface Minstrelsy and the American Working Class.* New York: Oxford University Press, 1995.

Bibliography

Lott, M. Ray. *Police on Screen: Hollywood Cops, Detectives, Marshall and Rangers.* Jefferson, NC: McFarland, 2006.
Lovell, Alan. *Don Siegel: American Cinema.* London: BFI, 1975.
Maenchen-Helfen, Otto J. *The World of the Huns: Studies in Their History and Culture.* Berkeley: University of California Press, 1973.
Maltby, Richard. *Hollywood Cinema.* Cambridge, MA: Blackwell, 1995.
Mappen, Marc. *Prohibition Gangsters: The Rise and Fall of a Bad Generation.* New Brunswick: Rutgers University Press, 2013.
Marchand, Roland. *Advertising the American Dream: Making Way for Modernity, 1920–1940.* Berkeley: University of California Press, 1985.
Marche, Jordan. *Theaters of Time and Space: American Planetaria, 1930–1970.* New Brunswick: Rutgers University Press, 2005.
Mason, F. *Hollywood's Detectives: Crime Series in the 1930s and 1940s from the Whodunnit to Hard-Boiled Noir.* New York: Palgrave Macmillan, 2012.
Matera, Dara. *John Dillinger: The Life and Death of America's First Celebrity Criminal.* New York: Carroll & Graf, 2004.
Mayer, Ruth. "In the Nick of Time? Detective Film Serials, Temporality, and Contingency Management, 1919–1926." *The Velvet Light Trap* 79, no. 1 (2017): 21–35.
McAdams, William. *Ben Hecht: The Man Behind the Legend.* New York: Scribner, 1990.
McGee, Scott. "Buster Keaton: Cops." Turner Classic Movies (TCM) film review. http://www.tcm.com/tcmdb/title/438357/Cops/articles.html.
McKay, James. *Dana Andrews: The Face of Noir.* Jefferson, NC: McFarland, 2010.
Merritt, Greg. *Celluloid Mavericks.* New York: Thunder's Mouth Press, 2000.
_____. *Room 1219: The Life of Fatty Arbuckle, the Mysterious Death of Virginia Rappe, and the Scandal That Changed Hollywood.* Chicago: Chicago Review Press, 2013.
Merton, Robert. "Anomie, Anomia, and Social Interaction." *Anomie and Deviant Behavior.* Ed. Marshall B. Clinard, 213–242. New York: Free Press, 1964.
_____. "Social Structure and Anomie." *American Sociological Review* 3 (1938).
Mintz, Steven, Randy W. Roberts, and David Welky. *Hollywood's America: Understanding History Through Film.* 5th edition. Malden, MA: Wiley Blackwell. 2016.
Mogulescu, M. "Tax Reform Act of 1976 and Tax Incentives for Motion Picture Investment: Throwing out the Baby with the Bath Water." *Southern California Law Review* 58 (1985): 839.
Munby, Jonathan. *Public Enemies, Public Heroes: Screening the Gangster from Little Caesar to Touch of Evil.* Chicago: University of Chicago Press, 1999.
Münsterberg, Hugo. *The Photoplay: A Psychological Study.* New York: D. Appleton, 1916.
Musser, Charles. *Before the Nickelodeon: Edwin S. Porter and The Edison Manufacturing Company.* Berkeley: University of California Press. 1991.
_____. *The Emergence of Cinema: The American Screen to 1907.* Los Angeles: University of California Press, 1990.
Naremore, James. "A Season in Hell or the Snows of Yesteryear?" Introduction to *A Panorama of American Film Noir (1941–1953),* by Raymond Borde and Etienne Chaumeton, xiv–xv, trans. Paul Hammond. San Francisco: City Lights, 2002.
Newburn, Tim. *Handbook of Policing: 2nd Edition.* Portland, OR: Willan, 2012.
Nichol, John Pringle. *A Cyclopædia of the Physical Sciences.* London: Richard Griffin and Company, 1857.
Nowell, Richard. *Blood Money: A History of the First Teen Slasher Film Cycle.* New York: Continuum, 2011.
Ohlheiser, Abby. "Most of America's Silent Films are Lost Forever: Seventy-five percent of silent-era films have been lost forever to history, according to a new

comprehensive study from the Library of Congress." *The Atlantic*, December 4, 2003. https://www.theatlantic.com/entertainment/archive/2013/12/most-americas-silent-films-are-lost-forever/355775/.

O'Kane, James. *The Crooked Ladder: Gangsters, Ethnicity, and the American Dream.* New Brunswick: Transaction, 1992.

———. *Wicked Deeds: Murder in America.* New Brunswick: Transaction, 2002.

Oliver, Willard M. *August Vollmer: The Father of American Policing.* Durham: Carolina Academic Press, 2017.

Orbach, Barak Y. "Prizefighting and the Birth of Movie Censorship." *Yale Journal of Law & the Humanities* 21, no. 2 (2009). http://digitalcommons.law.yale.edu/yjlh/vol21/iss2/3.

Osofsky, Gilbert. "Race Riot, 1900: A Study of Ethnic Violence." *The Journal of Negro Education* 32, no. 1 (Winter. 1963). http://www.jstor.org/stable/2294487.

Panek, LeRoy Lad. *The Origins of the American Detective Story: An Anthology.* Jefferson, NC: McFarland, 2006.

Pasley, Fred. *Al Capone: The Biography of a Self-Made Man.* Garden City, NY: Garden City Publishing Company, 1971.

Pautz, Michelle C., and Megan K. Warnement. "Government on the Silver Screen: Contemporary American Cinema's Depiction of Bureaucrats, Police Officers, and Soldiers." *PS: Political Science and Politics* 46, no. 3 (2013): pp. 569–579.

Peiss, Kathy. *Cheap Amusements: Working Women and Leisure in Turn-of-the-Century New York.* Philadelphia: Temple University Press, 1986.

———. *Hope in a Jar: The Making of America's Beauty Culture.* Philadelphia: University of Pennsylvania Press, 2001.

Pennington, Jody W. *The History of Sex in American Film.* Westport, CT: Praeger, 2007.

Peterson, Richard A. "Revitalizing the Culture Concept." *Annual Review of Sociology* 5 (1979): 137–166.

Peterson, Virgil W. *The Mob: 200 Years of Organized Crime in New York.* Ottawa, IL: Green Hill, 1933.

Pfeil, Fred. *White Guys: Studies in Postmodern Domination and Difference.* New York: Verso, 1995.

Platt, Richard. *Film.* New York: Alfred A. Knopf, 1992.

Pointer, Michael. "Earliest Holmes film." *Sherlock Holmes Journal* 8, no. 4 (Summer 1978): 138–140.

Polletta, Francesca, and Christine Tomlinson. "Date Rape after the Afterschool Special: Narrative Trends in the Televised Depiction of Social Problems." *Sociological Forum* 29, no. 3 (2014): 527–548.

Potter, Clare Bond. *War on Crime: Bandit, "G" Men, and the Politics of Mass Culture.* New Brunswick: Rutgers University Press, 1998.

Potter, Gary. "The History of Policing in the United States, Part 1." June 25, 2013. http://plsonline.eku.edu/insidelook/history-policing-united-states-part-1.

Poulsen, Ellen. *Don't Call Us Molls: Women of the John Dillinger Gang.* Oakland Gardens, NY: Clinton Cook, 2002.

Powers, Richard G. *Hoover's FBI in American Popular Culture.* Carbondale: Southern Illinois University Press, 1983.

Prassel, Frank Richard. *The Great American Outlaw: A Legacy of Fact and Fiction.* Norman: University of Oklahoma Press, 1993.

Prince, Stephen. *Classical Film Violence: Designing and Regulating Brutality in Hollywood Cinema, 1930–1968.* New Brunswick: Rutgers University Press, 2003.

Bibliography

Rafter, Nicole H. *Shots in the Mirror: Crime Films and Society.* New York: Oxford University Press, 2006.
Rafter, Nicole H., and Michelle Brown. *Criminology Goes to the Movies: Crime Theory and Popular Culture.* New York: New York University Press, 2011.
Ramaeker, P. "Realism, Revisionism and Visual Style: *The French Connection* and the New Hollywood *Policier.*" *New Review of Film and Television Studies* 8, no. 2 (2010): 144–163.
Randall, Richard S. *Censorship of the Movies: The Social and Political Control of a Mass Medium.* Madison: University of Wisconsin Press, 1968.
Ray, Robert B. *A Certain Tendency of the Hollywood Cinema, 1930–1980.* Princeton: Princeton University Press, 1985.
Regoli, Robert M., John D. Hewitt, and Anna E. Kosloski. *Exploring Criminal Justice: The Essentials.* 3rd edition. Burlington, MA: Jones & Bartlett, 2018.
Reiner, Robert, Sonia Livingstone, and Jessica Allen. "From Law and Order to Lynch Mobs: Crime News Since the Second World War." In *Criminal Visions: Media Representations of Crime and Justice.* Ed. Paul Mason, 13–32. Portland, OR: Willan, 2003.
Rejali, Darius. *Torture and Democracy.* Princeton: Princeton University Press, 2007.
Rhodes, Jane. "Television's Realist Portrayal of African-American Women and the Case of *L.A. Law.*" *Women and Language* 14, no. 1 (1991): 29–34.
Richards, Jeffery. "The British Board of Film Censors and content control in the 1930s: Images of Britain." *Historical Journal of Film, Radio and Television* 1, no. 2 (1981): 95–116.
Riordon, William L. *Plunkett of Tammany Hall.* New York: Dutton, 1963.
Robinson, David. *Chaplin: His Life and Art.* New York: McGraw-Hill, 1985.
_____. *From Peepshow to Palace: The Birth of American Film.* New York: Columbia University Press, 1996.
Roffman, Peter, and Jim Purdy. *The Hollywood Social Problem Film: Madness, Despair, and Politics from the Depression to the Fifties.* Bloomington: Indiana University Press, 1981.
Rollyson, Carl E. *Hollywood Enigma: Dana Andrews.* Jackson: University Press of Mississippi, 2012.
Romao, Tico. "Engines of Transformation: An Analytical History of the 1970s Car Chase Cycle." *New Review of Film and Television Studies* 1, no. 1 (2003): 31–54.
Rucker, Walter C., Jr., and James N. Upton, eds. *Encyclopedia of American Race Riots: Greenwood Milestones in African American History Volume 2 N-Z and Primary Documents.* Westpork, CT: Greenwood Press, 2007.
Ruth, David E. *Inventing the Public Enemy: The Gangster in American Culture, 1918–1934.* Chicago: University of Chicago Press, 1996.
Savage, Joanne. "The Role of Exposure to Media Violence in the Etiology of Violent Behavior: A Criminologist Weighs In." *American Behavioral Scientist* 51, no. 8 (2008): 1123–1136.
Scanlon, Jennifer. *Inarticulate Longings: The Ladies' Home Journal, Gender, and the Promises of Consumer Culture.* New York: Routledge, 1995.
Schrader, Paul. "Notes on Film Noir." *Film Comment* 8, no. 1 (1972): 581–591.
Segrave, Kerry. *Police Violence in America, 1869–1920: 256 Incidents Involving Death or Injury.* Jefferson, NC: McFarland, 2016.
Senate, New York. *Report and Proceedings of the Senate Committee Appointed to Investigate Police Corruption of the Police Department of the City of New York. Vol. 1.* Transmitted to the State Legislature January 18, 1895. Albany: James B. Lyon, State Printer, 1895.

Bibliography

Settle, William A. *Jesse James Was His Name: Or, Fact and Fiction Concerning the Careers of the Notorious James Brothers of Missouri.* Lincoln: University of Nebraska Press, 1977.
Shaffer, Marguerite. *See America First: Tourism and National Identity, 1880–1940.* Washington, D.C.: Smithsonian Books, 2001.
Sheerin, Jude. "'Fatty' Arbuckle and Hollywood's first scandal." *BBC News*, September 4, 2011. http://www.bbc.com/news/magazine-14640719.
Shiller, Gerald A. *It Happened in Hollywood: Remarkable Events That Shaped History.* Guilford, CT: Globe Pequot Press, 2010.
Skolnick, Jerome Herbert, and James J. Fyfe. *Above the Law: Police and the Excessive Use of Force.* New York: Simon & Schuster, 1994.
Slide, Anthony. *The New Historical Dictionary of the American Film Industry.* 2nd Edition. Lanham, MD: Scarecrow Press, 2001.
Slotkin, Richard. *Gunfighter Nation: The Myth of the Frontier in Twentieth-Century America.* Norman: University of Oklahoma Press, 1998.
Smith, Robert Barr. *The Last Hurrah of the James-Younger Gang.* Norman: University of Oklahoma Press, 2001.
Smith-Shomade, Beretta E. "'Rock-a-Bye, Baby!': Black Women Disrupting Gangs and Constructing Hip-Hop Gangsta Films." *Cinema Journal* 42, no. 2 (2003): 25–40.
Snyder, Robert W. *The Voice of the City: Vaudeville and Popular Culture in New York.* New York: Oxford University Press, 1989.
Spigel, Lynn. *Make Room for TV: Television and the Family Idea in Postwar America.* Chicago: University of Chicago Press, 1992.
Spitzer, Stephen. "The Rationalization of Crime Control in Capitalist Society." *Contemporary Crises* 3, no. 1 (1979).
Springhall, John. *Youth, Popular Culture and Moral Panics: Penny Gaffs to Gangsta-Rap, 1830–1996.* New York: St. Martin's Press, 1998.
Steckmesser, Kent Ladd. *The Western Hero in History and Legend.* Norman: University of Oklahoma Press, 1965.
Stephens, E.J., and Marc Wanamaker. *Early Warner Bros. Studios.* Mount Pleasant, SC: Arcadia Publishing, 2010.
Stiles, T.J. *Jesse James: Last Rebel of the Civil War.* New York: Vintage/Random House, 2003.
Stokes, Melvyn, and Richard Maltby. *Hollywood Spectatorship: Changing Perceptions of Cinema Audiences.* New York: Palgrave/BFI, 2001.
Strong, Josiah. "Perils—the Boss, the Machine, the Immigrant: A Nineteenth-Century View." *The City Boss in America: An Interpretive Reader.* Ed. Alexander B. Callow, Jr., 14–17. New York: Oxford University Press. 1976.
Sutherland, Edwin H. *On Analyzing Crime.* Ed. Karl Schuessler.Chicago: University of Chicago Press, 1973.
Swiencicki, Mark. "Consuming Brotherhood: Men's Culture, Style, and Recreation as Consumer Culture, 1880–1930." *Journal of Social History* 31, no. 4 (Summer 1998): 773–808.
Thompson, Dave. *Black and White and Blue: Adult Cinema from the Victorian Age to the VCR.* Toronto: ECW Press, 2007.
Thompson, Kristin. *Storytelling in Film and Television.* Cambridge: Harvard University Press, 2003.
_____. *Storytelling in the New Hollywood: Understanding Classical Narrative Technique.* Cambridge: Harvard University Press, 1999.

Bibliography

Todd, Drew. "The History of Crime Films." *Shot in the Mirror: Crime Films and Society*. Ed. Nicole Rafter, 21–59. New York: Oxford University Press, 2006.
Tolland, John. *The Dillinger Days*. New York: Random House, 1963.
Triplett, Frank. *The Life, Times, and Treacherous Death of Jesse James*. New York: Konecky & Konecky, 1970 (1882).
Tudor, Andrew. "Genre." *Film Genre Reader II*. Ed. Barry K. Grant, 3–10. Austin: University of Texas Press, 1995.
Turnbull, Sue. "Crime as Entertainment: The Case of the TV Crime drama." *Continuum* 24, no. 6 (2010): 819–827.
Tuska, Jon. *The Detective in Hollywood: The Movie Careers of the Great Fictional Private Eyes and Their Creators*. New York: Doubleday, 1978.
Tzanelli, Rodanthi, Majid Yar, and Martin O'Brien. "Con Me If You Can: Exploring Crime in the American Cinematic Imagination." *Theoretical Criminology* 9, no. 1 (2005): 97–117.
United States, Wickersham Commission. *Enforcement of the prohibition laws of the United States: Message from the President of the United States transmitting a report of the National Commission on Law Observance and Enforcement relative to the facts as to the enforcement, the benefits, and abuses under the prohibition laws, both before and since the adoption of the Eighteenth Amendment to the Constitution.* Available as a reprint of the University of Michigan Library (January 1, 1931), Ann Arbor.
Van Dine, S.S. *The Benson Case Murder*. Redditch, Worcestershire: Read Books, 2013.
Watkins, S. Craig. *Representing: Hip Hop Culture and the Production of Black Cinema*. Chicago: University of Chicago Press, 1998.
Wertheimer, John. "Mutual Film Reviewed: The Movies, Censorship, and Free Speech in Progressive America." *American Journal of Legal History* 37, no. 2 (1993): 158–189.
Whalen, Bernard, and David Doorey. "The Birth of the NYPD." *The Chief of Police: The Official Publication of the National Association of Chiefs of Police*. (March/April 1998). http://www.bjwhalen.com/article.htm.
White, Richard. "Outlaw Gangs of the Middle Border: American Social Bandit." *Western Historical Quarterly* 12, no. 4 (Winter 1981): 387–408.
Willemes, Cornelius William. *Behind the Green Lights*. New York: Alfred A. Knopf, 1931.
Williams, Linda Ruth. *The Erotic Thriller in Contemporary Cinema*. Bloomington: Indiana University Press, 2005.
Willis, Sharon. *High Contrast: Race and Gender in Contemporary Hollywood*. Durham: Duke University Press, 1997.
Wilson, Christopher P. *Cop Knowledge: Police Power and Cultural Narrative in Twentieth-Century America*. Chicago: University of Chicago Press, 2000.
Wilson, Ronald W. "Gang Busters: The Kefauver Crime Committee and the Syndicate Films of the 1950s." *Mob Culture: Hidden Histories of the American Gangster Film*. Eds. Lee Grieveson, Esther Sonnet, and Peter Stanfield, 67–89. New Brunswick: Rutgers University Press, 2005.
Witten-Keller, Laura. *Freedom of the Screen: Legal Challenges to State Film Censorship, 1915–1981*. Lexington: University Press of Kentucky, 2008.
Wright, Bradford W. *Comic Book Nation: The Transformation of Youth Culture in America*. Baltimore: Johns Hopkins University Press. 2001.
Yeatman, Ted P. *Frank and Jesse James: The Story Behind the Legend*. Nashville: Cumberland House, 2001.

Index

The Adventures of Superman 14, 125
Andrews, Dana 14, 105, 116
anomie theory 6, 66, 72, 91, 147, 149
Appointment by Telephone 49
Arbuckle, Roscoe "Fatty" 29, 77, 78, 80, 81
Astor, Mary 109
Augustus, Cesar 18

Bacall, Lauren 113
Bancroft, George 10, 86
The Bangville Police 72
Becker, Charles 67, 68
Behind the Green Lights 119, 131
The Big Heat 13, 105, 131
The Big Sleep 13, 105, 106, 113–116, 117, 120, 131
Billy the Kid 83, 147
The Birth of a Nation 66, 145
The Black Hand 5, 34, 57–59, 64
Black Maria see Edison, Thomas.
Black Mask 12, 106
Blake, Larry J. 127
Block v. City of Chicago 27
Bogart, Humphrey 109, 113
Bond, Ward 109
Bonnie and Clyde 83, 102, 147
Bowery Boys 21, 50
Breen, Joseph I. 10
brutality, police 2, 6, 7, 14, 34, 36–42, 45, 48, 54, 65–68, 75, 80, 81, 96, 111, 116–119
Bullets or Ballots 85
Byrnes, Thomas 6, 36, 40, 48, 55

Cabiria 66
Cagney, James 10, 32, 88, 99
Capone, Al 86, 87, 94–96, 102
Carter, Nick 7
celluloid 4, 24
censorship 1, 4, 10, 25–33, 51, 64, 67, 81, 94, 95, 99, 102
Chandler, Raymond 12, 106, 113
Chaplin, Charlie 8, 65, 67, 72–76, 80, 123
Charles, Nick 108

Chicago 20, 25–27, 46–47, 51, 68, 86, 93, 95, 98
Chinese Laundry see *Robetta and Doretto*
Cook, Elisha, Jr. 113, 115
Coon, Maurice 95
Cooper, Gary 15, 126, 127
Cops 6, 7, 65–68, 77–78, 80, 123, 131
A Corner in Wheat 2, 5, 34, 60–64, 132
corruption, police 5–7, 20–21, 26, 28, 34–42, 46–51, 61, 65, 67–68, 70, 72, 76, 97, 100, 116–120, 123, 127

da Fontana, Giovanni 22
Daguerre, Louis Jacques-Maude 23
Dalrymple, Louis 35, 36
The Dark Corner 13, 105, 132
Darrin, Sonia 114
Dempsey, Jack 87
Desperate Encounter Between Burglar and Police 57
Detective Story Magazine 12, 106
Devery, William "Big Bill" 6, 36, 38, 40, 45, 55, 72, 143
Dickson, William K.L. 4, 24
differential association 88, 148
differential opportunity theory 149
Dillinger, John 9, 83, 84, 102
D.O.A. 14, 104, 132
Dobson, F.A. 59
Don Juan 82
Doorway to Hell 89, 132
Double Indemnity 14, 104, 132
Dragnet 14–15, 29, 125, 132
A Drunkard's Reformation 28
Durkheim, Emile 91

Eastman, George 24
Easy Street 6–8, 65–68, 72–77, 80, 123, 132
Edison, Thomas A. 4, 5, 7, 24–26, 35, 41–43, 49, 54, 61
Ehrhart, S.D. 21
18th Amendment 8, 10, 86, 123
Estill, Robert 84

165

Index

Fairbanks, Douglas, Jr. 91
Farrell, Glenda 93
FBI 9, 88, 100–101
femme fatale 13, 14, 50, 104, 113, 125, 150
Fields, Stanley 92
Fights of Nations 5, 34, 47–48, 64
Finn, Mickey 51, 144
Flynn, Errol 29
Foster, Stephen 50, 144
Frank, Nino 12

"G" Men 11, 32, 85, 88–90, 97, 99–102, 124, 132
gangsters *see* organized crime
Gaunt, Percy 50, 51
Genovese, Vito 83
A Gesture Fight in Hester Street 5, 34, 47–48, 63, 132
Gish, Lillian 60
Gordon, Henry C. 96
The Great Train Robbery 5, 137, 140
Greenstreet, Sydney 109.112
Griffith, D.W. 2, 25, 59–61, 66

Hammett, Dashiell 12, 106, 108
Harrington, William 109
Hawks, Howard 113
Hays Code *see* Motion Picture Production Code
Hays, William H. 10, 32, 82, 95, 108
He Walked by Night 29, 132
The Heathen Chinee and the Sunday School Teacher 28
Heise, William 26
Hennessy, David C. 58
Heydt, Louis Jean 114
High Noon 15, 126–128, 132
Hollywood 25, 29, 31, 127
Holmes, Sherlock 43, 44
Homans, Robert 109
Hoover, J. Edgar. 95, 139
House Committee on Un-American Activities (HUAC) 127, 151
How They Do Things on the Bowery 5, 34, 49–50, 63, 133
How They Rob Men in Chicago 5, 34, 45–47, 63, 128, 133
Hoyt, Charles 50, 51
Hugens, Christian 23
Huston, John 108–109

The Inside of the White Slave Traffic 69

Jack and the Beanstalk 44
Jacson, Thomas E. 92
The James Boys in Missouri 27, 83
The Jazz Singer 82
The John C. Rice–Mary Irwin Kiss 25
Johnson, Al 82

Kaufmann, Reginald Wright 69
Keaton, Buster 67, 77–81, 123
Kelly, Grace 126
Keystone Kops 8, 66–67, 72–73, 123
Kinetoscope 41, 41, 43
The Kleptomaniac 2, 5, 34, 61, 64, 133

laterna magica 22, 23
Lexow Committee 6, 34–40, 42, 67
Life of an American Policeman 3, 5, 34, 40, 54–57, 64, 122, 126, 133
Little Caesar 10, 82, 85, 89–94, 99, 124, 133
Lorre, Peter 110
Los Angeles 29, 67, 80, 81
Lumière brothers 26

Madden, Karl 117
Mafia 58–59
The Maltese Falcon 12, 13, 105, 106, 108–113, 120, 125, 133
Marey, Etienne Jules 24
McAdoo, William 54, 55
McCutcheon, Wallace 3, 5, 45, 52, 54, 57, 87, 126
McDonald, Cassius 46
McDonald, Ian 126
McGurk's Suicide Hall 50
McLaughlin, Frank 45, 55
Méliès, Georges 5, 43
Merrill, Guy 117
Merton, Robert 91, 149
Metropolitan Police Act of 1829 19
Midnight Taxi 11, 85, 124, 133
The Moonshiners 5, 34, 52–53, 64, 134
Morrissey, John 21
Motion Picture Production Code 10, 31, 89, 90, 94, 99, 108, 124
Mounted Police Charge 26
Muni, Paul 96
Münsterberg, Hugo 23
The Musketeers of Pig Alley 5, 34, 39, 57, 59–60, 64, 134
Mutoscope 43, 46, 47, 49, 52, 59
Mutual Film Corporation v. Industrial Commission of Ohio 27, 28
Muybridge, Eadweard 23–24
My Wife's Gone Away 82

The Naked City 13, 105, 106, 134
Nast, Thomas 61, 62
National Board of Review 27
Nelson, "Baby Face" 83, 102, 147
New Orleans 20, 58
New York City 3, 6, 18–21, 25–26, 34–40, 44–49, 54–64, 67–69, 103, 106–108, 116–119, 126
New York City Police Riot of 1857 20

Index

New York City Race Riot of 1900 44, 45
Night Riders 27

Old California 25
organized crime 9, 46, 47, 57–60, 65, 83, 85–89, 96–98, 101, 123

Parkhurst, Charles 34
Pastor, Tony 4, 41, 143
Pawley, Edward 100
Peel, Robert 19
phenakistoscope 23
Porter, Edward S. 2–3, 5, 49, 51, 54, 57, 61, 126
The Postman Always Rings Twice 14, 104
Praetorian Gurad 18, 19, 21
Preminger, Otto 14, 116
Production Code *see* Motion Picture Production Code
Progressive Era 3, 63–65, 75, 122–123
Prohibition 9, 77, 86–89, 98, 102, 108, 119, 122–123, 128
The Public Enemy 10, 89, 94, 99, 124, 134
Public Hero Number 1 11, 124, 134

Raft, George 96
Rappe, Virginia 77, 78
Reagan, Ronald 83
Ridgley, John 116
Robbins, James 54, 55
Robetta and Doretto 4, 34, 36, 41–43, 63, 134
Robinson, Edward G. 85, 91
Roosevelt, Theodore 40
Runaway in the Park 145

St. Valentine's Day Massacre 95
Sandow, Eugene 42, 43
Scarface 10, 32, 89, 90, 94–98, 124, 135
Sherlock Holmes Baffled 4, 34, 43–45, 63, 135
Siegel, Benjamin "Bugsy" 83, 102
The Silver Wedding 34, 59, 135
Simon, Robert F. 118
Smalley, Phillips 53, 145
social bond theory 149
Statute of Winchester (1285) 19
Stevens, Craig 117
Stevens, Landers 92
Stone, Herbert 25
Suspense 5, 34, 52–53, 64, 135
Sutherland, Edwin 88, 148

Tammany Hall 6, 20, 21, 35, 38, 45
tenderloin district 21, 39, 44
thaumatrope 23
The Thin Man 108, 135
third degree 6, 14, 96, 116, 118–119, 125, 129
36 Hours to Kill 11, 85, 123, 135
This Gun for Hire 14, 104
Thorpe, Robert 44, 45
Tierney, Gene 117
Toomey, Regis 100, 114
Traffic in Souls 6, 7, 17, 65–72, 80, 135
A Trip to Chinatown 50
Tschernoff, Ivan 42, 43
Tucker, George Loane 18, 67, 69, 80
Turner, William 18

Underworld 6, 10, 86, 89, 90, 94, 100, 135

Vance, Philo 106–108, 110
Vickers, Martha 113
Volstead Act. *See* Prohibition
Von Eltz, Theordore 113
von Sternberg, Josef 10, 86
von Zell, Harry 117

Waldron, Charles 113
Warner Bros 12, 82, 99, 106, 108
Wayne, John 15, 127
Webb, Jack 29
Weber, Lois 53, 69, 145
Weiss, Hyme 83, 102
What Happened to Mary 7, 135, 139
Where Are All My Children 69
Where the Sidewalk Ends 13–14, 97, 103, 105, 116–120, 135
Whipsaw 11, 85, 124, 136
White, Betty 83
White, James H. 26
Wickersham Commission 14, 118, 119, 139
Willemese, Cornelius Wilham 103, 119
Williams, Alexander "Clubber" 6, 34, 36, 38–40, 48, 55
The Woman in the Window 14, 104
Women's Christian Temperance Union (WCTU) 28
writ of habeus corpus 97, 98
Wynn, Marty 29

zoetrope 23

www.ingramcontent.com/pod-product-compliance
Lightning Source LLC
Chambersburg PA
CBHW032048300426
44117CB00009B/1230